Ludwig von Auer

Dynamic Preferences, Choice Mechanisms, and Welfare

 Springer

Author

Ludwig von Auer
University of Magdeburg
Fakultät für Wirtschaftswissenschaften
Volkswirtschaftslehre IV
Internationale Wirtschaft
Postfach 4120
D-39016 Magdeburg, Germany

Library of Congress Cataloging-in-Publication Data

Von Auer, Ludwig, 1966-
    Dynamics preferences, choice mechanisms, and welfare / Ludwig von
Auer.
       p.   cm. -- (Lecture notes in economics and mathematical
systems ; 462)
    Includes bibliographical references (p.   ).
    ISBN 3-540-64320-6 (Springer-Verlag Berlin Heidelberg New York :
pbk. : alk. paper)
    1. Utility theory--Mathematical models. 2. Decision-making-
-Mathematical models.   I. Title.   II. Series.
HB201.V66   1998
658.4'033--dc21   98-16029
                                                                 CIP

ISSN 0075-8442
ISBN 3-540-64320-6 Springer-Verlag Berlin Heidelberg New York

© Springer-Verlag Berlin Heidelberg 1998
Printed in Germany

The use of general descriptive names, registered names, trademarks, etc. in this publication does not imply, even in the absence of a specific statement, that such names are exempt from the relevant protective laws and regulations and therefore free for general use.

Typesetting: Camera ready by author
SPIN: 1064928   43/3142-543210 - Printed on acid-free paper

Lecture Notes in Economics and Mathematical Systems

462

Springer
Berlin
Heidelberg
New York
Barcelona
Budapest
Hong Kong
London
Milan
Paris
Santa Clara
Singapore
Tokyo

To all those

who steered me through troubled waters

Acknowledgements

I am indebted to Professor Seidl and to Professor Herberg who made extensive comments on an earlier draft. I would like to thank my former colleague U. Schmidt who carefully went through the manuscript and gave me numerous helpful suggestions.

Furthermore, I am grateful to Jonathan Köhler and Kathrin Fach who improved the language style of this work and detected a number of typesetting errors. I gained much from stimulating discussions with F. Bulthaupt, K. Ehlers, P. Hammond, R. Lütz, R. Menges, M. Salge, M. Thiede, and S. Traub and from the excellent atmosphere in which I had the privilege to work. A good part of responsibility for this pleasant environment goes to G. Rahn.

Magdeburg, October 1997

Ludwig v. Auer

Contents

II Preferences, Choice, and Welfare in Universal Utility Models   99

1

Introduction

For most economic aspects of human behaviour, static decision models provide an insufficient description. More specifically,
they ignore the fact that preferences may change over time and
that at each point of time current preferences depend on aspects
which are associated with the past or the future. The neglect of
these phenomena may lead to results which have little in common with real life.

Dynamic decision models were developed in order to cope
with these complications. Spurred by the availability of new
mathematical tools such as optimal control theory and dynamic
programming, dynamic utility models mushroomed over the last
two decades. Various frameworks were developed featuring different restrictions on the way agents form preferences in an intertemporal environment.

Unfortunately, no systematic reappraisal of this literature exists. The survey provided in part I of this thesis attempts to
fill in this gap. It introduces a comprehensive classification system which allows for a coherent organization of all studies of
intertemporal choice under certainty and complete information.

The latter implies that the individual knows in advance all future preferences and choice possibilities.

In this survey we show that all dynamic utility models can be viewed as special cases of the class of *universal utility models*. It is therefore desirable to investigate intertemporal decision making in terms of this least restrictive framework. Accordingly, all findings of part II of this thesis are derived for the class of universal utility models.

Part II addresses fundamental aspects of intertemporal decision making which, in our view, have not been subjected to satisfactory scrutiny:

- How do agents decide in the presence of changing preferences, that is, how do they transform dynamic preferences into actual choices? Which difficulties arise from indifference and how can they be resolved?

- Is it possible to identify significant properties of choice which characterize an agent's actual choice behaviour?

- Under which conditions can dynamic decision problems be simplified to static ones without loosing any relevant information?

- Where are points of contact between the "traditional" theory of intertemporal choice and game theoretic equilibrium concepts?

Moreover, we address a fundamental question which interlinks the theory of dynamic utility and welfare theory:

- Is it possible to make judgements on an individual's welfare, even though preferences change over time?

The only existing study which tries to identify conditions for an affirmative answer to the last question, is by v. Weizsäcker (1971). Our exposition shows that he adopts a flawed line of reasoning.

The plan of this thesis is as follows: The survey presented in part I begins with a synopsis of dynamic utility models under certainty (chapter 2). It classifies all models into four broad classes. *Myopic utility models* represent the most restricted class. This framework is discussed in chapter 3. Myopic utility models are special cases of the more general class of *additive utility models*. A review of the latter is provided in chapter 4. Chapter 5 discusses the class of *recursive utility models*. Myopic, additive, and recursive models are nested in the class of *universal utility models*. In chapter 6, all those universal utility models are discussed which cannot be assigned to any of the other three classes.

This completes part I of this thesis. Both parts are self–contained. Hence, the reader interested only in the considerably more technical part II of this thesis may well skip over part I.

The opening chapter of part II (chapter 7) develops the universal utility framework in terms of decision tree terminology and introduces fundamental concepts such as *choice sets* and *choice mechanisms*. Moreover, it relates choice mechanisms to the notion of subgame perfection. Chapter 8 presents various properties which are attractive for the characterization of an agent's observed choice behaviour. One such property is denoted as *contractibility*. We demonstrate that the satisfaction of this property possesses far–reaching implications. Chapter 9 investigates whether contractibility allows to judge on an individual's welfare even though preferences change over time. Since contractibility is of great significance, one may ask how dynamic preferences have to look like in order to exhibit contractibility? This question is investigated in chapter 10. Up to here the analysis is restricted to deterministic decision problems. Chapter 11 extends the findings of chapters 7 to 10 to the case of uncertainty. Chapter 12 provides some concluding remarks.

Part I

A Survey of Intertemporal Choice under Certainty

2
Elements of Intertemporal Choice

2.1 Preliminaries

There are many ways to survey the intertemporal choice literature. In our view, a good comprehension of intertemporal choice first of all requires a well structured synopsis of dynamic utility models. Only then it is possible to assess a model's generality, and hence to appreciate its findings. To the best of our knowledge, no such classification of dynamic utility models and, in fact, no such survey exists in the literature.

Intertemporal decision making is a long established area of economic research. Hence, one would expect a number of comprehensive review articles. Surprisingly, only one such review exists. It is written by Shefrin (1996) and takes a route which differs from the one favoured in this thesis. Most importantly, it provides no classification system for dynamic utility models.

In our own survey we begin by establishing a framework which allows us to group together the existing models into a number of basic classes. It is appealing to classify intertemporal choice models according to the dynamic utility function they are based upon. We are going to identify four classes. Once these classes' main features are analysed and their relationships are highlighted, one may proceed to discuss the various issues appearing in the literature on intertemporal choice (e.g. dynamic consistency).

However, not all issues are uniformly interesting across the different classes of dynamic utility and some issues are specific to a certain class. For this reason, we separately analyse each class and discuss its related issues. If the same issue is also relevant in a different class we point this out and come back to it in the respective class.

A number of topics has been discussed in the literature only in the context of a particular class of dynamic utility model. Some issues, however, would be equally applicable to other classes. Our comprehensive approach allows to identify such deficiencies and to comment on them. For instance, the important issue of making welfare judgements in the presence of changing preferences has been discussed only in the simplest class of utility models. However, it could be analysed also in the context of more complex classes.

Another challenge to writing surveys is the question of notation. We use uniform notation throughout this survey, and in fact, throughout this thesis. It is the purpose to apply a notational standard which corresponds as closely as possible to common practice – if anything of this sort exists.

Furthermore, in this survey some assumptions are stated in a formulation which differs from the original. This is necessary in order to relate these assumptions to similar or identical ones appearing in other studies. As a side–effect, though, checking with the original sources may require a little more effort. However, in all cases it should be easy to see the equivalence between our formulation and the original.

2.2   A Basic Overview

Before we develop a more elaborate synopsis of all dynamic utility models we first point out some fundamental connections. We distinguish between the following four frameworks, each representing a particular class of dynamic utility model:

1. Universal Utility Models,

2. Recursive Utility Models,

3. Additive Utility Models,

4. Myopic Utility Models.

The most basic relationship between these models is depicted in Figure 2.1. The class of universal utility models is the most general type. Imposing additional restrictions, we can transform universal utility models into the other three classes. Some models exist which fall into both the additive and the recursive class. A subset of this intersection is known in the literature as the discounted utility model. In our survey the discounted utility model is discussed in the context of additive utility models. Another subclass of additive utility models we denote as myopic models. A small subset of myopic models is recursive, too. Having presented the broad categorization we can now become more detailed.

2.3   Dynamic Utility – A Synopsis

2.3.1   A Simple Example

In order to illustrate the implications of the various dynamic utility functions and functionals we sometimes refer to a simple example:

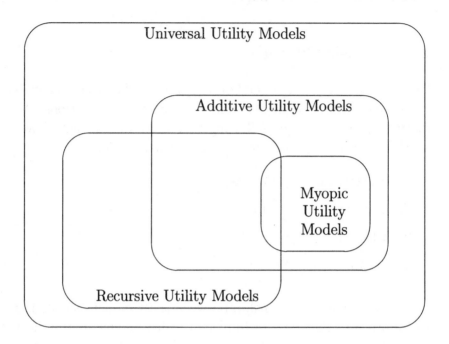

FIGURE 2.1. Four Classes of Dynamic Utility Models.

Example 2.1 *At each morning a Wall Street broker has to de-cide whether he wants his coffee white or black.*[1]

For simplicity, suppose there are only two mornings in the broker's life. For our categorization of models, the time hori-zon is irrelevant. The broker's dynamic decision problem can be represented in the decision tree of Figure 2.2. At the beginning of the first period (period 0), the broker finds himself at the initial decision node n_0. Deciding for white coffee brings him to decision node n_1, whereas deciding for black coffee brings him to n_1'. If, at n_1, he drinks another milky coffee, then he ends up

---

[1] We are aware of the fact that a Wall Street broker might be confronted with more important decision problems than that. Yet, the wrong morning drink may adversely affect his daily business.

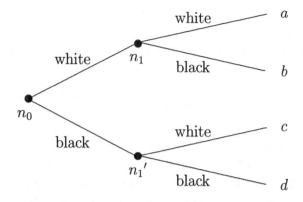

FIGURE 2.2. The Broker's Coffee Problem.

in a, and if he switches to black coffee, he finds himself in b. In this section, though, we are not concerned with the broker's decisions but exclusively with his preferences. The decisions which result from these preferences will be discussed in section 2.4.

2.3.2 Models without Instantaneous Utility

All *universal utility models* assume that at each decision nodethe agent's preferences form an ordering which can be represented by an (ordinal) intertemporal utility function. In Example 2.1 this makes three utility functions, one related to period 0 and two related to period 1. Note that the broker located at n_1, looks back at a different history than the broker at n_1'. Hence, the functional form of the respective utility functions may also differ and it may not be possible to merge them. Preferences between the options available at some given decision node may depend on all past and future periods. In period 1, for instance, the preference between white and black coffee may depend on period 0's coffee.

Let x_t indicate consumption in period t and x the complete consumption profile:[2]

$$x = (\ldots, x_{-1}, x_0, x_1, \ldots).$$

---

[2]It would be equally appropriate to interpret x_t as activities or characteristics. For simplicity, though, we usually refer to x_t as consumption.

The feasible set X, that is the set of all possible consumption profiles x, is assumed to be compact.

The intertemporal utility function of universal models can be written as

$$U_{\bar{h}_t} = U_{\bar{h}_t}(x_t, x_{t+1}, \ldots), \quad t \geq 0. \tag{2.1}$$

The subscript $\bar{h}_t = (\ldots, x_{t-2}, x_{t-1})$ is a *vector* which stands for "habits" in a broad sense. Habits capture consumption of past periods. Here habits enter the intertemporal utility function either as *parameters* or they even affect the *functional form* of $U_{\bar{h}_t}$.[3] As a consequence, the broker's universal utility function related to n_1 may differ from the one related to n_1'. Furthermore, comparisons across different nodes (cross–history comparisons) are not necessarily feasible.

Note that in universal utility models the utility function (2.1) is defined exclusively on options available in the respective period (the opportunity set). More specifically, no preferences are formed on options which were feasible in the past but are no longer in the opportunity set.[4]

The universal utility model with its utility function (2.1) is the framework part II of this thesis is based upon. It is the most general existing framework and should be credited to Hammond (1976a). However, his analysis is confined to the case of *strict preferences* and finite opportunity sets. The intertemporal utility function (2.1) also appears at the head of Figure 2.3 which together with Figures 2.4 and 2.5 provides a graphical companion to this section's discussion. As one moves downwards in these diagrams, additional restrictions on the utility function are imposed.

---

[3] This is not to say that consumption during future periods (x_{t+1}, x_{t+2}, ...) is irrelevant for the individual's decision. However, future consumption bundles are *arguments* of $U_{\bar{h}_t}$ and not *parameters* and they do not affect the *functional form* of $U_{\bar{h}_t}$.

[4] Allowing for such "retrospective preferences" could provide new and interesting insights. However, such an investigation would be outside the scope of this analysis (the universal utility model) and would complicate a coherent presentation. Furthermore, in order to derive tractable results for retrospective utility models, it appears inevitable that other restrictions must be imposed which are not necessary for the analysis of universal utility models. In the field of non–expected utility theory such an approach is

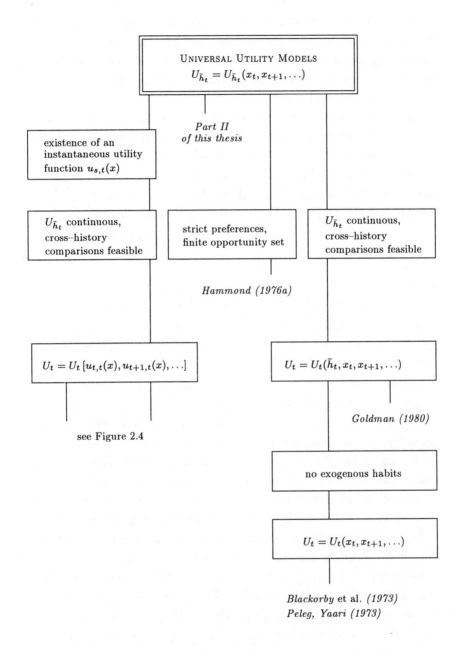

FIGURE 2.3. Dynamic Utility Models – Part I

Most dynamic utility models furthermore assume that (2.1) is a functional with *instantaneous utility functions* as its arguments. These models are investigated in due course. For the moment, the discussion is kept to those models which do without instantaneous utility.

Often it is assumed that intertemporal utility functions related to the same period are identical and directly comparable. As a consequence, in each period only one intertemporal utility function exists and cross–history comparisons are possible. Accordingly, habits $\bar{h}_t$ do not affect the *functional form* and they should be treated as *arguments* rather than *parameters*. This leads to the following intertemporal utility function:

$$U_t = U_t(\bar{h}_t, x_t, x_{t+1}, \ldots), \quad t \geq 0, \qquad (2.2)$$

where $\bar{h}_t = (\ldots, x_{t-2}, x_{t-1})$ is a vector of past consumption bundles (habits). In addition, these models postulate that the intertemporal utility function is continuous. Such a function is used in Goldman's (1980) brief study on implications of indifference on dynamic choice.

Habits can be interpreted as memories of past consumption. They are a device for modelling complementarities. The vector $\bar{h}_t$ in (2.2) emphasizes the fact that the satisfaction extracted from x_t, x_{t+1}, $\ldots$, may depend on past consumption encoded in $\bar{h}_t$. In Example 2.1, for instance, $\bar{h}_0$ captures aspects of the past, that is of periods -1, $-2, \ldots$. These are *exogenous habits* in the sense that the individual's decision at node n_0 can not change these aspects. In (2.2), $\bar{h}_t$ captures exogenous habits.

Such complementarities may also exist between x_t and x_{t+1}, say. For instance, the broker located at n_0 (that is the broker with habits $\bar{h}_0$) may develop a taste for black coffee upon drinking black coffee during period 0. This could be an aspect which favours option d (black coffee, black coffee) as compared to option c (black coffee, white coffee). These complementarities, too, are modelled by "habits".[5] Here, by choosing a particular path,

---

taken in the "regret theory" of Bell (1982) and Loomes and Sugden (1982), and also in Loomes and Sugden's (1986) "disappointment theory".

[5] They will be further formalized in section 2.3.3.

the broker can determine which habits he *wants to develop* in the future. Choosing black coffee for period 0, the broker may want to develop a habit for black coffee. Such habits are denoted as *endogenous habits*, in order to deliminate them from the exogenous type of habits discussed in the preceding paragraph.

Some theorists allow for endogenous though not for exogenous habits. As a consequence, (2.2) simplifies to

$$U_t = U_t(x_t, x_{t+1}, \ldots), \quad t \geq 0.$$

This states that the broker's intertemporal utility as evaluated in period 1 (U_1) is completely unaffected by his period 0 drink. Prominent studies applying this intertemporal utility function are Blackorby *et al.* (1973) and Peleg and Yaari (1973).

2.3.3   Models Based on Instantaneous Utility

Most dynamic utility models postulate that intertemporal utility can be represented by some functional U_t which can be perceived as the aggregate of a sequence of instantaneous utility functions. The latter are specified as

$$u_{s,t}(x) = u_{s,t}(\bar{h}_s, x_s, x_{s+1}, \ldots), \quad s \geq t, \qquad (2.3)$$

where $\bar{h}_s = (\ldots, x_{s-2}, x_{s-1})$ is a vector of past consumption bundles.[6]

(2.3) indicates that the instantaneous utility functions depend on both the period to which the *intertemporal* utility function is related, t, and the period of consumption, s. Changes of preferences over time which are induced by changing functional forms, are referred to as being exogenous. Conversely, if preferences change due to a change in the consumption profile x, one usually speaks of endogeneous preference changes.

The restriction $s \geq t$ merely says that intertemporal utility U_t depends on the instantaneous utility functions related to periods $t, t+1, \ldots$, and not on the instantaneous utility functions

---

[6] Only as a special case, a habit function h_s exists which maps each vector $\bar{h}_s$ into a numerical value. To this case we turn in due course.

of previous periods $(t-1, t-2, \ldots)$. Note, however, that this *does not* prevent past consumption bundles $x_{t-1}, x_{t-2}, \ldots$, from affecting intertemporal utility U_t. Since the argument of each instantaneous utility function is the complete consumption profile $x = (\bar{h}_s, x_s, x_{s+1}, \ldots)$, habit formation effects (complementarities) occur *within* the instantaneous utility functions. In short, $s \geq t$ does not preclude habits from affecting intertemporal utility. Habits (endogenous or exogenous) affect intertemporal utility indirectly via their impact on instantaneous utility. Note again that the existence of habit effects does not necessarily imply that some habit *function* can be established (see also page 18).

All models featuring instantaneous utility functions postulate that cross–history comparisons are feasible and that both $u_{s,t}(x)$ and U_t are continuous. One obtains the following intertemporal utility functional:

$$U_t = U_t\left[u_{t,t}(x), u_{t+1,t}(x), \ldots\right], \quad t \geq 0, \qquad (2.4)$$

where the first subscript of $u_{s,t}(x)$ indicates the period of consumption, s, and the second the period of the intertemporal utility function, t. From here two different routes can be taken, one leading to the class of additive models, the other leading to the class of recursive models (see Figure 2.4).

Recursive utility models assume that the instantaneous utility functions in (2.4) are independent of the period of consumption s. They only depend on the period of evaluation t, that is on the period of the intertemporal utility functional U_t. More importantly, the future is assumed to be separable from the present and past. Such a postulate bans any sort of habits. Specifically, recursive utility models can be expressed in the following form:

$$U_t = W_t\left[u_t(x_t), \hat{U}_t(x_{t+1}, x_{t+2}, \ldots)\right]. \qquad (2.5)$$

This says that intertemporal utility related to period t is a function of instantaneous utility from current consumption and aggregate utility derived from all future consumption. Recursive models are ususally based on an infinite time horizon. In these

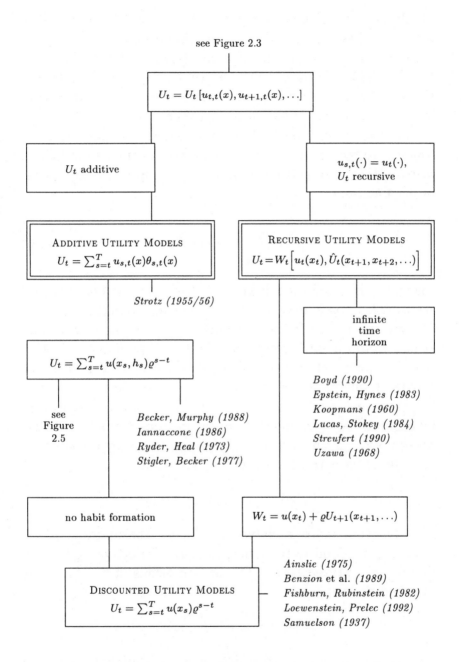

see Figure 2.3

$$U_t = U_t\left[u_{t,t}(x), u_{t+1,t}(x), \ldots\right]$$

U_t additive

$$u_{s,t}(\cdot) = u_t(\cdot),$$
$$U_t \text{ recursive}$$

ADDITIVE UTILITY MODELS
$$U_t = \sum_{s=t}^{T} u_{s,t}(x)\theta_{s,t}(x)$$

RECURSIVE UTILITY MODELS
$$U_t = W_t\left[u_t(x_t), \hat{U}_t(x_{t+1}, x_{t+2}, \ldots)\right]$$

Strotz (1955/56)

$$U_t = \sum_{s=t}^{T} u(x_s, h_s)\varrho^{s-t}$$

infinite
time
horizon

Boyd (1990)
Epstein, Hynes (1983)
Koopmans (1960)
Lucas, Stokey (1984)
Streufert (1990)
Uzawa (1968)

see
Figure
2.5

Becker, Murphy (1988)
Iannaccone (1986)
Ryder, Heal (1973)
Stigler, Becker (1977)

no habit formation

$$W_t = u(x_t) + \varrho U_{t+1}(x_{t+1}, \ldots)$$

DISCOUNTED UTILITY MODELS
$$U_t = \sum_{s=t}^{T} u(x_s)\varrho^{s-t}$$

Ainslie (1975)
Benzion et al. (1989)
Fishburn, Rubinstein (1982)
Loewenstein, Prelec (1992)
Samuelson (1937)

FIGURE 2.4. Dynamic Utility Models – Part II

problems it is common to stipulate that $\hat{U}_t$ and U_t are identical functions. The function W_t is called the *aggregator*.

Prominent studies in this field are Boyd (1990), Epstein and Hynes (1983), Lucas and Stokey (1984), Streufert (1990), and Uzawa (1968). The foundations to recursive utility theory were laid by Koopmans' (1960) seminal paper.

Additive utility models provide an alternative approach. In contrast to recursive models, they do not abstract from habits. Instead, they assume that (2.4) is additive in its instantaneous utility functions:

$$U_t = \sum_{s=t}^{T} u_{s,t}(x)\theta_{s,t}(x), \qquad (2.6)$$

where $\theta_{s,t}$ is usually referred to as the *discount function* and the time horizon T may or may not be infinite. In Example 2.1, the broker's utility U_0 can be modelled as the discounted sum of instantaneous utility experienced during periods 0 and 1. If the discount function is independent of consumption, then one arrives at the framework of Strotz's (1955/56) seminal study.

In additive utility models it is often assumed that instantaneous utility is independent of future consumption and that consumption in the past, $\bar{h}_s$, can be aggregated by a stationary *habit function* with habits evolving according to

$$h_s = h(\bar{h}_s) = h(x_{s-1}, h_{s-1}).$$

This function maps each vector of past consumption $\bar{h}_s = (\ldots, x_{s-2}, x_{s-1})$ into a numerical value h_s. Periods preceding period 0 are captured by h_0. The instantaneous utility functions can then be stated as

$$u_{s,t}(x) = u_{s,t}(h_s, x_s).$$

If the instantaneous utility functions are stationary (i.e. only endogenous changes in instantaneous utility may occur) and the discount function is exponential and depends exclusively on the time distance between the period of evaluation of intertemporal utility, t, and the period of consumption, s, then the intertemporal utility function (2.6) can be expressed as

$$U_t = \sum_{s=t}^{T} u(x_s, h_s)\varrho^{s-t}, \tag{2.7}$$

where ϱ is a constant discount factor.[7] Some important contributions which fall into this class of utility models are Becker and Murphy (1988), Iannaccone (1986), Ryder and Heal (1973), and Stigler and Becker (1977).

Following (2.7), the broker's intertemporal utility from the complete life span can be decomposed into instantaneous utility from period 0 and instantaneous utility from period 1. The former depends on the coffee in period 0 and habits inherited from his pre–broker life, and the latter depends on period 1's coffee and the habits effective in period 1 which, in turn, may well be effected by period 0's coffee.

If one is willing to accept an additional assumption one can transform (2.7) into the *discounted utility model*:

$$U_t = \sum_{s=t}^{T} u(x_s)\varrho^{s-t}. \tag{2.8}$$

This functional shows that instantaneous utility no longer depends on habits. Some influential studies related to this type of model are Fishburn and Rubinstein (1982) and Samuelson (1937). The work of Ainslie (1975), Benzion *et al.* (1989), and Loewenstein and Prelec (1992), however, cast serious doubt on the discounted utility model's descriptive validity.

Note that the discounted utility model can also be viewed as a special type of recursive model. Suppose the aggregator happens to be

$$W_t = u(x_t) + \varrho U_t(x_{t+1}, x_{t+2}, \ldots).$$

In view of (2.5), this yields

$$U_t = u(x_t) + \varrho[u(x_{t+1}) + U_t(x_{t+2}, x_{t+3}, \ldots)]$$

---

[7] The significant implications of these additional restrictions are explored in Strotz (1955/56). His work is discussed in section 4.3.

$$\begin{aligned} &= \ u(x_t) + \varrho u(x_{t+1}) + \varrho U_t(x_{t+2}, x_{t+3}, \ldots) \\ &= \ \ldots \\ &= \ u(x_t) + \varrho u(x_{t+1}) + \varrho^2 u(x_{t+2}) + \ldots, \end{aligned}$$

which is the discounted utility model (2.8).

Our framework makes it particularly transparent that the class of *myopic utility models*, too, is a subset of the additive class (see Figure 2.5). One merely has to postulate that in (2.7)

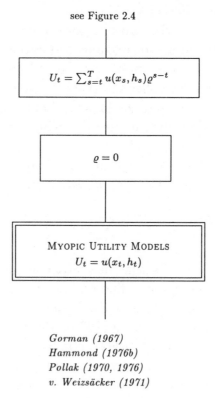

see Figure 2.4

$$U_t = \sum_{s=t}^{T} u(x_s, h_s)\varrho^{s-t}$$

$$\varrho = 0$$

MYOPIC UTILITY MODELS
$$U_t = u(x_t, h_t)$$

Gorman (1967)
Hammond (1976b)
Pollak (1970, 1976)
v. Weizsäcker (1971)

FIGURE 2.5. Dynamic Utility Models – Part III

the discount factor takes the value 0. One then arrives at

$$U_t = u(x_t, h_t),$$

which defines the class of myopic utility models.

In Figure 2.2 this implies that at n_0 the broker is indifferent between options a and b as well as between options c and d. He perceives life span utility U_0 solely in terms of period 0. Some well known studies related to this class of models are Gorman (1967), Hammond (1976b), Pollak (1970, 1976), and v. Weizsäcker (1971).

Before a separate exposition is provided for each class, one has to clarify a second fundamental aspect of intertemporal choice.

2.4   From Dynamic Utility to Actual Choices

The preceding section was exclusively concerned with the underlying preferences and their representation in the form of utility functions or functionals. Nothing was said about how these preferences lead to actual choices. In static models the rule for this transformation is a trivial thing. One simply chooses the most preferred option (provided this option is unique). In dynamic decision problems, however, sequences of orderings exist which may contradict each other, that is preferences may not be constant over time:[8]

Definition 2.1 *Preferences are constant if and only if for all consumption profiles* $(x_t, x_{t+1}, x_{t+2}, \ldots)$ *and* $(x_t, x'_{t+1}, x'_{t+2}, \ldots)$, *with at least one pair of bundles* $x_s \neq x'_s$, $s > t$:

$$U_{\bar{h}_t}(x_t, x_{t+1}, x_{t+2}, \ldots) \geq U_{\bar{h}_t}(x_t, x'_{t+1}, x'_{t+2}, \ldots) \qquad (2.9)$$

implies that

$$U_{\bar{h}_{t+1}}(x_{t+1}, x_{t+2}, \ldots) \geq U_{\bar{h}_{t+1}}(x'_{t+1}, x'_{t+2}, \ldots), \qquad (2.10)$$

where in (2.10) x_t *is an element of* $\bar{h}_{t+1}$.

As compared to static models, in dynamic models in which preferences may change it is more complex to determine a *rule*

---

[8]Some authors would speak of consistent preferences. Since this terminology may give rise to confusion with the notion of consistent *choice*, we prefer to speak simply of constant preferences. In Strotz (1955/56) such preferences are labelled as the "harmony case".

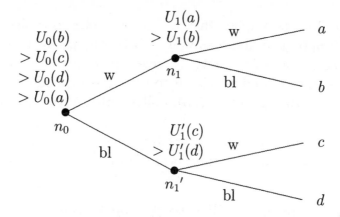

FIGURE 2.6. The Broker's Preferences.

for transforming preferences into actual choices. We denote such a rule as a *choice mechanism.*

Suppose the broker's preferences are as depicted in Figure 2.6. He knows the complete decision tree including all preferences. The path along which the broker moves through this decision tree, is determined by the sequences of orderings *and* the applied choice mechanism. Here it suffices to illustrate two such choice mechanisms: *naive* and *sophisticated* choice.[9] Both were introduced by Strotz (1955/56).

The broker applying a *naive* choice mechanism will, at each decision node, embark on the path which currently seems best. At n_0 this is b and at n_1 it is a. Hence, he ends up with white coffee throughout his short broker life. Notice that viewed from n_0 this is the worst of all possible choices.

The *sophisticated* broker takes account of his future decisions. In his consideration at n_0 he incorporates the fact that at n_1 his optimal choice is to move to a and at n_1' to follow c. Hence, c and a are the only options which will actually be followed and only a and c are relevant for his decision at n_0. Since $U_0(c) > U_0(a)$, he moves to n_1' and from there $U_1'(c) > U_1'(d)$ brings him to c. Note that again his actual choice (c) is not the option which at n_0 is his favourite one.

---

[9] Section 7.3 provides a comprehensive analysis of possible choice mechanisms.

Every intertemporal choice model applies some choice mechanism. Unfortunately, it is not always explicitly stated which one. Under certain assumptions on the intertemporal utility function the naive and the sophisticated choice mechanisms lead to identical actual choices. In these cases it is irrelevant which of the two mechanisms is used.

2.5   Recapitulation

In this chapter dynamic utility models were classified into four broad categories. The all embracing general class was denoted as the class of universal utility models. Under a set of additional assumptions one arrives at the class of recursive utility models. An alternative set of assumptions leads to the class of additive utility models and additional assumptions to the class of myopic utility models.

It was the purpose of this chapter to provide a sufficiently firm basis for a more detailed analysis of intertemporal choice models. The following chapters are each dedicated to one of the four classes of dynamic utility models and discuss the associated issues. The exposition begins with the most restrictive class which is the class of myopic models. In chapter 4 we turn to the more general class of additive utility models including the discounted utility model. Recursive models are presented in chapter 5. Chapter 6, finally, discusses all those universal models which cannot be assigned to any of the other three classes.

3
Myopic Utility Models

3.1 Preliminaries

Most utility models take account of the fact that utility derived from the current consumption bundle x_t is affected by past consumption patterns $\bar{h}_t = (\ldots, x_{t-2}, x_{t-1})$. Memories of past consumption are usually referred to as *habits*. The process in which past consumption is transformed into habits is called *habit formation*. Usually, habit formation is formalized by some stationary function h.

Myopic utility models are an extreme case of additive utility models in that they assume that future instantaneous utility is completely discounted. The myopic intertemporal utility function can be expressed in the form

$$U_t = U(x_t, h_t) = u(x_t, h_t), \qquad (3.1)$$

where

$$h_t = h(\bar{h}_t) = h(x_{t-1}, h_{t-1}), \qquad \frac{\partial h_t}{\partial x_{t-1}} > 0. \qquad (3.2)$$

As outlined on page 18, the variable h_t in (3.1) indicates habits effective in period t and accumulated in previous periods. We speak of (3.2) as the *habit function*. It maps each vector of past consumption $\bar{h}_t$ into a numerical value h_t. Note that the functional forms of U_t and h_t are assumed to be stationary over time.

The intertemporal utility function (3.1) is *degenerate* in the sense that it is an instantaneous utility function. The consumer who finds himself in period t cares only for the current period. Consumption in later periods is completely irrelevant.

In any dynamic choice problem the sequence of utility functions must be transformed into actual choice behaviour. Which choice mechanism prevails in myopic utility models? As illustrated in section 2.4, sophisticated choice involves some far ahead looking strategies which take into account future preferences. It would be paradoxical to apply such a far–sighted choice mechanism to short–sighted agents who care exclusively for current consumption. It is therefore not surprising, that all myopic utility models assume a naive agent.

Recall that a naive choice mechanism postulates that the decision maker ignores *future preferences*. In each period, the individual selects the option which, according to the preferences valid in that period, seems best. Translated into a consumer problem, in each period, a naive consumer simply maximizes the currently valid utility function (3.1) subject to the current budget constraint.

Note that current consumption x_t affects future utility U_{t+1}. The transmitter of these effects is the habit variable h_{t+1}. Since for the optimization in period t the naive agent cares exclusively for current utility U_t, he ignores the effect of x_t on h_{t+1}, and thus, on U_{t+1}.

Habits might be *harmful* in the sense that they raise necessary minimum quantities of some goods (e.g. tobacco) or they might be *beneficial* in the sense that the consumer learns to extract more satisfaction from a given quantity (e.g. listening to classical music). More generally, we define habits h_t^i (that is, habits which affect the satisfaction from consumption of commodity i) in the following way:

Definition 3.1 *Habits h_t^i are*

$$\text{harmful,} \quad \textit{if} \quad \frac{\partial u}{\partial h_t^i} < 0,$$

and they are

$$\text{beneficial,} \quad \textit{if} \quad \frac{\partial u}{\partial h_t^i} > 0.[1]$$

Myopic utility models are short–sighted with respect to two dimensions. Firstly, they postulate that the agent's intertemporal preferences do not depend on future periods, and secondly, they apply a choice mechanism which ignores future preferences. As a consequence, it is not sensible to use a myopic utility model as a durable goods consumption model. Such a model would require a more far–sighted agent.

Before we review the various studies, it is worthwhile to illustrate their underlying theme. For this purpose, a simple two–good example is introduced. Consider a myopic agent with the intertemporal utility function[2]

$$U = \ln(x_t^1 - \frac{1}{2}x_{t-1}^1) + \ln(x_t^2 - \frac{1}{2}x_{t-1}^2). \tag{3.3}$$

As throughout this study, subscripts indicate the period and superscripts indicate the commodity. Hence, a consumption bundle is denoted as $x_t = (x_t^1, x_t^2)$. Current utility is affected by last

---

[1] Note that in most models past consumption of some commodity i generates habits, h_t^i, that is habits which affect the satisfaction from current consumption of commodity i. However, past consumption of commodity i exerts no impact on h_t^j, $j \neq i$. In other words, the satisfaction derived from commodities j is independent from commodity i's past consumption. For instance, listening to classical music may increase our capacity to appreciate classical music in the future ($\frac{\partial u}{\partial h_t^i} > 0$). However, it does not affect our smoking habits (h_t^j). Some models exist, however, which allow for such cross effects (see section 3.2).

[2] In the literature degenerate intertemporal utility functions are often denoted as *short–run utility functions*.

period's consumption but not by earlier periods ($h_t^i = x_{t-1}^i$).
Suppose periodic income m_t and prices $p_t = (p_t^1, p_t^2)$ are constant over time. Maximization of (3.3) subject to

$$p^1 x_t^1 + p^2 x_t^2 = m \tag{3.4}$$

yields the first order conditions

$$\frac{1}{2(x_t^i - \frac{1}{2}x_{t-1}^i)} = \lambda p^i, \qquad i = 1, 2, \tag{3.5}$$

with λ being the Lagrange–multiplier. (3.5) leads to the *short–run demand functions*

$$
\begin{aligned}
x_t^i &= \frac{1}{2}x_{t-1}^i + \frac{1}{2p^i}(m - \sum_{j=1,2} \frac{1}{2}x_{t-1}^j) \\
&= \frac{1}{2}x_{t-1}^i + \frac{m}{4p^i}, \qquad i = 1, 2. \tag{3.6}
\end{aligned}
$$

Note that short–run demand x_t^i depends on previous consumption (habits) of both goods. As long as these habits change over time also short–rund demand x_t^i will change. Hence, for a stationary equilibrium of short–run demand, habits must remain constant, that is $h_{t-1} = h_t$. Since constant habits generate constant consumption, an equilibrium is characterized by $x_t = x_{t-1} = \ldots = \bar{x}$.

Suppose that in period $t - 1$ the consumption bundle was $x_{t-1} = \bar{x}$. Then (3.6) directly leads to the equilibrium demand functions

$$\bar{x}^i = \frac{m}{2p^i}, \qquad i = 1, 2. \tag{3.7}$$

These demand functions are usually denoted as *long–run demand functions.*[3] We follow this convention.

These long–run demand functions were derived by a two step procedure. To start with, first–order conditions (3.5) were derived from the maximization of utility function (3.3) subject

---

[3] Obviously, the derivation of long–run demand functions necessitates an infinite time horizon.

to the budget constraint (3.4). Solving these conditions under the equilibrium condition $x_t = x_{t-1} = \ldots = \bar{x}$, generated the long–run demand functions (3.7).

One may ask whether it is possible to arrive at these long–run demand functions in a more direct fashion. More specifically, can one create a function $Q(\bar{x})$, such that its maximization subject to the budget constraint (3.4) leads to the long–run demand functions (3.7), in the same way as the maximization of "short–run" utility function (3.3) subject to (3.4) leads to the short–run demand functions (3.6)? This is the classical "integrability problem". In our example,

$$Q = \ln \bar{x}^1 + \ln \bar{x}^2 \tag{3.8}$$

represents such a function. Maximization of (3.8) subject to (3.4) yields

$$p^1 \bar{x}^1 = p^2 \bar{x}^2.$$

Using (3.4), this condition leads to the long–run demand functions (3.7). Hence, these long-run demand functions can be "integrated".

Utility function (3.3) can be viewed as a conducive device for coding information about the individual's *short–run* demand behaviour. This information can be elicited by maximization of (3.3) subject to the budget constraint. Analogously, in $Q(\bar{x})$ information is encoded on the agent's *long–run* demand behaviour. This information, too, can be elicited by maximization subject to the budget constraint. For this reason, Gorman (1967) denotes $Q(\bar{x})$ as a *long–run demand indicator*.[4]

All studies of myopic utility models investigate the relationship between the utility function, $U(h_t, x_t)$, and the long–run demand indicator, $Q(\bar{x})$. Apart from Hammond (1976b), these studies are exclusively concerned with the consumer's typical choice problem: Choose the optimal consumption bundle x_t from an infinite compact budget set X_t.

---

[4] As will be explainded in section 3.3, the term is much better than the misleading term "long–run utility function", a terminology which was introduced by Pollak (1970). Paradoxically, Pollak (1976) provides a strong argument for abandoning the idea that the "long–run utility function" indicates any sort of satisfaction.

3.2 Utility Functions and Long–Run Demand Indicators

3.2.1 The Two–Good Case

Peston (1967):

In his brief contribution, Peston discusses the optimizing behaviour of a consumer whose preferences are represented in the following Cobb–Douglas utility function:

$$U = \bar{k} x_t^{1 \, h_t^1} x_t^{2 \, h_t^2}, \tag{3.9}$$

where $\bar{k}$ is some constant and

$$h_t^1 = h^1 \left(\frac{x_{t-1}^1}{x_{t-1}^2} \right), \tag{3.10}$$

$$h_t^2 = h^2 \left(\frac{x_{t-1}^1}{x_{t-1}^2} \right). \tag{3.11}$$

The habit functions (3.10) and (3.11) are assumed to be stationary over time, single valued, continuous, and, for $\frac{x_{t-1}^1}{x_{t-1}^2}$ non–negative, they are assumed to be positive and finite. Income m and prices $p = (p^1, p^2)$ are exogenously given and also remain constant over time. In each period the consumer maximizes (3.9) subject to the budget constraint

$$p^1 x_t^1 + p^2 x_t^2 = m.$$

The first order conditions of this naive optimization behaviour leads to

$$\frac{h_t^1}{h_t^2} = \frac{x_t^1 p^1}{x_t^2 p^2}.$$

The corresponding *long–run* (or equilibrium) first order conditions must lead to

$$\frac{h^1 \left(\frac{\bar{x}^1}{\bar{x}^2} \right)}{h^2 \left(\frac{\bar{x}^1}{\bar{x}^2} \right)} = \frac{\bar{x}^1 p^1}{\bar{x}^2 p^2}. \tag{3.12}$$

Peston shows that (3.12) implies the existence of long–run demand functions $\bar{x}^1(p, m)$ and $\bar{x}^2(p, m)$.[5] Can these demand functions be "integrated", that is, can they be rationalized by a long–run demand indicator? As alluded to before, such an indicator must generate condition (3.12). Peston asserts that this is possible. However, no justification is given for this statement. That Peston is right, though, is shown by v. Weizsäcker (1971).

Finally, Peston analyses how long–run demand reacts to changes in the relative prices p. He demonstrates that price vectors may exist, such that the (possibly unique) corresponding long–run demand vector $\bar{x}(p, m)$ is dynamically unstable.

v. Weizsäcker (1971):

In contrast to Peston, v. Weizsäcker does not presuppose any specific form of utility function. He considers the general class of utility functions leading to short–run demand functions

$$x_t^i = x_t^i(p, m, x_{t-1}^1, x_{t-1}^2). \tag{3.13}$$

Here, consumption in the previous period affects current demand (and utility), but consumption in the more distant path is irrelevant:

$$h_t^i = h^i(x_{t-1}), \qquad i = 1, 2. \tag{3.14}$$

As in Peston's model, income m is exogenously given. In his study v. Weizsäcker shows that if the utility function leads to short–run demand functions such that $-(1-\varepsilon) < \frac{\partial x_t^1}{\partial x_{t-1}^1} + \frac{\partial x_t^2}{\partial x_{t-1}^2} < 1 - \varepsilon$, everywhere for some $\varepsilon > 0$, then long–run demand functions exist which are stable and, to each price–income vector, yield a unique equilibrium $\bar{x}$. Furthermore, a long–run demand indicator $Q(\bar{x})$ exists which can be represented by a consistent set of isoquants in x^1, x^2–space.[6]

---

[5] Prof. Herberg pointed out to me that Peston's conditions are not sufficient, since equation (3.12) does not necessarily lead to a solution: $h^2 = 1$, $h^1 = 1 + \bar{x}^1/\bar{x}^2$, and $p^1/p^2 \leq 1$.

[6] To each set of prices and the associated income (that is to each budget constraint) the tangential point of the budget line to the $Q(\bar{x})$ isoquants indicates the individual's long–run demand.

Since the model considered by Peston is a special case of (3.13) and (3.14), v. Weizsäcker's results verify Peston's assertion that to his model a long–run demand indicator exists.

In his study, v. Weizsäcker presumes that his findings carry over to the case $n > 2$. Pollak (1976) rejects this view. He points out that in the two–good case demand functions which satisfy the budget constraint and are homogenous of degree zero always satisfy the Slutsky symmetry condition. These considerations suggest proceeding to models allowing for more than two goods.

3.2.2 The Many–Good Case

Gorman (1967):

Gorman discusses the same questions as Peston and v. Weizsäcker. He considers a naive agent with the following utility function:

$$U = U\left(x_t^1, x_t^2, \ldots, x_t^n, h_t^1, h_t^2, \ldots, h_t^q\right) = U(x_t, h_t), \qquad (3.15)$$

where q indicates the number of goods subject to habit formation. It is furthermore assumed that utility is differentiable in (x_t, h_t), and strictly increasing and strictly quasi concave in x_t. The habit functions h_t^j are assumed to be differentiable and to depend only on last period's consumption:

$$h_t^j = h^j(x_{t-1}), \qquad j = 1, 2, \ldots q. \qquad (3.16)$$

Since it is assumed that $q < n$, the class of utility functions analysed by Peston and v. Weizsäcker are not a subset of (3.15).[7]

Maximization of (3.15) subject to the budget constraint

$$\sum_{i=1}^{n} p^i x^i = m \qquad (3.17)$$

---

[7] (3.16) indicates that possibly all n commodities are involved in the *generation* of h_t^j, the habits affecting the satisfaction derived from commodity j. In other words, all commodities i may contribute to habit formation. Not all commodities i, however, are *subject* to habit formation. That is, not all commodites i possess a habit variable h_t^i (see also this chapter's footnote 1).

yields the standard first order conditions

$$\frac{\partial U(x_t, h_t)}{\partial x_t^i} = \lambda p^i, \qquad i = 1, 2, \ldots, n. \qquad (3.18)$$

The corresponding long–run first order conditions are

$$\frac{\partial U(\bar{x}, h(\bar{x}))}{\partial \bar{x}^i} = \bar{\lambda} p^i, \qquad i = 1, 2, \ldots, n.[8] \qquad (3.19)$$

Suppose a long–run demand indicator exists. By definition, maximization of such a long–run demand indicator $Q(\bar{x})$ subject to the linear budget constraint (3.17) must generate the first order conditions

$$\frac{\partial Q(\bar{x})}{\partial \bar{x}^i} = \bar{\lambda} p^i, \qquad i = 1, 2, \ldots, n,$$

which corresponds to (3.19). Otherwise the long–run demand indicator would indicate demand functions which are differnt from those derived from (3.19).

Gorman points out that it is not possible to make precise statements about such long–run demand indicators. In particular, he cannot show that it is a well behaved function. Instead, he considers the behaviour of the utility function (3.15) at stationary equilibrium points $\bar{x}$ and analyses first order approximations of the utility function in the neighbourhood of these equilibria.

Houthakker and Taylor (1970):

In chapter 5 of their book they consider a quadratic utility function formulated in *continuous* time:

$$U = x'k + h'b + \frac{1}{2}x'Kx + x'Bh + \frac{1}{2}h'Ch, \qquad (3.20)$$

where all members of the row vectors x' and h' are functions of time. Habits are related to consumption through

$$\dot{h} = \frac{\partial h}{\partial t} = x - Dh.[9] \qquad (3.21)$$

---

[8] Note that λ in (3.18) depends on h_t, that is on past consumption. Thus, it must be distinguished from the Lagrange multiplier $\bar{\lambda}$ in (3.19) which is derived on the presumption that past consumption equals current consumption.

[9] Integration of (3.21) yields as general solution:

$$h = e^{-tD_{ii}} \left(h_0 + \int_0^t x e^{tD_{ii}} \, dt \right),$$

All elements of the matrices B, C, D, K, and of the column vectors k and b are constants. K, B, and D are assumed to be diagonal and nonsingular, which implies that there is no substitution or complementarity in the utility function.

Peston (1967), Gorman (1967), and v. Weizsäcker (1971) consider habits related to good i (h_t^i) as being dependent upon *previous period's* consumption of *all* goods ((3.10), (3.11), (3.14), and (3.16)). In contrast, the habit formation hypothesis expressed in (3.21) says that h_t^i is a function of good i's past consumption $x_{t-1}^i, x_{t-2}^i, \ldots$. That is, (3.21) is more general with respect to the time dimension but less general with respect to the commodity dimension.

Maximization of (3.20) subject to the budget constraint

$$p'x = m$$

leads to the short–run demand vector

$$x = K^{-1}(\kappa p - k - Bh), \tag{3.22}$$

where

$$\kappa = \frac{m + p'K^{-1}k + p'K^{-1}Bh}{p'K^{-1}p}. \tag{3.23}$$

Short–run demand is linear in habits h and income m, though not in prices p. Houthakker and Taylor show that for short–run demand x to converge to an equilibrium $\bar{x}$ it is sufficient that

$$K_{ii} < 0 \tag{3.24}$$

$$\text{and} \quad K_{ii}D_{ii} + B_{ii} < 0, \tag{3.25}$$

where K_{ii}, B_{ii}, and D_{ii} are the diagonal elements of K, B, and D, respectively. The coefficients K_{ii} determine the change in *marginal* utility caused by a change of x_i. Since this change is usually decreasing, (3.24) is in line with static theory. Because D_{ii} is positive, (3.25) postulates that the harmful effect

---

where h and x are functions of time (see, for instance, Gandolfo (1996), p.162) and D_{ii} is a diagonal element of the diagonal matrix D. Note that if consumption were constant, then, as t becomes infinite, h would converge to $\frac{x}{D_{ii}}$.

of habits, B_{ii}, should not be so strong as to offset the combined effect of diminishing marginal utility and the depreciation rate.

Houthakker and Taylor (p.197–199) show that (3.22) and (3.23) imply that all commodities are substitutes (in the Slutsky sense) and that the same must be true for long–run demand $\bar{x}$. Their work is not concerned with the existence of a long–rund demand indicator.

The ultimate objective of Houthakker and Taylor is the estimation of consumer demand in the U.S. . In a later paper, however, Taylor and Weiserbs (1972) conclude that "..., the empirical results leave little question but that the linear expenditure system is a better vehicle of analysis than the additive quadratic model (p.464)." To the linear expenditure system we turn next.

Pollak (1970):

Gorman's (1967) work indicates that if one wishes to derive well–defined long–run demand indicators, one has to consider more narrowly defined classes of utility functions and habit functions. Pollak investigates a class of utility functions which is characterized by two properties: additivity (in goods) and quasi–homotheticity (i.e. linear Engel curves).[10] The simplest representative of this class is the Stone–Geary utility function

$$U = \sum_{i=1}^{n} \beta^i \log \left(x_t^i - h_t^i \right), \qquad (3.26)$$

with $x_t^i - h_t^i > 0$, $\beta^i > 0$, and $\sum_{i=1}^{n} \beta^i = 1$. (3.26) implies that habits are harmful (see Definition 3.1).

As do Houthakker and Taylor (1970), Pollak assumes that h_t^i is solely a function of good i's past consumption $(x_{t-1}^i, x_{t-2}^i, \dots)$. More specifically, the habit formation function is defined as

$$h_t^i = \alpha^i + \gamma^i g_t^i \qquad (3.27)$$

---

[10] These utility functions are modified versions of the Bergson family of utility functions. For a more detailed exposition of this class see Pollak (1971).

where $0 \leq \delta < 1$ and $0 \leq \gamma^i < 1$. (3.27) says that habits h_t^i depend linearly on g_t^i, a geometrically weighted average of past consumption. One may interpret α^i as the physiologically necessary quantity of good i and $\gamma^i g_t^i$ as the psychologically necessary quantity. For $\delta = 0$ and $\alpha^i = 0$, one would obtain the simple habit formation hypothesis that good i's stock of habits is proportional to this good's consumption during the previous period: $h_t^i = \gamma^i x_{t-1}^i$.[11]

If prices $p = (p^1, p^2, \ldots, p^n)$ and income m are constant over time, then maximization of (3.26) subject to (3.17) leads to the first order conditions

$$\frac{\beta^i}{x_t^i - h_t^i} = \lambda p^i, \qquad i = 1, 2, \ldots, n. \tag{3.29}$$

Solving these conditions yields the well known linear expenditure system.[12] The corresponding short–run demand functions are

$$x_t^i = h_t^i + \frac{\beta^i}{p^i} \left(m - \sum_{j=1}^{n} p^j h_t^j \right), \qquad i = 1, 2, \ldots, n. \tag{3.30}$$

Of each good, the agent purchases the "necessary quantity" h_t^i. The remaining budget $(m - \sum_{j=1}^{n} p^j h_t^j)$, transformed in real terms, is proportionally allocated to all goods. The factors of proportionality are the "weights" in the utility function, β^i.

From (3.30) it can be seen that short–run demand for good i depends on past consumption of all other goods, not only of good i's past consumption. Since $\beta^i \leq 1$ and in (3.27) $\gamma^i \geq 0$, the higher the consumption of good i in the past, the higher current consumption of good i and the lower current consumption of all other goods.

---

[11] Note that in (3.28) δ is identical for all goods. McCarthy (1974) shows that this assumption is not necessary for the derivation of Pollak's results.

[12] Estimations of the parameters in Pollak's model are provided in Pollak and Wales (1969). Phlips (1978) estimates an extended version in which income is no longer exogenously given but determined by maximization of a utility function which has "hours of leisure" as one of its arguments.

Next we turn to the long–run properties. As alluded to before, in a stationary equilibrium it must hold that $x_{t-1} = x_{t-2} = \ldots = \bar{x}$. Thus, (3.27) and (3.28) simplify to

$$h_t^i = \alpha^i + \gamma^i \bar{x}^i.$$

Substituting into (3.29) and using $\sum_{i=1}^n p^i \bar{x}^i = m$ leads to the long–run demand functions

$$\bar{x}^i = \tilde{h}^i + \frac{\tilde{\beta}^i}{p^i}\left(m - \sum_{j=1}^n p^j \tilde{h}^j \right), \qquad i = 1, 2, \ldots, n, \qquad (3.31)$$

where

$$\tilde{h}^i = \frac{\alpha^i}{1 - \gamma^i}$$

$$\text{and} \quad \tilde{\beta}^i = \frac{\frac{\beta^i}{1-\gamma^i}}{\sum_{j=1}^n \frac{\beta^j}{1-\gamma^j}}.$$

Note the similarity between the long–run demand functions (3.31) and the short–run demand functions (3.30).

Can (3.31) be "integrated"? That is, can one find some long-run demand indicator $Q(\bar{x})$ such that its maximization subject to the budget constraint (3.17) yields the long–run demand functions (3.31)? Obviously, a possible long–run demand indicator is

$$Q(\bar{x}) = \sum_{i=1}^n \tilde{\beta}^i \log\left(\bar{x}^i - \tilde{h}^i \right).$$

This long–run demand indicator is of the same functional form as utility function (3.26). Its parameters, however, depend on both the intertemporal utility function's parameters and those of the habit formation functions.

Pollak shows that long–run demand (3.31) is locally stable. He also investigates all alternative utility functions which are both additive (in goods) and quasi–homothetic. For those, too, he establishes local stability of the long–run demand functions and derives the long–run demand indicator.

he establishes local stability of the long–run demand functions and derives the long–run demand indicator.

In Pollak (1976), he proves that among the quasi–homothetic utility functions the additive ones are the only ones which generate long–run demand functions which can be "integrated".[13]

El–Safty (1976a), (1976b):

El Safty (1976a) generalizes Pollak's (1970) model. The utility function is assumed to be weakly separable:

$$U = U \left[z^1(x_t^1, h_t^1), z^2(x_t^2, h_t^2), \ldots, z^n(x_t^n, h_t^n) \right].$$

The habit formation functions take the form:

$$h_t^i = h^i(g_t^i), \tag{3.32}$$

$$g_t^i = (1 - \delta^i) \sum_{s=0}^{\infty} \delta^{is} x_{t-1-s}^i, \qquad i = 1, 2, \ldots, n. \tag{3.33}$$

For the special case that δ^i is identical for all i and that h_t^i depends linearly on g_t^i, we get (3.27) and (3.28), the habit formation hypothesis employed by Pollak (1970).

First, El–Safty considers two extreme cases:

$$\text{a)} \qquad z^i(x_t^i, h_t^i) = x_t^i - k^i \cdot h_t^i, \tag{3.34}$$

$$\text{b)} \qquad z^i(x_t^i, h_t^i) = l^i \cdot h_t^i \cdot x_t^i, \tag{3.35}$$

where k^i and l^i are positive constants. Case a) is denoted as the "pure habit forming case" and b) as the "pure learning case". Note that the pure habit forming case implies harmful habits and the pure learning case implies beneficial habits (see Definition 3.1). For these two cases, El–Safty presents properties characterizing the short–run demand functions.

For the general case, he provides sufficiency conditions for short–run demand to be stable, that is to converge to some long–run demand vector $\bar{x}$. He furthermore shows the uniqueness of this long–run demand vector.

---

[13] In his proof, though, he assumes that $h_t^i = \gamma^i x_t^i$. He asserts that the proof is valid also for the habit formation hypothesis (3.27) and (3.28).

It remains to answer the "integrability question". Can long–run demand be directly derived from some long–run demand indicator $Q(\bar{x})$? El–Safty proves that if stability is satisfied, then the long–run demand functions can be rationalized by a long–run demand indicator, if and only if the utility function is of the form

$$U = F\left[z^1(x_t^1, h_t^1) + z^2(x_t^2, h_t^2) + \ldots + z^q(x_t^q, h_t^q)\right]$$
$$+Z\left(x_t^{q+1}, x_t^{q+2}, \ldots, x_t^n\right),$$

where $q(\leq n)$ indicates the number of commodities which experience habit effects. Note that this finding is consistent with Pollak's (1970) result when $q = n$ and $z^i(x_t^i, h_t^i) = \beta^i \log(x_t^i - h_t^i)$.

In a companion paper, El–Safty (1976b) considers utility functions which satisfy two properties: They generate stable and unique long–run demand indicators, and they are of the form

$$U = U\left(x_t^1, x_t^2, \ldots, x_t^n, h_t^1, h_t^2, \ldots, h_t^q\right), \qquad q \leq n.$$

Habit formation is still given by (3.32) and (3.33). For these utility and habit functions, he derives necessary and sufficient conditions for the long–run demand functions to be rationalizable by a long–run demand indicator.

3.2.3   A Generalization to Choice Sets

Hammond (1976b):

All studies of myopic utility models presented so far, analyse basically the same choice problem: A consumer maximizes utility subject to an infinite compact budget set, that is a compact budget set with all commodities being freely divisible. This optimization results in demand functions. Hammond's work generalizes the idea of demand functions to the notion of choice sets. Such a concept allows him to extend the analysis to choice problems which are beyond the scope of consumer theory.

Hammond's approach is based on the general utility function (3.1) and the habit functions

$$h_t^i = h^i(x_{t-1}), \qquad i = 1, 2, \ldots, n. \tag{3.36}$$

$A \subseteq X$ denote the opportunity set from which the agent can choose. Suppose some option x_{t-1} was chosen in the previous period. If and only if for some $x_t \in A \subseteq X$ and for all $\tilde{x}_t \in A$ it is true that

$$U(\underbrace{x_t, x_{t-1}}_{h_t}) \geq U(\underbrace{\tilde{x}_t, x_{t-1}}_{h_t}),$$

then x_t is in the *choice set* $\hat{C}_{x_{t-1}}(A)$, where the subscript x_{t-1} indicates the option chosen in the *previous* period. Hammond denotes the sequence of choice sets $\hat{C}_{x_s}(A)$ with $s = t-1, t, t+1, \ldots$, as being *conservative* if the agent in each period sticks to the previous period's option, unless an alternative option exists which would make the agent strictly better off.

Two further concepts are introduced by Hammond. The *long–run preference relation* $\hat{P}$ between two options x_t and x_{t-1} is defined as follows:

$$x_t \hat{P} x_{t-1} \qquad \text{if and only if} \qquad U(x_t, x_{t-1}) > U(x_{t-1}, x_{t-1}).$$

This says that x_{t-1} was chosen in the previous period, and that x_t is chosen in the current period, even though x_{t-1} is still available. Obviously, if only for $\tilde{x}_t = x_{t-1}$ it is true that $\tilde{x}_t \hat{P} x_{t-1}$, then the agent has reached a stationary equilibrium. This is formalized by the notion of a *long–run choice set*:

$$\hat{C}(A) = \{\bar{x} \in A \mid \tilde{x} \hat{P} \bar{x}, \; \tilde{x} \in X \Rightarrow \tilde{x} \notin A\}.$$

Note that the long–run choice set $\hat{C}(A)$ may well be empty.

Hammond shows that the long–run preference relation $\hat{P}$ is acyclical if and only if for any *finite* set A, any conservative choice sequence converges. Naturally, the limit must be a long–run choice $\bar{x}$. Note that this result does not prove the existence of a long–run preference *ordering*. Furthermore, Hammond points out that for *compact* sets A his result does not necessarily go through. He his able to show, though, that for compact sets A together with $\hat{P}$ being acyclical, $\bar{x}$ is the unique long–run choice from A if and only if every conservative choice sequence converges to $\bar{x}$.

Hammond demonstrates how these results can be extended to the case in which the habit function (3.36) is replaced by Pollak's (1970) habit formation hypothesis (3.27) and (3.28).

In Pollak's (1970) model only those consumption bundles are feasible which satisfy $x_t^i - h_t^i > 0$ (see equation (3.26)). This implies that his model's consumption sets are not exogenously given, but change endogenously depending on past consumption. Suppose that X is a subset of the n–dimensional Euclidean space. Hammond discusses conditions under which the previous results carry over to the case of endogenously changing sets X. He shows that the long–run demand functions (3.31) derived by Pollak are globally stable. Pollak was merely able to prove local stability.

3.3 The Interpretation of Long–Run Demand Indicators

Since maximization of the long–run demand indicator leads to long–run demand functions, one might be tempted to interpret the long–run demand indicator as a "long–run utility function", representing an agent's "overall preferences" or welfare. In v. Weizsäcker (1971) the following justification for this interpretation is provided.

Consider the v. Weizsäcker framework (see section 3.2.1). Let x_0 and x_T indicate two consumption bundles such that

$$Q(x_0) > Q(x_T). \tag{3.37}$$

Is it possible to find a sequence of consumption bundles $(x_0, x_1, \ldots, x_T)$, such that

$$U(x_1,h_1) > U(x_0,h_1), U(x_2,h_2) > U(x_1,h_2), \ldots, U(x_T,h_T) > U(x_{T-1},h_T)? \tag{3.38}$$

The satisfaction of (3.38) assures that it is possible to go from x_0 to x_T in a finite number of periods such that in each period the consumer considers the move to the new bundle as an improvement. Provided a long–run demand indicator exists, v.

Weizsäcker is able to prove the following result: For all pairs of bundles x_0 and x_T, if and only if (3.37) is satisfied, then a sequence (3.38) exists.

He claims that this result serves as a satisfactory justification for viewing the long–run demand indicator as a yardstick for some "overall preferences". In this view, (3.37) would say that the move from x_0 to x_T makes the consumer (overall) better off.

Is v. Weizsäcker's argument convincing?[14] In our own view, it is not. Suppose a sequence such as (3.38) exists. What significance does such a sequence possess? As v. Weizsäcker himself points out, simultaneously to (3.38) an alternative sequence might exist, such that

$$U(x_0,h_1) > U(x'_1,h_1), U(x'_1,h'_2) > U(x'_2,h'_2), \ldots, U(x'_{T-1},h'_T) > U(x_{\tilde{T}},h'_{\tilde{T}}),$$
(3.39)

where x_T and $x_{\tilde{T}}$ are identical consumption bundles. Here, each move from x_0 to $x_{\tilde{T}}$ (the same pair of bundles as in (3.38)) makes the agent *worse* off. This is an extremely disturbing result and undermines Weizsäcker's justification. In the presence of some sequence (3.39), the existence of some sequence (3.38) is a very weak justification for interpreting the move from x_0 to x_T as an overall improvement.[15]

This argument can be easily illustrated by a simple example:

$$U = \frac{1}{2}\ln(x_t^1 - \frac{2}{3}x_{t-1}^1) + \frac{1}{2}\ln(x_t^2 - \frac{2}{3}x_{t-1}^2).$$
(3.40)

This utility function belongs to the class of utility functions considered by v. Weizsäcker. Maximizing (3.40) subject to

$$x_t^1 + x_t^2 = m$$

(that is $p^1 = p^2 = 1$), leads to the short demand functions

$$x_t^1 = \frac{2}{3}x_{t-1}^1 + \frac{1}{2}\left[m - \frac{2}{3}(x_{t-1}^1 + x_{t-1}^2)\right],$$

---

[14] The question considered by v. Weizsäcker is related to that analysed by Strotz (1955/56): Can a sequence of intertemporal utility functions be aggregated to some "overall utility function"?

[15] Notice that the starting point for both sequences (3.38) and (3.39) is x_0 and h_0. Hence, in period 1, also h_1 is identical in both sequences. Of course, the values for h_2, h_3, etc., differ in both sequences.

$$x_t^2 = \frac{2}{3}x_{t-1}^2 + \frac{1}{2}\left[m - \frac{2}{3}(x_{t-1}^1 + x_{t-1}^2)\right],$$

and the long–run demand functions:

$$\bar{x}^i = \frac{1}{2}m, \qquad i = 1, 2.$$

A corresponding long–run demand indicator is

$$Q = \bar{x}^1\bar{x}^2.$$

Let x^1 indicate kilograms of low–calorie food and x^2 kilograms of high–calorie food. Suppose that, on the one hand, the consumer does not want to put any weight on, on the other hand, he has this perpetual feeling of hunger. Consider the two bundles $x_0 = (12, 8)$ and $x_T = (10, 10)$, with $m = 20$. We get

$$Q(x_T) > Q(x_0).$$

Furthermore, it is easy to verify that if in the previous period consumption was x_0, then in the current period x_0 is preferred to x_T. This says that, being used to (12,8), in a binary choice situation the individual would not switch *directly* to (10,10).[16] Thus, the sequence (x_0, x_T) satisfies (3.39). However, if the individual moves from x_0 to x_T in a sequence of sufficiently small changes, then the new bundle is always preferred to the old one. In other words, we can generate a sequence satisfying (3.38) and v. Weizsäcker would claim that x_T is overall preferred to x_0.

In our own view, the existence of a sequence of improvements such as (3.38) is necessary for making statements about overall preferences x_0 and x_T, but it is not sufficient. It must be complemented by the following requirement: It is not possible to move from x_0 to x_T in a finite number of steps without any deterioration. In short, for x_0 and x_T no sequence must exist

---

[16] Conversely, if in the previous period x_T was the consumption bundle, then x_T is preferred also in the current period. Hence, in both cases the consumer prefers to continue former consumption rather than to switch *directly* to a new bundle.

such as (3.39).[17] This additional requirement may sound trivial. Yet, this merely reinforces the criticism against v. Weizsäcker's argument.

Pollak's criticism of v. Weizsäcker's conjecture points in the same direction: "... congruence with binary choice is the sine qua non of a utility function representing preferences,... (Pollak (1976), p.294)". Pollak concludes that a long–run demand indicator which does not square with binary choice situations is no more and no less than a convenient device for coding information about demand behaviour. It is inappropriate for representing an individual's overall preferences.

3.4 Recapitulation

Myopic utility models are short–sighted with respect to two dimensions: Current preferences do not depend on future consumption (degenerate intertemporal utility function) and for the selection of a particular path the decision maker ignores future preferences (naive choice mechanism).

All myopic utility models are primarily concerned with the derivation of long–run demand functions from some given (degenerate intertemporal) utility function. Most studies investigate whether these long–run demand functions can be derived more directly by the maximization of some so–called long–run demand indicator. In v. Weizsäcker's (1971) study it is proposed to interpret the long–run demand indicator as a yardstick for some notion of "overall preferences". We rejected this view. Our argument was similar to the objection expressed by Pollak (1976). In fact, Pollak's discussion caused some disenchantment with myopic utility models and initiated a number of studies which investigate the phenomenon of habit formation in more elaborate classes of models. Much work in this respect has been

---

[17] The property of *contractibility*, which will be introduced in chapter 8 of this study, takes account of this requirement. In any choice situation the "overall preferred" bundle would be chosen.

done in the context of additive utility models to which we turn next.

4
Additive Utility Models

4.1 Preliminaries

In additive utility models, intertemporal utility is specified as
a functional which is additive in its instantaneous utility functions:

$$U_t = \sum_{s=t}^{T} u_{s,t}(x)\theta_{s,t}(x), \tag{4.1}$$

where $u_{s,t}(x)$ denotes instantaneous utility and $\theta_{s,t}(x)$ is called
a discount function. The time horizon T may or may not be infinite. This functional postulates that instantaneous utility and
the discount rate related to period s may depend on present,
past, and future consumption bundles as well as on the vantage
point of evaluation t.

In most studies instantaneous utility in each period s is taken as being independent from future periods and from the perspective of evaluation t. The impact of past consumption on current instantaneous utility is usually captured in a stationary habit function of the form

$$h_t = h(\bar{h}_t) = h(\ldots, x_{t-2}, x_{t-1}).^1$$

Periods preceding period 0 are taken care of by h_0. If it is furthermore assumed that instantaneous utility is stationary and that the discounting solely depends on the *time distance* $s - t$, then (4.1) simplifies to:

$$U_t = \sum_{s=t}^{T} u(x_s, h_s)\theta_{s-t}.$$

In studies analyzing the phenomenon of addiction the discount function is usually taken to be exponential:

$$U_t = \sum_{s=t}^{T} u(x_s, h_s)\varrho^{s-t}, \tag{4.2}$$

where the *discount factor* ϱ is constant. If no habit formation takes place, (4.2) can be written as

$$U_t = \sum_{s=t}^{T} u(x_s)\varrho^{s-t}, \tag{4.3}$$

which is the discrete analogue to the *discounted utility model* as introduced by Samuelson (1937).

In myopic utility models (chapter 3) periodic income m was exogenously given. In additive utility models the budget constraint is given by some life–time wealth w_0 which has to be

---

[1] In order to deliminate their work from studies of habit formation embedded in a myopic utility framework (see chapter 3), many of the authors applying an additive utility model speak of *rational habit formation* (e.g. Pollak (1975), Stigler and Becker (1977), Spinnewyn (1981), Becker and Murphy (1988), Becker *et al.* (1991)). Since the diversity of applications has eroded the deliminating power of the label "rational", we avoid to use it in this survey.

allocated over time. Obviously, for myopic utility models this would be a pointless assumption. As long as utility is strictly increasing in consumption, the individual would spend complete life–time wealth in the first period.

The plan of this chapter is as follows: We begin by highlighting experimental studies testing the validity of the simplest additive utility model which is the discounted utility model (4.3). The exposition is kept to a minimum since Seidl (1996a) and Shefrin (1996) provide careful surveys of this issue. Referring to the work of Strotz (1955/56), the notions of changing preferences and dynamically consistent choice behaviour are discussed. Dynamic consistency is a basic assumption in all studies concerned with addiction and satiation. We provide a fairly detailed review of this literature. A different string of studies discusses questions arising from an econometric point of view. Since a detailed exposition can be found in Phlips (1983), we merely provide a sketchy account of this part of the literature.

4.2   The Discounted Utility Model and its Experimental Falsification

The simple utility functional (4.3) is known as the discounted utility model. It is additively separable over time. Both the instantaneous utility function and the discount function are stationary over time.

Numerous studies, though, challenge its descriptive validity. Most of these studies contribute their observation to the inappropriateness of the simple form of discounting. Accordingly, in order to make the underlying model consistent with the observations, they propose a modified discount function (e.g. Ainslie (1975)). Some studies preserve simple discounting but challenge the presumption that instantaneous utility is independent of both past consumption (habits) and anticipation of future consumption. Examples for this latter approach are Loewenstein (1987, 1988) and Loewenstein and Prelec (1992). Note, that the additive functional form of U_t remains unquestioned.

Reading through the literature, one may identify five major effects causing deviations from (4.3). For most of these effects, counterparts exist in the experimental literature challenging expected utility theory. This is hardly surprising, since both types of models feature the same additive structure.

In our discussion, we point out experimental studies which confirm the relevance of these effects. We do not describe, though, the various experimental designs. Summaries of most experiments can be found in Loewenstein and Thaler (1989), Loewenstein and Prelec (1992) and Seidl (1996a).

Perhaps the most prominent and best documented effect is the

- *Common Difference Effect*: It says that an individual might prefer a can of beer today to two cans tomorrow, but at the same time prefers two cans in a year and a day to one can in a year. More generally, preferences at date t between outcomes which accrue at different dates s and r possibly switch when both dates s and r are further delayed by a constant time interval.

  This effect calls in question the validity of the stationarity property which is crucial in Koopmans' (1960) and Fishburn and Rubinstein's (1982) axiomatic derivations of the discounted utility model.[2]

  The common difference effect suggests that the discount rate $(1-\varrho)$ decreases with an increasing time delay. This is confirmed, for instance, in Benzion *et al.* (1989). In Ainslie (1975, 1991) the phenomenon of decreasing discount rates is captured by a hyperbolic discount function.[3]

Hyperbolic discounting leads to complications with respect to an agent's choice behaviour. This aspect will be discussed in

---

[2] Also the studies of Dolmas (1995) and Harvey (1986) are concerned with the discounted utility model's axiomatic underpinnings.

[3] A very general form of hyperbolic discounting was proposed by Loewenstein and Prelec (1992). The relationship between the various forms of hyperbolic discounting is described in Seidl (1996a).

section 4.3 which presents the work of Strotz (1955/56). The following two effects are not related to Strotz's analysis.

- *Magnitude Effect*: This effect says that discount rates decline with the size of rewards. Empirical evidence is provided, for example, by Thaler (1981) and Benzion *et al.* (1989).

- *Gain–Loss Asymmetry*: This effect captures the phenomenon that discount rates for gains usually exceed those for losses. An experiment exhibiting this feature can be found in Loewenstein and Prelec (1992). As shown by Thaler (1981) and Benzion *et al.* (1989), this asymmetry is most pronounced for small rewards.

  In an experiment with non–monetary rewards reported by Loewenstein (1987) the subjects preferred an immediate loss over a delayed loss of equal value, whereas a delayed gain was preferred to an immediate gain of equal value.

The findings of Thaler (1981) and Benzion *et al.* (1989) suggest that correlations exist between the magnitude effect and the gain–loss asymmetry. Loewenstein's (1987) observation on the gain–loss asymmetry directly leads to the next phenomenon.

- *Negative Time Preference*: If the instantaneous utility functions in (4.3) are appropriate, then Loewenstein's (1987) result suggests negative discount rates. Similar findings are reported in Loewenstein and Prelec (1991). Work by Loewenstein and Sicherman (1991) on workers' preferences for wage profiles points in the same direction: workers prefer increasing wage profiles.

  It appears more likely, however, that these results indicate a misspecified instantaneous utility function rather than a negative discount rate. As pointed out by Loewenstein (1987), anticipation of future rewards (savouring and dread) or the memory of past rewards (habit formation) may affect current (instantaneous) utility. The preference

for increasing wage profiles, for instance, can be easily justified by a utility function which takes account of harmful
habits.

- *Delay–Speedup Asymmetry:* It states that the amount required to compensate for delaying a reward, from date s to
date r say, is much greater than the amount subjects are
willing to sacrifice to expedite this reward from r to s. In
other words, discount rates for delaying a gain are higher
than for speeding–up that gain. Such a result is reported,
for instance, in Loewenstein (1988).

The experiment by Benziol *et al.* (1989) also encompasses a
joint analysis of the delay–speedup and the gain–loss asymmetry. It is shown that losses have high discount rates for speed–
ups and low discount rates for delays, whereas gains exhibit low
discount rates for speed–ups and high discount rates for delays.
Note that the Loewenstein (1988) result is in line with the findings of Benziol *et al.* (1989).

Both asymmetry effects can be viewed as framing effects. Options are perceived as deviations from some reference level, an
idea which also lies at the heart of the habit formation literature
based on the Stone–Geary utility function (e.g. Pollak (1970)).

The studies presented cast serious doubts on the descriptive
relevance of the discounted utility model. More elaborate representations of preferences have to be developed. The rest of this
chapter is concerned with models which preserve the basic additive structure but modify the instantaneous utility function or
the discount function.

4.3 Dynamic Consistency and Pareto Optimality

Strotz (1955/56) analyses a consumer whose preferences, at each
period of time, can be represented by an intertemporal utility
function of the form

$$U_t = \sum_{s=t}^{T} u(x_s)\theta_{s-t}. \tag{4.4}$$

This model deviates from the discounted utility model only in terms of the discount function. Discounting still depends exclusively on the time interval $s - t$, but the dependence is not necessarily an exponential one.

Let w_0 indicate life time wealth and suppose that prices in all periods equal 1 and that the interest rate is zero. In each period t the individual who applies a *naive* choice mechanism maximizes (4.4) with respect to the sequence of consumption bundles $x_t, x_{t+1}, \ldots, x_T$, subject to the budget constraint

$$\sum_{s=t}^{T} x_s = w_t, \tag{4.5}$$

where

$$w_t = w_{t-1} - x_{t-1}. \tag{4.6}$$

Since in period t, x_{t-1} and w_{t-1} are given, w_t is exogenous. The corresponding first order conditions are

$$u'(x_s)\theta_{s-t} = u'(x_{s+1})\theta_{s+1-t}, \qquad \forall\, s \mid t \le s \le T - 1.$$

This says that discounted marginal (instantaneous) utility must be identical for all periods.

Suppose a sequence of consumption bundles exists which solves this optimization problem. We denote this sequence as $(x_t^{*t}, x_{t+1}^{*t}, \ldots, x_T^{*t})$, where the superscripts $*t$ indicate the sequence's optimality related to period t. This consumption profile should be interpreted as the naive agent's *planned choices*. In period t the naive consumer embarks on this sequence, that is, the consumer selects x_t^{*t}. In period $t + 1$ the subject is free to re-evaluate the sequences of consumption still open to him. Formally, in period $t + 1$,

$$U_{t+1} = \sum_{s=t+1}^{T} u(x_s)\theta_{s-t+1}$$

is maximized subject to

$$\sum_{s=t+1}^{T} x_s = w_t - x_t^{*t}.$$

Let the solution to this optimization be given by $(x_{t+1}^{*t+1}, x_{t+2}^{*t+1}, \ldots, x_T^{*t+1})$, where the superscript indicates that this consumption profile is optimal from the perspective of period $t+1$.

The question which lies at the heart of Strotz's analysis is the following: Is the sequence of consumption which is optimal from the perspective of period t, also optimal when evaluated from the perspective of period $t+1$? To put it differently, do *planned choices* change over time? More formally, we have to check whether

$$x_s^{*t} = x_s^{*t+1}, \qquad \forall\, s\,|\, t+1 \le s \le T. \tag{4.7}$$

Strotz shows that unless the discount function is an exponential function of the form

$$\theta_{s-t} = \varrho^{s-t},$$

(4.7) is not satisfied. If (4.3) is valid, however, then naive choice satisfies (4.7), regardless of w_0. He furthermore demonstrates that this result extends to more general models than (4.4)–(4.6). For instance, instantaneous utility could depend on past and future consumption or on features which are specific to period s.[4] Also the budget constraint may take more complex forms. It is crucial, however, that instantaneous utility and the budget constraint remain invariant with respect to the period of evaluation t.

Suppose the discount function is not exponential, and hence, (4.7) is violated. This implies that in some period t $(x_t^{*t}, x_{t+1}^{*t}, \ldots, x_T^{*t})$ is preferred to $(x_t^{*t}, x_{t+1}^{*t+1}, \ldots, x_T^{*t+1})$, but in period $t+1$ $(x_{t+1}^{*t+1}, x_{t+2}^{*t+1}, \ldots, x_T^{*t+1})$ is preferred to $(x_{t+1}^{*t}, x_{t+2}^{*t}, \ldots, x_T^{*t})$, with at least one pair of bundles such that $x_s^{*t} \ne x_s^{*t+1}$, $s > t$. This constitutes a *change of preference* (see Definition 2.1).

An agent applying a naive choice mechanism, in each period follows the path which currently seems best. If preferences

---

[4] To illustrate the latter possibility, Strotz uses the example of drinking champagne which at calendar date s, the subject's birthday, may cause greater satisfaction than at other dates.

change in each period, then the resulting sequence of actual choices is $(x_t^{*t}, x_{t+1}^{*t+1}, \ldots, x_T^{*T})$. Here, planned consumption must be modified in each period. The literature characterizes this phenomenon as *dynamically inconsistent choice behaviour*. In other words, in the presence of changing preferences (non–exponential discounting), a naive choice mechanism leads to inconsistent choices.[5]

Applying a *sophisticated* choice mechanism avoids inconsistent choice behaviour. That is, the agent sticks to his original planned consumption even though preferences are changing over time.[6]

Strotz attempts to derive a general procedure for calculating the sequence of consumption bundles which corresponds to the sophisticated choice mechanism. If the individual's discount function is non–exponential, then the subject should substitute the true discount function by an exponential one which, at $t = 0$, has the same slope as the true one. Strotz claims that the consumption profile which maximizes this modified utility functional is the sophisticated solution. It is correct that this procedure removes any inconsistency in the subject's choice behaviour, but as shown by Pollak (1968), it does not necessarily yield the sophisticated solution.

Note that dynamic consistency of naive choice leads to actual choices which are identical to those generated by a sophisticated choice mechanism. In other words, if naive choice is dynamically consistent, then there is nothing to learn from analyzing sophisticated choice behaviour.

The only other study which addresses inconsistency in the context of a theoretical additive utility model is by Phelps and Pollak (1968). They consider a growth model with two polar cases. As one extreme, it is assumed that generation 0 (the ana-

---

[5] In chapter 6 we will return to this issue in more detail.

[6] Strotz denotes the sophisticated choice mechanism as the "strategy of consistent planning (p.173)". As an alternative route to consistent choice behaviour, Strotz suggests that the agent should choose an option of precommitment. Unfortunately, he remains vague as to what he precisely means by precommitment. We will briefly discuss this issue on page 115.

logue to the individual decision maker in period 0, or the "current self") may commit the following generations (the analogue to the "future selves") on the behaviour which is optimal for generation 0.[7] Alternatively, the generation may have no impact on the decisions of future generations. It then pursues a second best strategy. It maximizes its own utility taking future decisions as given. This corresponds to the sophisticated choice mechanism.

Consider a consumption profile generated by consistent choices. Is this consumption profile Pareto optimal? Shefrin (1996) shows that if discounting is hyperbolic, then it is possible to construct a consumption profile which in each period exhibits lower consumption than the sophisticated consumption profile but Pareto–dominates the latter in the sense that at each point in time it is judged superior to the sophisticated profile.

What can be said about dynamic consistency in myopic utility models? In this class of models the agent in each period t is indifferent between those sequences of consumption bundles which start with the same bundle x_t. Constancy of preferences requires that, after having consumed x_t, the agent is indifferent between *all* options still available in period $t+1$. We know, however, that the agent in period $t + 1$ is indifferent only between those options which share the same consumption bundle $\hat{x}_{t+1}$. In short, myopic utility models exhibit changing preferences which, in turn, lead to dynamically inconsistent naive choices.

Having discussed the notion of consistency, one can turn to other aspects of dynamic utility models. A central issue is the economic rationale for phenomena like satiation and addiction.

---

[7]Notice that this case anticipates what McClennen (1990) introduces as the resolute choice mechanism. We will discuss this mechanism in section 6.2.1

4.4   Addiction and Satiation

4.4.1   Basic Concepts

Models investigating conditions for addiction and satiation preserve the discount function of the discounted utility model, but
generalize the instantaneous utility function. The typical intertemporal utility functional is (4.2). Its analogue in continuous
time is

$$U_t = \int_t^T u(x, h) \exp\left\{-\rho(s - t)\right\} ds, \qquad (4.8)$$

where x and h are shorthand writings for $x(s)$ and $h(s)$, the
continuous counterparts to x_s and h_s. The parameter ρ indicates the *rate of time preference*. The exponential form of the
discount function ensures dynamically consistent naive choices.
Hence, the applied choice mechanism (naive, sophisticated) is
of no relevance. All mechanisms lead to the same actual choices
and choice behaviour is consistent.

The earliest study which touches upon the notions of addiction and satiation is by Ryder and Heal (1973). The merit of
Stigler and Becker's (1977) work is to elaborate these issues and
to give more structure to the forces at work.[8] In their work they
emphasize that a phenomenon such as addiction is not necessarily the consequence of preferences which change over time. It
may occur even in the presence of constant preferences. In other
words, an individual may purposely get addicted. Becker and
Stigler's work paved the road for studies like Iannaccone (1984,
1986), Becker and Murphy (1988), and Becker *et al.* (1991),
which lend more formal stringency to the ideas expressed in
Stigler and Becker (1977).[9]

---

[8] Stigler and Becker (1977) make a big point of reformulating (4.8) as

$$U_t = \int_t^T u(z)e^{-\rho(s-t)} ds, \qquad (4.9)$$

where $z = z(x, h)$. They claim that (4.8) expresses the conventional view that tastes may
change whereas (4.9) represents unchanging tastes. In our own view, this is a semantic
over–subtlety. We continue to speak of changing tastes irrespective of whether it is $u(z(\cdot))$
which changes or $z(\cdot)$. Further problems arising from the Stigler and Becker approach
are discussed in Cowen (1989).

[9] A recent study which investigates the role of uncertainty is Orphanides and Zervos
(1995).

It is worthwhile to give a more detailed account of these later contributions. To begin with, we introduce the fundamental notions of addiction and satiation as introduced by Stigler and Becker (1977) and Iannaccone (1984, 1986). They characterize commodities according to the sign of $\dot{x}$ and $\dot{h}$ along the optimal path.[10]

Definition 4.1 *A commodity is*

> addictive, *if* $\dot{h}$ *and* $\dot{x}$ *have the same sign,*

and it is

> satiating, *if* $\dot{h}$ *and* $\dot{x}$ *have opposite sign.*

We add another definition.

Definition 4.2 *A commodity is*

> absorbing,   *if* $\dot{x} > 0$,

and it is

> abating,   *if* $\dot{x} < 0$.

The labels "addiction" and "satiation" may give rise to some misinterpretation. An addictive commodity does not necessarily lead to getting hooked to it. In other words, addiction is not necessarily absorbing. Correspondingly, satiation is not necessarily abating. This is illustrated in Figure 4.1

Suppose the individual has to allocate life time wealth over time and may spend it either on commodity i or on some other commodity j. Suppose further that habit formation occurs only with respect to commodity i, and that these habits h^i are harmful. Recall from Definition 3.1 that we denote habits related to commodity i as harmful if $u_{h^i} < 0$, and as beneficial if $u_{h^i} > 0$ (as long as we work in continuous time, the subscripts can be used to indicate partial derivatives). It is assumed that the other good j is neither subject to the formation of habits nor does it generate habits with respect to commodity i. In the following

---

[10]As usual, a dot on the variable indicates its derivative with respect to time. For simplicity, we suppress the superscript i.

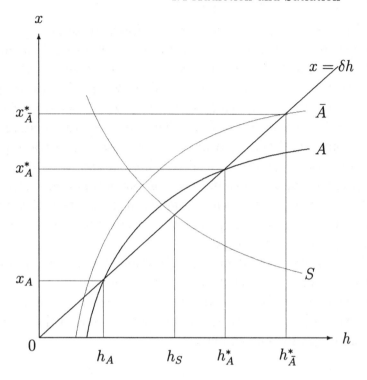

FIGURE 4.1. Phase Diagram of Present and Past Consumption.

discussion (and in Figure 4.1) we suppress the superscript i: $x^i = x$ and $h^i = h$.

Let $\dot{h} = x - \delta h$. Then the straight line $x = \delta h$ represents the *loci* of steady states, that is of *long–run demand*. If good x is addictive, then the optimal relation between current consumption x (short–run demand) and habits h might be as arbitrarily depicted by the increasing curve A. For stocks of habits below h_A, the individual consumes less and less of the *addictive* good! The addictive commodity is abating.

If good x is satiating, then the relation between x and h might be as depicted in curve S. Habits below h_S cause the individual to consume more and more of the *satiating* commodity! The satiating commodity is absorbing. The labels "addiction" and "satiation" correspond to intuition only for $\dot{h} > 0$, that is for $h > h_A$ if good x is addictive, and for $h > h_S$ if it is satiating.

The same figure can be used to illustrate some aspects discussed in Becker and Murphy (1988). Suppose x is a harmful addictive good. An initial stock below h_A leads to the stable steady state 0 and initial stocks above h_A to the stable steady state (h_A^*, x_A^*). The steady state (h_A, x_A) is unstable. Suppose the consumer is in (h_A^*, x_A^*). A fall in the price of x (or an increase in income) shifts curve A upwards to $\bar{A}$, say. As a consequence, current consumption vertically jumps on the new path $\bar{A}$ and then moves along this path towards the new stable steady state $(h_{\bar{A}}^*, x_{\bar{A}}^*)$. This expresses a fundamental implication of habit formation: The long–run response to price or income changes exceeds the short–run response.

The stronger the degree of addiction, the steeper is path A and the more pronounced is the long–run response to a price or income change. This would contradict the commonly held belief that the demand for strongly addictive goods is fairly insensitive to price and income changes.

4.4.2   Optimal Control Models

For a more rigorous analysis of addiction and satiation, optimal control theory is a natural candidate. An early application of optimal control to habit formation can be found in Ryder and Heal (1973).[11] Also the econometrically oriented paper by Lluch (1974) exploits this convenient tool.[12]

Iannaccone (1986) develops an optimal control model which allows for a more stringent investigation of the relationship between the notions of harmful (beneficial) and addictive (satiating) commodities. He considers the intertemporal utility func-

---

[11] They analyse optimal growth under habit formation. A related model is in Boyer (1978). Growth models featuring other forms of intertemporally dependent preferences were introduced by Chakravarty and Manne (1968), Wan (1970), Samuelson (1971), and Majumdar (1975).

[12] For a study which applies dynamic programming techniques rather than optimal control see Orphanides and Zervos (1994).

tional (4.8).[13] Habits h are determined by the equation of motion

$$\dot{h} = f(x, h) - Dh,$$

where $f(x, h)$ are gross additions to the habit stock and depreciation D is a non–negative diagonal matrix with diagonal elements δ^i.[14] The other equation of motion specifies how wealth w evolves over time:

$$\dot{w} = rw - px.$$

Prices p and the interest rate r are assumed to be constant. The boundary conditions are

$$
\begin{aligned}
h(0) &= h_0, \\
w(0) &= w_0, \\
\text{and} \quad w(T) &\geq 0.
\end{aligned}
$$

The current–value Hamiltonian is

$$H = u(x, h) + \mu[f(x, h) - Dh] + \xi[rw - px],$$

where μ indicates the current value shadow price of having an additional unit of habit stock, and ξ the current value shadow price of wealth. The necessary conditions for a maximum are

$$H_x = u_x + \mu f_x - \xi p = 0 \tag{4.10}$$

and the respective costate equations and transversality conditions:

$$
\begin{aligned}
\dot{\xi} &= -H_w + \rho\xi, & (4.11) \\
\dot{\mu} &= -H_x + \rho\mu, & (4.12) \\
\xi(T)w(T) &= 0, & (4.13) \\
\mu(T)h(T) &= 0, & (4.14)
\end{aligned}
$$

---

[13] In optimal control models the derivation of tractable solutions very much hinges on the specific concavity and convexity assumptions. It is worthwhile, therefore, to list Iannaccone's assumptions: Instantaneous utility $u(x, h)$ is assumed to be concave in (x, h) jointly and to be twice differentiable with $u_{x^i} > 0$ and $u_{x^i x^i} < 0$. In addition, for each good i, either $u_{h^i} > 0$ or $u_{h^i} < 0$. In order to rule out corner solutions, Iannaccone assumes that $\lim_{x^i \to 0} u_{x^i} = \infty$.

[14] Gross additions $f = (f^1, f^2, \ldots, f^m)$, are assumed to be non–negative and twice continuously differentiable with $f^i_{h^j} \geq 0$, $f^i_{x^j} \geq 0$, for all i and j. Furthermore, $f^i_{h^j} > 0$ if and only if $sgn(u_{h^j}) = sgn(u_{h^i})$, and $f^i_{h^j} = 0$ otherwise. Finally, it is assumed that $f^i_{h^i h^i} \leq 0$ if h^i is beneficial and $f^i_{h^i h^i} \geq 0$ if h^i is harmful.

where T is finite and ρ is the rate of time preference appearing in (4.8). Since $h(T) > 0$ and $\xi(T) > 0$ (due to $p_T > 0$), (4.13) and (4.14) become $w(T) = 0$ and $\mu(T) = 0$.

Equation (4.10) says that at each point of time marginal utility derived from an additional unit of commodity i must be identical to the joint effect of this unit on the decrease of wealth (ξp^i) and on habits (μf_{x^i}). Note that in myopic utility models the latter effect drops out and we would obtain the standard first order conditions $u_x = \xi p$.

Using former results by Léonard (1981), Iannaccone shows that any consumption path which solves the system (4.10) to (4.14) is optimal, continuous, and differentiable with respect to time. For beneficial habits h^i, the corresponding shadow price μ^i is positive and for harmful habits it is negative. The shadow price of wealth ξ is non–negative and, unless all habits h^i are harmful, it is strictly positive.

In order to derive further results Iannaccone assumes that habits are *commodity specific*.[15] Before stating Iannaccone's main results one has to explain another characteristic of commodities. It is related to the change in marginal intertemporal utility caused by a commodity's consumption. *Adjacent complementarity* describes the fact that an increment in consumption at some date t raises the marginal intertemporal utility of this commodity at nearby dates relative to distant dates. An individual whose consumption during his youth is increased would shift consumption away from his old days towards his midlife period. With *distant complementarity* consumption would be shifted from midlife to old age.[16]

Recall that in a steady state there is neither addiction nor satiation. These two notions merely provide information about

---

[15] In his model this implies that $f_{x^j}^i = 0$ and $f_{h^j}^i = 0$ for all $j \neq i$ and that the ratio of u_{x^i} and u_{h^i} depends only on x^i and h^i. Note that in the myopic utility models of Pollak (1970, 1976) and in the simple illustration of section 4.4.1 habits are commodity specific, too. The same is true for a study by Spinnewyn (1981) which we will briefly discuss in section 4.5.

[16] Since the intertemporal utility is captured by a functional the above sort of statement involves the concept of Volterra derivatives. For an illuminating exposition and application to dynamic utility see Ryder and Heal (1973).

the path on which steady states are possibly reached. Iannaccone shows that in the neighbourhood of a stable steady state commodity i is addictive (satiating) if it is characterized by adjacent (distant) complementarity.[17]

For $D = 0$, he relates his results to the work of Pollak (1970, 1976), Spinnewyn (1981), and Stigler and Becker (1977). In Pollak (1970, 1976) and Spinnewyn (1981) h^i and x^i enter utility in additive form: $z^i = x^i - h^i$ (the pure–habit forming case, see El–Safty (1976a)). Imposing the same additional conditions as in Spinnewyn (1981) or Pollak (1970, 1976) one arrives at the simple result that good i is addictive (satiating) if it is harmful (beneficial).

Stigler and Becker (1977) consider the case in which z^i is a multiplicative function of x^i and h^i (the learning case). Let the elasticity $\sigma^i = -u_{z^i z^i} \frac{z^i}{u_{z^i}}$ measure intertemporal substitutability of z^i. Then, imposing the additional conditions of Stigler and Becker, Iannaccone shows that for commodity i with beneficial habits h^i, $\sigma^i > 1$ is necessary for addiction and $\sigma^i \leq 1$ is sufficient for satiation. For a commodity with harmful habits, $\sigma^i > 1$ is necessary for satiation and $\sigma^i \leq 1$ is sufficient for addiction.

Becker and Murphy (1988) analyse a model which in many respects is similar to Iannaccone's (1986), though they restrict it to the two–good case.[18] They consider an individual who has to allocate life time wealth over time. Habits are commodity specific and only occur with respect to one commodity but not with respect to the other. Let us denote the commodity which is subject to habit formation as commodity x. It is assumed that x is characterized by harmful habits. Another important modification in comparison to Iannaccone, is the dropping of the assumption: $\lim_{x \to 0} u_x = \infty$. Now boundary solutions may occur.

---

[17]Obviously, steady state analysis requires to transform (4.10)–(4.14) into an infinite time horizon problem. For questions of existence and stability see Iannaccone (1984).

[18]The reader of Becker and Murphy (1988) should be warned that equation (5) is correct only if $\sigma = r$. Furthermore, in the second condition of (6) a minus sign is missing.

We begin by considering a *myopic* utility model with per period income m which is assumed to be constant over time. The
derivative $u_{xh} > 0$ says that higher past consumption of x increases marginal utility of current consumption. As a consequence, x rises with increasing habit stocks h, and x falls with
decreasing stocks h. In either case, the two variables x and h
move in the same direction and the commodity can be characterized as being addictive (see Definition 4.1).

In additive utility models such as (4.8) the agent no longer
simply weighs marginal utility of x against marginal utilty of
the alternative good, but incorporates into the optimization the
adverse consequences of higher current consumption on future
habit stocks (see equation (4.10)). Hence, for addiction, u_{xh}
must be greater than these adverse consequences.[19]

It is shown in Becker and Murphy (1988) and Becker (1992)
that, for $\dot{h} = x - \delta h$ and a list of further assumptions on the
shape of u and the equations of motion, a necessary and sufficient condition for addiction near a steady state is

$$\tilde{u}_{xh} > -\frac{\tilde{u}_{hh}}{\rho + 2\delta}, \qquad (4.15)$$

where $\tilde{u}_{xh}$ and $\tilde{u}_{hh}$ are local approximations near the steady
state. If one imposes the (debatable) assumption that the harm-
ful effect of habits becomes more pronounced as the stock of
habits rises $(\tilde{u}_{hh} < 0)$, then $\tilde{u}_{xh} > 0$ is a necessary condition for
addiction. (4.15) suggests that the stronger the decision maker
discounts the future, ρ, and the more pronounced the depreciation of past stocks, δ, the more likely is addiction.[20]

---

[19] Iannaccone (1984, p.21) defines a good as *reinforcing* if $u_{xh} > 0$, and as *moderating*
if $u_{xh} < 0$. The reader of Becker *et al.* (1991) should be warned that in their paper
reinforcement is used synonymously with addiction, where the latter is defined as in
Definition 4.1.

[20] For a model in which all goods are beneficial rather than harmful see Boyer (1983).
He shows that under certain assumptions the infinite time horizon problem can be re-
duced to a two–period problem. Under some additional assumptions it is possible to
investigate the stability of steady states.

4.5   Econometric Aspects

From an econometrician's point of view, an additive utility model is useful if it is amenable to the estimation of certain parameters of demand. Two aspects are of particular relevance:

(a) How do consumers allocate life–time wealth over time? Obviously, this involves saving decisions.

(b) Given some period's total expenditure, how is it spread over the various commodities or classes of commodities?

A study which analyses certain habit formation hypothesis in the context of *myopic* decision making is Pollak and Wales (1969). Recall, however, that in the myopic class of utility models in each period some income m is exogenously given *and spent*. In each period exogenous income m automatically equals total expenditures. No saving decisions are considered.

In contrast, additive utility models do allow for saving decisions. Lluch (1973), for instance, extends the linear expenditure system by introducing a saving decision. Habits, however, are assumed to be fixed (no habit formation). The same is true for a related paper by Phlips and Spinnewyn (1982). They propose a model which allows for a two stage optimization. In a first step, for each period total expenditure is determined (the savings decision), and in a second step these expenditures are allocated among the various goods.

In a similar model, Boyer (1983) adds a habit formation hypothesis. Boyer's study, however, is not the first which generates measurable demand equations reflecting habit formation and saving decisions. The first model is due to Lluch (1974). He, too, allows for habit formation and saving decisions and derives complete demand systems, though not in a two stage process. Two forms of instantaneous utility functions are considered by Lluch, the Stone–Geary form and the quadratic form. Aggregating period t's demand over all goods yields total expenditures in period t. These, in turn, allow Lluch to infer the saving decisions. Estimations of the influence of habit formation on labour supply are provided in Bover (1991), Hotz *et al.* (1988), and Kennan (1988).

Spinnewyn (1981) shows that models in which instantaneous utility depends only on "uncommited consumption", $z^i = x^i - h^i$, can be transformed into decision models without habit formation. In other words, that part of Lluch's (1974) analysis which is based upon the Stone–Geary utility function is redundant. Spinnewyn furthermore demonstrates that myopic optimization behaviour (with habit formation) is empirically indistinguishable from intertemporal optimizing behaviour. Pashardes (1986) points out that this observational equivalence goes through only for the linear expenditure system. In the almost ideal demand system, for instance, equivalence requires that the instantaneous utility functions must be of the Cobb–Douglas type.

4.6   Endogenously Changing Discount Factors

Strotz's (1955/56) work shows that if the discount function depends on the time interval $s-t$ (that is, on the distance between the period at which instantaneous utility accrues and the period of intertemporal utility evaluation) and the discount factor ϱ is fixed, then any non–exponential discount function leads to inconsistent naive choices. In order to avoid this complication, models of addiction and satiation (section 4.4) and econometrically oriented studies (section 4.5) preserve the simple discounting rule of the discounted utility model. Experimental deviations from the discounted utility model are then taken care of by generalizing the instantaneuous utility function.

Alternatively one could preserve the simple instantaneous utility function but modify the discount function. For instance, it may no longer be exogenously given by s and t but may depend on aggregated past consumption. These endogenous changes can be formalized by making the discount factor ϱ a function of habits.

The intuitive underpinnings for this approach date back to Fisher: "It has been noted that a person's rate of preference for present over future income, given a certain income stream, will be high or low according to the past habits of the individual. If he has been accustomed to simple and inexpensive ways, he finds it fairly easy to save and ultimately to accumulate a little property. ... Reversely, if a man has been brought up in the lap of luxury, he will have a keener desire for present enjoyment than if he had been accustomed to the simple living of the poor (1930, p.337)."

A recent study taking this approach is Shi and Epstein (1993). For a single-good economy, they analyse the following functional:

$$U_0 = \int_0^\infty u(x) \exp\left\{-\int_0^t h[g(s)]\, ds\right\} dt. \qquad (4.16)$$

In this functional $g(s)$ denotes a weighted average of past consumption with weights declining exponentially into the past:

$$g(s) = \delta \int_{-\infty}^s x \exp\left\{\delta(r - s)\right\} dr, \qquad (4.17)$$

where $g(0) = g_0 \geq 0$ and $\delta > 0$.[21] Note that this model assumes an infinite time horizon. Recall that in additive utility models ϱ is called the *discount factor*. It indicates the marginal rate of substitution between consumption at two adjacent dates s and $s + 1$. If this factor is constant, then the *rate of time preference*, $\rho = \varrho^{-1} - 1$, is constant too. In the Shi and Epstein model, however, the discount factor is not constant and the derivation of the rate of time preference becomes more involved. It is shown in their study that the rate of time preference depends on past, present and future consumption.

Shi and Epstein investigate how wealth accumulates in an economy with heterogenous agents. The result differs considerably from the one obtained in models based on the discounted

---

[21] Note that (4.16) implies that $s \geq 0$. This does not preclude earlier consumption from affecting the discount function. (4.17) expresses the fact that to each date's habit index, $g(s)$, the arguments x extend infinitely into the past.

utility model such as Becker's (1980). He shows, for instance, that in an economy with heterogenous households and constant discounting, in the steady state all capital is held by the household with the lowest rate of time preference. In the Shi and Epstein model, all consumers can own positive levels of wealth.

It is furthermore demonstrated that x is an addictive good. Shi and Epstein also use their model for a discussion of questions arising in the theory of international trade.

4.7   Recapitulation

Additive utility models are general enough to encompass a wide range of questions arising in the context of intertemporal decision making. The additivity assumption ensures that these questions can be analysed by a comparatively modest mathematical apparatus. Techniques such as the calculus of variations and its modern generalizations (optimal control theory and dynamic programming) are sufficient for the derivation of economically meaningful results.

In this chapter we surveyed experiments challenging the descriptive validity of the discounted utility model. This lead us to investigate richer additive utility models. Such models, however, are prone to dynamically inconsistent behaviour. We outlined conditions for consistency. This set the stage for a review of the literature on addiction and satiation. Furthermore we provided a brief account of econometrically oriented studies and discussed a model with endogenously changing discount factors.

Critics of additive utility models object that for some purposes the simple summation of instantaneous utility is unnecessarily restrictive and leads to questionable results. In the following chapter we discuss a class of dynamic utility models which circumvents additivity. As was pointed out in chapter 2, however, dispensing with additivity is not costless. In order to obtain tractable non–additive models one has to impose alternative restrictions.

5
Recursive Utility Models

5.1 Preliminaries

In section 4.2 a number of studies was reviewed which challenge
the descriptive validity of the discounted utility model. The ré-
sumé to be drawn from that review is that in a number of choice
situations the simple discounted utility model is a poor reflection
of an agent's actual behaviour. In order to capture choice behaviour more accurately one must look for less restrictive utility
models.

The approach followed in the rest of chapter 4 was to preserve
the basic additive structure of the intertemporal utility functional but to modify the instantaneous utility function or the
discount function. In sections 4.4 and 4.5 models with modified
instantaneous utility functions were presented. In section 4.6 we

discussed the Shi and Epstein (1993) model, which sticks to the discounted utility model's simple instantaneous utility function but dispenses with the idea of constant discount factors.

Recursive utility models follow a route which is similar to the one taken by Shi and Epstein. Recursive models, too, allow the discount factor to change over time. However, they impose new restrictions. Instantaneous utility must be independent of the time of consumption s and it must be possible to express the intertemporal utility functional as

$$U_t = W_t[u_t(x_t), \hat{U}_t(x_{t+1}, x_{t+2}, \ldots)]. \tag{5.1}$$

If $U_t = \hat{U}_t$, then (5.1) leads to to

$$U_t = W_t\{u_t(x_t), W_t[u_t(x_{t+1}), W_t(x_{t+2}, \ldots)]\}.^1$$

Following Koopmans (1960) terminology, W_t is called the *aggregator*. (5.1) says that intertemporal utility can be expressed as a function of current consumption and aggregated (sub–)utility from future periods. This expresses the fact that future consumption is weakly separable from consumption in previous periods.[2] The marginal rate of substitution between x_{t+1} and x_{t+2}, say, is independent of "past" consumption x_t. Such a separability property precludes any habits.

In (5.1), the subscript t attached to U and W intimates that all functions are related to an agent who evaluates consumption profiles from the perspective of time t.[3]

In recursive utility models the consumer's time horizon is commonly supposed to extend to infinity.[4] Such an assumption avoids the difficulties connected with the inclusion of bequests. An infinite time horizon is particularly convenient for Koopmans' (1960) axiomatic derivation of these models. The cost, however, is in terms of technical complications. For instance,

---

[1] In many models $u_t(x_t) = u(x_t) = x_t$. Some authors refer to the instantaneous utility function as *felicity function*.

[2] Notice that for the discounted utility model also the reverse is true. Past consumption is weakly separable from future consumption.

[3] This aspect is stressed also in Koopmans *et al.* (1964, p.85).

[4] An exception is the recursive model formulated in Blackorby *et al.* (1973).

the tools of dynamic optimization (optimal control theory and dynamic programming) have to be adapted to it.

The foundations of recursive utility can be attributed to Koopmans (1960). He formalizes a method used by Fisher (1930) who points out that the *rate of time preference* should depend on the consumption profile.[5] Due to the separability property, however, the rate of time preference must be independent of *past* consumption. However, it may depend on present and future consumption.[6]

Besides descriptive reasons also theoretical considerations suggest a non–constant rate of time preference. In optimal growth models, for instance, fixed rates of time preference and interest imply that consumers either save or borrow without limit. Only for the knife–edge case in which the interest rate equals the rate of time preference, one obtains an interior steady state. As mentioned above (section 4.6), a model by Becker (1980) shows that in an economy with heterogeneous households, in the steady state all capital is held by the household with the lowest rate of time preference. A variable rate of time preference leads to more appealing results.

Thanks to their attractive features (dynamic consistency, amenability to dynamic programming) recursive utility models flourished over the last fifteen years. They have been applied to a number of areas. Optimal growth is studied, for instance, in Becker *et al.* (1989), Benhabib *et al.* (1987), Boyd (1990), Dolmas (1996), Hertzendorf (1995), Lucas and Stokey (1984), and Uzawa (1968). Based on the Uzawa (1968) model, Calvo and Findlay (1978), Findlay (1978), and Obstfeld (1981, 1982) investigate issues of international trade.[7]

Recently, two surveys of recursive utility have been published, one by Becker and Boyd (1993) and one by Streufert (1996).

---

[5]Recall that in additive utility models with constant *discount factor*, ϱ, the *rate of time preference* is $\rho = \varrho^{-1} - 1$ which is a constant, too.

[6]Recall that in the Shi and Epstein (1993) model discussed in section 4.6, discounting depends on *past*, present, and future consumption.

[7]Recursive utility has been applied also to models featuring uncertainty. Some recent contributions are Epstein and Melino (1995), Joshi (1995), and Ma (1993).

Both surveys provide a thorough exposition of the complex technicalities involved in recursive utility models. This allows us to put this chapter's emphasis on different matters.

Based on more specific forms of the utility functional we illustrate the nature of recursive utility and how one can distil the rate of time preference. Moreover, we investigate the descriptive validity of recursive utility models and relate it to the discounted utility model. Finally, we discuss the aggregator approach to recursive utility which deviates from the original path taken by Koopmans (1960) and Uzawa (1968), and examine whether recursive models satisfy dynamic consistency.

5.2   The Aggregator and the Rate of Time Preference

For the sake of expository clearness, we continue to look at the discrete time form. It is common practice to define the local rate of time preference as

$$\rho(\bar{x}) = \frac{\frac{\partial U}{\partial x_t}}{\frac{\partial U}{\partial x_{t+1}}} - 1, \qquad (5.2)$$

evaluated at $x_t = x_{t+1} = \bar{x}$. The consumer is indifferent between $\bar{x}$ now and $(1 + \rho)\bar{x}$ next period. Note that for homothetic preferences the local rate of time preference is independent of the level of consumption $\bar{x}$.

Suppose that preferences based on a recursive utility model lead to dynamically consistent naive choices.[8] As we explained in section 4.3, dynamically consistent choices imply that a consumer, who is free to revise his plan, today will find that path optimal which in the previous period was regarded as optimal. It therefore suffices to consider the agent's optimization in period 0:

$$U_0 = W_0[u(x_0), \hat{U}_0(x_1, x_2, \ldots)]. \qquad (5.3)$$

---

[8] This assumption will be qualified in section 5.4.

The subscript 0 attached to U, u, and W indicates that all functions are related to an agent who evaluates consumption profiles from the perspective of period 0. In order to avoid clustering the notation, we suppress this subscript in the rest of this section. Recursive models with inifinite time horizon usually stipulate that $\hat{U} = U$. Now, (5.3) can be expressed as

$$U = W[u(x_0), U(x_1, x_2, \ldots)]. \tag{5.4}$$

A particularly simple recursive utility model is the discounted utility model. The aggregator corresponding to (4.3) is

$$W = u(x_0) + \varrho U(x_1, x_2, \ldots).$$

For $x_t = x_{t+1}$, one obtains $\frac{\partial u}{\partial x_t} = \frac{\partial u}{\partial x_{t+1}}$, and hence, $\frac{\partial U}{\partial x_t} / \frac{\partial U}{\partial x_{t+1}} = \varrho^{-1}$. Then, according to (5.2), the discounted utility model's rate of time preference is

$$\rho = \varrho^{-1} - 1.$$

We now proceed to more complex frameworks. Perhaps the most important class of recursive utility models is defined as follows:

$$U = \sum_{t=0}^{\infty} v(x_t) \exp\left\{ -\sum_{s=0}^{t} u(x_s) \right\}, \tag{5.5}$$

where both $u(\cdot)$ and $v(\cdot)$ can be interpreted as instantaneous utility functions. Two important special forms can be derived from (5.5).[9] If $u(x_s)$ is set equal to $\pi[v(x_s)]$, where $\frac{\partial \pi}{\partial v} > 0$, then one arrives at

$$U = \sum_{t=0}^{\infty} v(x_t) \exp\left\{ -\sum_{s=0}^{t} \pi[v(x_s)] \right\}. \tag{5.6}$$

This is the discrete time form of Uzawa's (1968) model.[10] He was the first to apply the idea of recursive utility to a continuous time framework.

---

[9]Such a model's connection to optimal control theory is demonstrated in Hayakawa and Ishizawa (1993).

[10]The relationship between the continuous analogue to (5.6) and Uzawa's original formulation is documented in Epstein and Hynes (1983).

Alternatively, if it is postulated that $v(x_t) = -1$ for all t, then one obtains from (5.5) the discrete analogue to the continuous model elaborated by Epstein and Hynes (1983):

$$U = -\sum_{t=0}^{\infty} \exp\left\{-\sum_{s=0}^{t} u(x_s)\right\}, \qquad (5.7)$$

where $u > 0$, $\frac{\partial u}{\partial x} > 0$, and $\frac{\partial^2 u}{(\partial x)^2} < 0$. Notice that $U < 0$ and if $x_t > x'_t$ for all t, then $U(x_0, x_1, \ldots) > U(x'_0, x'_1, \ldots)$. Functional (5.7) could equivalently be written as

$$U = \exp\{-u(x_0)\}\left[-1 - \underbrace{\sum_{t=1}^{\infty} \exp\left\{-\sum_{s=1}^{t} u(x_s)\right\}}_{U(x_1, x_2, \ldots)}\right], \qquad (5.8)$$

which highlights the recursive structure expressed in (5.4). (5.8) reflects the fact that recursive utility models dispense with the time–additive structure of the intertemporal utility functional.Obviously, the relative evaluation between two consumption paths x and x' which are identical with respect to bundle x_0, depends only on periods later than period 0. Furthermore, subutility from these latter periods is defined by the functional U, that is by the same functional as utility from the complete time horizon (5.7).

What does functional (5.7) imply for the rate of time preference? From (5.8) one obtains:

$$\frac{\partial U}{\partial x_0} = -\exp\{-u(x_0)\}\frac{\partial u}{\partial x_0}[-1 + U(x_1, x_2, \ldots)]$$

$$\frac{\partial U}{\partial x_1} = \exp\{-u(x_0)\}\frac{\partial u}{\partial x_1}U(x_1, x_2, \ldots),$$

which, for $x_0 = x_1$, leads to

$$\rho = -\frac{1}{U(x_1, x_2, \ldots)} . \qquad (5.9)$$

This demonstrates that the rate of time preference at period 0 is a function of aggregate future consumption. Specifically, future consumption is aggregated by the utility functional U. Since the assumptions imposed on (5.7) imply that this functional is negative, we observe positive discounting. Delaying a given consumption profile by some time distance decreases U (that is, increases its absolute value).

Note that in this model the rate of time preference is a function of *future* consumption but not of *present* consumption. One may argue that the rate of time preference should depend also on current consumption. A hungry individual discounts given future five–course meals quite differently from an individual currently enjoying a luxurious free buffet. For the continuous framework, though, this criticism must be toned down. In Uzawa's (1968) continuous model the rate of time preference is a function of future *and* present consumption, but the relationship is much more complex than (5.9).

More importantly, (5.9) says that the larger aggregate future consumption, the larger the rate of time preference. The same is true for the rate of time preference derived in Uzawa's (1968) and in Lucas and Stokey's (1984) studies. In our view, this feature lacks some intuitive appeal. A very poor man, who faces the risk of starvation is relatively unconcerned with future consumption. The more likely the man's survival, the more weight will be put on the future and the lower the discount rate. Epstein (1987) and Obstfeld (1990), though, argue that for higher consumption levels it is reasonable to assume that the discount rate starts rising again.

5.3   Descriptive Validity

Authors of recursive utility models claim that their models represent a significant improvement as compared to the discounted utility model. Since the surveys by Becker and Boyd (1993) and Streufert (1996) are written by protagonists of recursive utility, one cannot expect to come across a critical assessment of the above claim. This section provides some remarks on this issue.

In order to write the intertemporal utility functional as in
(5.1) one has to swallow rather restrictive assumptions, which
are illustrated in the following simple two–period example:

Example 5.1 *In the first period an individual can choose between a fat meal (fish and chips) and a light meal (a selection
of fresh fruit). In the second period, which immediately follows
the meal, the choice is given between vodka and green tea.*

Recursivity expressed in (5.1) implies that, if the individual
prefers the option (fish and chips, vodka) to (fish and chips, tea),
then (fruit, vodka) is preferred to (fruit, tea).[11] It is needless to
point out the vastly different effects vodka entails in a stomach
stuffed with fat food and a stomach filled with fruit.

We saw in chapters 3 and 4 that myopic and additive models
may take account of such effects by introducing habits. Recursive models, in contrast, abstract from habits. In this respect
they fall behind the richer additive models discussed in sections
4.4 and 4.5.

Recall, however, that the *discounted utility model*, too, ab-
stracts from habits. Is it true, then, that compared to the discounted utility model, recursive models constitute a major advance? Discounted utility models have their domain in the theory of capital accumulation and optimal growth. Most of their
popularity they owe to their simple structure and normative
appeal. Nevertheless, some theorists propose to abandon discounted utility models in favour of recursive models. In their
view, the latter allow for more realistic modelling. A number
of authors justify recursive utility by pointing out that it leads
to more appealing *results* than the discounted utility model. In
our own view, this is a debatable argument. A more important
yardstick for "realistic modelling" is whether the recursive utility models' *assumptions* on economic actors correspond more
closely to *observed behaviour* than do the assumptions of the

---

[11] In Koopmans' (1960) axiomatic derivation of recursive utility this is the Independence Assumption (3b) (p.292). Streufert (1996) denotes this assumption as "strictly
after-1 separability". Note that (5.1) furthermore implies that if (fish and chips, vodka)
is preferred to (fruit, vodka), then (fish and chips, tea) is preferred to (fruit, tea).

discounted utility model. Unfortunately, no experimental studies exist examining the descriptive validity of recursive models.

Nevertheless, there is scope for judgement on the descriptive validity of recursive utility models. Our optimism is due to the fact that central axioms necessary for the derivation of the discounted utility model are also necessary for the derivation of the recursive utility model.[12]

In section 4.2 we described a number of effects challenging the validity of the discounted utility model. The defense of recursive utility models is well–grounded only if the various experimental violations of the discounted utility model do not apply to recursive models.

The work of Koopmans (1960, 1972) and Fishburn and Rubinstein (1982) show that "stationarity" is a crucial assumption in the axiomatic derivation of both, the recursive and the discounted utility model. Stationarity says that delaying two consumption paths by the same time interval and filling the gap by consumption bundles which are identical for both paths, does not alter the ranking between the two consumption paths. As pointed out in section 4.2, the *common difference effect* captures the phenomenon that preferences between two rewards may switch when both rewards are delayed by a constant time interval. Hence, the common difference effect casts serious doubts on the validity of stationarity. In other words, the common difference effect not only questions the discounted utility model but also the recursive utility model.

The *magnitude effect* suggests that the rate of time preference declines with the size of reward. This phenomenon could be captured by recursive utility models. We saw in section 5.2, however, that most recursive models exhibit *just the opposite*. The rate of time preference increases with the size of the reward (e.g. Epstein and Hynes (1983), Uzawa (1968), Lucas and Stokey (1984))! Our impression is that the assumption of increasing rates of time preference is a concession towards the derivation of *stable* steady states rather than a concession to reality. In

---

[12]For details see Koopmans (1972).

other words, appealing behavioural assumptions are sacrificed for appealing findings.

The *gain–loss asymmetry* implies that the rates of time preference for gains are higher than those for losses. This effect is reflected in recursive utility models. In (5.9), for instance, U takes a larger *absolute* value for losses than for gains. In view of $U(\cdot) < 0$, the rate of time preference for gains exceeds those for losses.

Do recursive models allow for *negative time preference*? In section 4.2 we pointed out that negative time preference might be due either to anticipation of future rewards or to the memories of past rewards. As mentioned above, weak separability expressed in (5.1) requires that the past exerts no effect on the rate of time preference. Hence, recursive utility models can incorporate anticipation of future consumption but not memories of the past. Notice that Epstein and Hynes (1983) and Uzawa (1968) exclude negative rates of time preference.

The *delay–speedup asymmetry* suggests that the rates of time preference for delaying some gain from period 0 to period 1, say, are higher than for speeding up that gain from 1 to 0. Recursive utility models predict that no such asymmetry exists. In (5.9), for instance, ρ applies to both a delay and a speedup. The rates of time preference depend only on consumption profiles.

In sum, we feel that this account cannot support the claim that recursive utility models represent a significant step towards more behavioural plausibility. Only the gain–loss asymmetry is captured more accurately. The magnitude effect, in contrast, diametrically contradicts the recursive utility hypothesis. In our view, this appears insufficient to outweigh the costs of recursive models in terms of additional analytical complexity and obscured interpretation.

5.4   Further Aspects

5.4.1   The Aggregator Approach

In his original work, Koopmans' (1960) derives conditions which ensure that a utility functional U_t can be represented by some aggregator W_t. Besides two fairly uncontroversial technical postulates on continuity and sensitivity, he imposes an independence and a stationary condition. The restrictive nature of the independence condition was illustrated in Example 5.1 (p.76) and the stationary condition was discussed on page 77 in connection with the common difference effect.

Even if all these "Koopmans conditions" are satisfied, it could be an ambitious task to derive the corresponding aggregator. This difficulty can be avoided, if one starts with the aggregator.

Boyd (1990) argues that such an aggregator approach is appealing for several reasons. Firstly, it is much easier to specify an aggregator than a recursive utility function. Koopmans *et al.* (1964), for instance, propose an aggregator which reflects a certain hypothesis on agent's behaviour (increasing marginal impatience). The corresponding utility functional, though, does not possess a closed form expression. Secondly, it might be simpler to incorporate behavioural constraints in aggregators than in utility functionals. Finally, it is simpler to ensure dynamic consistency.

Unfortunately, the aggregator approach obscures the actual utility functional. It is, therefore, desirable to construct the corresponding utility functional. Studies by Boyd (1990) and Streufert (1990) derive conditions on the aggregator which ensure that the utility functional can be recovered.

Becker and Boyd (1993) point out that the idea to take the aggregator as primitive can be traced back to Fisher (1930) and Hayek (1941). The first modern paper to start with the aggregator rather than with the utility functional is Lucas and Stokey (1984).

5.4.2 Weak Separability and Dynamic Consistency

It has been pointed out by various writers (e.g. Becker and Boyd (1993, p.60,62), Epstein and Hynes (1983, p.612)) that the recursive structure of (5.1) ensures constant preferences, and hence, dynamically consistent choice behaviour. In contrast, Koopmans *et al.* (1964, p.85–86) emphasize that the aggregator W_t, and hence u_t and U_t, in (5.1) are specifically related to an agent who evaluates options from the perspective of period t. In period $t+1$ a completely different aggregator W_{t+1} may apply which ranks options different from W_t and U_t.

What is required in order to ensure constant preferences (see Definition 2.1)?

Theorem 5.1 *Given (5.1) is valid for all t, a necessary and sufficient condition for constant preferences is*

$$U_{t+1} = F(\hat{U}_t), \qquad (5.10)$$

where $F(\cdot)$ is some monotonicly increasing transformation of $\hat{U}_t$.[13]

PROOF:

[1] In view of (5.1), (2.9) of Definition 2.1 can be expressed as

$$W_t[u_t(x_t), \hat{U}_t(x_{t+1}, x_{t+2}, \ldots)] \geq W_t[u_t(x_t), \hat{U}_t(x'_{t+1}, x'_{t+2}, \ldots)].$$

As a consequence,

$$\hat{U}_t(x_{t+1}, x_{t+2}, \ldots) \geq \hat{U}_t(x'_{t+1}, x'_{t+2}, \ldots),$$

which implies that for all $F(\cdot)$:

$$F[\hat{U}_t(x_{t+1}, x_{t+2}, \ldots)] \geq F[\hat{U}_t(x'_{t+1}, x'_{t+2}, \ldots)]. \qquad (5.11)$$

If for some $F(\cdot)$, (5.10) is satisfied, then (5.11) implies that

$$U_{t+1}(x_{t+1}, x_{t+2}, \ldots) \geq U_{t+1}(x'_{t+1}, x'_{t+2}, \ldots), \qquad (5.12)$$

---

[13] A related result which covers the case of finite time horizon can be found in Blackorby *et al.* (1973).

and no $F(\cdot)$ can be found which violates (5.12).

[2] Conversely, if no $F(\cdot)$ exists, such that (5.10) is satisfied, then this would necessitate that for any $F(\cdot)$ a pair of consumption profiles $(x_t, x_{t+1}, x_{t+2}, \ldots)$ and $(x_t, x'_{t+1}, x'_{t+2}, \ldots)$ can be found, such that (5.11) is valid but

$$U_{t+1}(x'_{t+1}, x'_{t+2}, \ldots) > U_{t+1}(x_{t+1}, x_{t+2}, \ldots).$$

However, this would contradict Definition (2.1).   ‖

Typically, $U_{t+1} = U_t$ and for infinite time horizon $\hat{U}_t = U_t$. Then (5.1) simplifies to

$$U = W[u(x_t), U(x_{t+1}, x_{t+2}, \ldots)],$$

which ensures constant preferences.

Requirement (5.10) implies that weak separability of future consumption from past consumption is not sufficient for constant preferences. Note that it is neither necessary. Consider the non–recursive functional (4.2). As shown by Strotz (1955/56), this functional implies constant preferences.

Constant preferences are an attractive property since they make recursive utility models amenable to dynamic programming. We take (5.10) to be an implicit assumption in all the recursive utility models employing this tool of optimization.

5.5   Recapitulation

The recursive utility approach is a modest generalization of the discounted utility model in that it dispenses with separability of future consumption from past and present consumption. In recursive models the intertemporal utility functional can be transformed into an aggregator which expresses utility as a function of current consumption and subutility from future consumption. Often subutility is defined by the same functional as the intertemporal utility functional. Such a structure is particularly amenable to dynamic consistency and hence to standard dynamic optimization tools.

We expressed our scepticism concerning the descriptive validity of recursive utility models. In particular, the neglect of the past leads to behavioural predictions which are less plausible than those implied by a discounted utility model which is augmented by habits. In other words, if one wishes to make the discounted utility model more akin to observed decision making, then one should rather take account of the past (as in the richer additive models of sections 4.4 and 4.5) than of the future (as in recursive utility models).

Additive and recursive utility models are special types of universal utility models in that they are based on some notion of instantaneous utility function. In the following chapter we turn to all those universal utility models which exhibit no instantaneous utility functions.

6
Universal Utility Models

6.1 Preliminaries

Universal utility models are the most general class of dynamic
utility models. Myopic, additive, and recursive models are special cases of universal models. In contrast to the frameworks
discussed there, in this chapter we consider only those models, which abstain from presupposing any form of instantaneous
utility. The intertemporal utility function employed in universal
models is defined as

$$U_{\bar{h}_t} = U_{\bar{h}_t}(x_t, x_{t+1}, \ldots).\tag{6.1}$$

This function highlights the fact that, in contrast to myopic,
additive, and recursive models, for any period t more than one
intertemporal utility function may exist. Each of these functions

depends on a vector of past consumption captured by the subscript $\bar{h}_t$. As a consequence, any pair of options $(x_t, x_{t+1}, \ldots)$ and $(x'_t, x'_{t+1}, \ldots)$ which connect to different histories $\bar{h}_t$ and $\bar{h}'_t$ may not be comparable from the perspective of period t (see the introductory illustration on page 12).

A subclass of universal utility models exists, though, which postulates that such cross–history comparisons are feasible and that the finite intertemporal utility function is continuous:

$$U_t = U_t(\bar{h}_t, x_t, x_{t+1}, \ldots, x_T), \tag{6.2}$$

where $\bar{h}_t = (x_0, \ldots, x_{t-2}, x_{t-1})$ is a vector of past consumption and the domain of U_t is the T-dimensional non-negative Euclidean orthant.

In section 6.2, models are reviewed which are based on (6.1). Models defined on (6.2) are discussed in section 6.3.

6.2   Models Doing Without Continuous Preferences

6.2.1   Basic Concepts

This class of dynamic utility models was introduced by Hammond (1976a). It is based on choice sets (defined below) rather than on maximization of a continuous utility function and it does not require cross–history comparisons. Since a good grasp of Hammond's seminal work also supports the understanding of part II of this work, we devote comparatively much space to this class of utility model.

Hammond uses a decision tree where choices can be made only at discrete times $t = 0, 1, 2, \ldots, T$. The finite set of terminal nodes $X = \{a, b, c, \ldots\}$ constitutes the set of all possible terminal nodes an agent can reach (see Figure 6.1). By definition, in a tree branches cannot re–join. For this reason, associated with terminal node a, say, is a unique complete branch (option) $a(n_0)$.

A complete branch $a(n_0)$ can be divided up into portions a_t. At the beginning of each portion a_t, there is a decision node n_t at which the agent can choose among the truncated options still available to him. The truncated part of branch $a(n_0)$ which, at n_t, is still open to the agent is denoted as $a(n_t) = (a_t, a_{t+1}, a_{t+2}, \ldots)$.

Instead of using intertemporal utility functions we state preferences directly in terms of the underlying intertemporal preference ordering. In universal utility models associated with each decision node is a weak ordering $R(n_t)$. To indicate that at some node n_t the truncated branch $a(n_t)$ is weakly preferred to the truncated branch $b(n_t)$, we are going to write $aR(n_t)b$, instead of the more precise but also more cumbersome $a(n_t)R(n_t)\,b(n_t)$. In Figure 6.1, for instance, $bR(n_0)a$ would say that at the initial node the complete option $b(n_0)$ is weakly preferred to the complete option $a(n_0)$, and $aP(n_1)b$ would say that at node n_1 the truncated option leading to terminal node a is strictly preferred to the one leading to terminal node b. Finally, $aI(n_1)b$ indicates indifference.

Recall that in all universal utility models, orderings $R(n_t)$ are defined exclusively on those options available at the respective node n_t. The agent at node n_1 of Figure 6.1, for instance, does not form retrospective preferences over option $c(n_0)$ versus $a(n_0)$ or $b(n_0)$. Furthermore, the following form of "independence of irrelevant alternatives" is invoked: Any preference $aR(n_t)b$ remains unaltered as some option $c(n_s)$ is added to or excluded from the decision tree. This assumption is implicit in the postulate that related to each decision node a preference *ordering* exists. $X(n_0)$ indicates the underlying set *of all* options (branches)

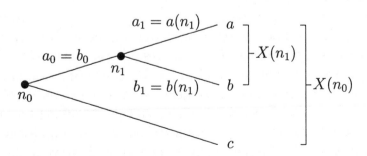

FIGURE 6.1. A Simple Decision Tree.

of a decision problem. Then, let $A(n_0) \subseteq X(n_0)$ denote the compact *opportunity* set of an agent located at the initial decision node. Similarly, $X(n_t)$ represents the set of all (truncated) options beginning at node n_t, and $A(n_t) = X(n_t) \cap A(n_0)$ is the agent's opportunity set at node n_t.

In any type of universal utility model the agent has full information. This implies that the agent not only knows the complete structure of the decision problem but also his future preferences and decisions.

Choice sets are defined in the following way:

Definition 6.1 *Imagine an agent located at n_t who faces the opportunity set $A(n_t)$. $C(A)(n_t)$ denotes the set of options this agent may find himself choosing.*

Obviously, $C(A)(n_t) \subseteq A(n_t)$. It should be emphasized that in a dynamic framework a choice set *is not* necessarily the set of options an agent willingly chooses. It is rather the set of options the agent ends up with! Of course, in a single choice situation the decision maker can end up with only one option. It is customary, however, to allow for choice sets which may contain more than one element. If a choice set contains two options, then this says that the agent may end up with any of those two.

$C(A)(n_0)$ describes the entire sequence of decisions taken by an agent who starts at node n_0. Analogously, the sequence of decisions taken by an agent who starts at node n_1 is represented by $C(A)(n_1)$.

We described in section 2.4 that it is a general feature of dynamic choice problems, that at various points in time the agent forms preference orderings over the options available to him at this point in time. He transforms this sequence of orderings into decisions. These decisions finally result in actual choices, that is in choice sets. The mechanism for this transformation of preferences into actual choices we denoted as a *choice mechanism*. In other words, a choice mechanism is a rule specifying how choice sets $C(A)(n_t)$ are to be obtained from a given opportunity set of options $A(n_t)$ as well as given present and future preferences. Any model of dynamic choice implicitly or explicitly applies such a mechanism. The most prominent choice mechanisms are naive and sophisticated choice which were introduced in chapter 2.4.

In order to illustrate the relationship between opportunity sets, choice mechanisms and choice sets let us consider the following example:

Example 6.1 *A teenager contemplates her afternoon occupation. Suppose she has three options:*

a) *spending the first and the second part of the afternoon at her home computer, trying to increase her personal record score of her favourite computer game,*

b) *spending the first part of the afternoon at the computer and for the rest of the afternoon joining her boy friend at a nearby lake,*

c) *spending the complete afternoon with her boy friend at the lake.*

This choice problem can be represented in the decision tree depicted in Figure 6.2. Let us assume that at n_0 she likes best

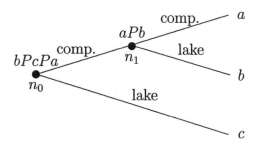

FIGURE 6.2. A Teenager's Choice of Leisure Occupations.

option b, that is starting the afternoon with computer games and finishing it with her boy friend. Spending the whole time at the lake (option c) she prefers to doing computer games for the whole afternoon (option a): $bP(n_0)cP(n_0)a$. However, upon spending the first part of the afternoon at the computer she gets possessed with it. Her initial preference between a and b gets reversed such that, at n_1, she prefers a to b: $aP(n_1)b$. Note that already at the outset the teenager is well aware of this preference change.

What are the actual choices generated by the preferences we just described? If the teenager applies a naive choice mechanism, then she always moves along the option she currently likes best. Confronted with $A(n_0) = \{a(n_0), b(n_0), c(n_0)\}$, the teenager moves from n_0 to n_1, since option $b(n_0)$ is the one she likes best at n_0. At n_1 she follows option $a(n_1)$, the favourite option at node n_1. Thus, she ends up in a: $C^n(\{a(n_0), b(n_0), c(n_0)\}) = \{a(n_0)\}$, where superscript n indicates "naive". In contrast, a sophisticated agent anticipates that moving to n_1 would bring her to a. Since at n_0 she prefers $c(n_0)$ to $a(n_0)$ she decides to move towards c. Hence, the sophisticated teenager would end up in c: $C^s(\{a(n_0), b(n_0), c(n_0)\}) = \{c(n_0)\} \neq C^n(\{a(n_0), b(n_0), c(n_0)\})$, where superscript s indicates "sophisticated". This little example illustrates that a choice set crucially depends on the applied choice mechanism.

It is important to keep in mind that the choice set $C(A)(n_0)$ indicates with which option the agent starting at node n_0 would *end up with*, and not which option at n_0 she chooses to follow. $C^n(\{a(n_0), b(n_0), c(n_0)\}) = \{a(n_0)\}$ says that the naive teenager finds herself ending up with $a(n_0)$, which is not the option she initially chose to follow. At the outset she was willing to choose option $b(n_0)$.[1]

McClennen (1990) introduces a third mechanism which he labels as *resolute choice*. This mechanism can be viewed as the antagon to sophisticated choice. The sophisticated teenager of Example 6.1 regards her preference at n_1 as binding for her move at n_1. Anticipating that she would end up in a, at n_0 she overrules her currently valid preference $bP(n_0)c$ and decides to move along $c(n_0)$. The resolute teenager, in contrast, takes her

---

[1] For those consulting Hammond's (1976a) work, a word of warning seems in place. In his study, Hammond first refers to a choice set as a set of options the agent "...is willing to choose (p.160,165)." This is somewhat misleading, since when analysing property α Hammond interprets a naive and a sophisticated choice set as the set of options the agent "...may find himself choosing (p.168)", that is the set of options he may end up with. As we just illustrated, this is very different from the set of options he is willing to choose.

initial preferences as binding and at n_1 overrules the preference $aP(n_1)b$. We obtain $C^r(\{a(n_0), b(n_0), c(n_0)\}) = \{b(n_0)\}$.[2]

Which of the three choice mechanisms is the most appealing one? Most authors argue that the sophisticated choice mechanism is the only mechanism which deserves to be viewed as "rational". The typical reasoning can be found, for instance, in Yaari (1977, p.76). Related to our own example his argument runs as follows: for the teenager arriving at n_1 bygone is bygone. The only relevant aspect for the decision in n_1 is the current preference between $a(n_1)$ and $b(n_1)$. Hence, everything else than moving along $a(n_1)$ is implausible. The teenager who is still located at n_0 anticipates that once she is at n_1 she will make precisely these considerations. Therefore, option $b(n_0)$ is not feasible and she cannot do better than to choose $c(n_0)$.

Being familiar with the concepts of choice sets and choice mechanisms, it is straightforward to define a *choice function*.

Definition 6.2 $C(n_t)$ *indicates the choice function associated with node n_t. It attributes to any set $A(n_t)$, which is a non-empty compact subset of $X(n_t)$, a non-empty choice set $C(A)(n_t) \subseteq A(n_t)$.*

Since choice sets depend on the applied choice mechanism also a choice functions does. The naive choice function $C^n(n_0)$ of the teenager yields:[3]

$$C^n(\{a(n_0), b(n_0), c(n_0)\}) = \{a(n_0)\} \qquad (6.3)$$
$$C^n(\{a(n_0), b(n_0)\}) = \{a(n_0)\} \qquad (6.4)$$
$$C^n(\{a(n_0), c(n_0)\}) = \{c(n_0)\}$$
$$C^n(\{b(n_0), c(n_0)\}) = \{b(n_0)\}.$$

The sophisticated choice function yields

$$C^s(\{a(n_0), b(n_0), c(n_0)\}) = \{c(n_0)\} \qquad (6.5)$$

---

[2]In section 7.3.2, p.115 it is explained which difference McClennen makes between resolute choice and Strotz's notion of precommitment.

[3]It is trivial that the choice set of an opportunity set containing only one option x is this option x.

$$C^s(\{a(n_0), b(n_0)\}) = \{a(n_0)\} \qquad (6.6)$$
$$C^s(\{a(n_0), c(n_0)\}) = \{c(n_0)\}$$
$$C^s(\{b(n_0), c(n_0)\}) = \{b(n_0)\},$$

and the resolute choice function is given by

$$C^r(\{a(n_0), b(n_0), c(n_0)\}) = \{b(n_0)\}$$
$$C^r(\{a(n_0), b(n_0)\}) = \{b(n_0)\}$$
$$C^r(\{a(n_0), c(n_0)\}) = \{c(n_0)\}$$
$$C^r(\{b(n_0), c(n_0)\}) = \{b(n_0)\}.$$

6.2.2 Important Findings Based on Strict Preferences

For the derivation of his essential results, Hammond (1976a) stipulates that at each decision node the agent has a *strict* preference ordering on $X(n_t)$. As a consequence, each choice set is a singleton.

Hammond's work centers around the question whether or not the choice functions $C^n(n_0)$ and $C^s(n_0)$ satisfy property α.[4] Property α requires that adding new options to an opportunity set should not have the effect that a previously rejected option suddenly becomes favourable.[5] In a dynamic choice context this is expressed by the following definition:

Definition 6.3 *A choice function satisfies property α if and only if for all A, $\tilde{A}$, and n_t, with $\tilde{A}(n_t) \subseteq A(n_t) \subseteq X(n_t)$:*

$$C(A)(n_t) \cap [\tilde{A}(n_t) \setminus C(\tilde{A})(n_t)] = \emptyset.$$

Note that $[\tilde{A}(n_t) \setminus C(\tilde{A})(n_t)]$ indicates the set of previously rejected options in $\tilde{A}(n_t)$, and $C(A)(n_t)$ indicates the choices from the enlarged opportunity set.

Do $C^n(n_0)$ and $C^s(n_0)$ of Example 6.1 satisfy property α? For the naive teenager, adding $b(n_0)$ to $\{a(n_0), c(n_0)\}$ generates

---

[4] The terminology is adopted from Sen (1969). The property goes back, however, to Chernoff (1954), p.429, who presents it as his postulate 4 for rational choice. Hammond (1976a) was the first to adopt it for dynamic choice problems. There it is stated in a different formulation and labelled as "coherence".

[5] For an illustration see section 8.2.1.

a violation of property α, since $a(n_0) \notin C^n(\{a(n_0), c(n_0)\})$ but $a(n_0) \in C^n(\{a(n_0), b(n_0), c(n_0)\})$. Also $C^s(n_0)$ exhibits a violation of property α: $c(n_0) \notin C^s(\{b(n_0), c(n_0)\})$ but $c(n_0) \in C^s(\{a(n_0), b(n_0), c(n_0)\})$.

Hammond analyses how the decision tree and the associated preferences must look like in order to produce choice functions which satisfy property α. He arrives at the following finding:

Theorem 6.1 *[Hammond (1976a, p.168)] A naive or sophisticated choice function $C(n_t)$ satisfies property α if and only if there is no triple of options $\{a(n_0), b(n_0), c(n_0)\}$, such that*

$$(i) a P(n_t^{ac}) b P(n_t^{ac}) c$$
$$(ii) b(n_s^{ab}) a, \qquad s > t,$$

where n_t^{ac} indicates the node at which options $a(n_0)$ and $c(n_0)$ split and analogously n_s^{ab}. Figure 6.2 is an example for a violation of the conditions in Theorem 6.1.[6]

6.2.3 H–Consistency and H–Ordinality

In section 4.3 we discussed the property of dynamic consistency as introduced by Strotz (1955/56). Hammond (1976a, p.166,167) proposes the following more fundamental formulation:

Definition 6.4 *Choice is H–consistent if and only if for all $A(n_t)$ and $A(n_0)$ in $X(n_0)$, with $A(n_t) \subseteq A(n_0)$ and $A(n_t) \cap C(A)(n_0) \neq \emptyset$:*

$$C(A)(n_t) = A(n_t) \cap C(A)(n_0).^7 \qquad (6.7)$$

Hammond does not use the label "H–consistency" but simply speaks of consistency. We attach the "H" in order to highlight

---

[6] Hammond labels this preference configuration as "essentially inconsistent".

[7] It is important to recall that $A(n_t)$ evolves according to $A(n_t) = X(n_t) \cap A(n_0)$. That is, options automatically drop out as one moves to consecutive nodes. They are not selectively excluded from $A(n_0)$ as was the case in our derivation of choice functions related to Example 6.1 (p.89).

that consistency in the sense of Strotz is, in general, different from H–consistency, a fact which went largely unnoticed by the literature.

First of all, it is important to recognize that depending on the definition of a choice set, H–consistency postulates very different things. Suppose, for instance, choice sets are defined as in Definition 6.1, that is as the agent's *actual choices*. If $a(n_0) \in C(A)(n_0)$, then (6.7) postulates that *for all $A(n_t)$, which evolve along $a(n_0)$*, it must be true that the agent who starts with $A(n_t)$ should end up in terminal node a. In Figure 6.2, for instance, we observe $C^s(\{a(n_1), b(n_1)\}) = \{a(n_1)\}$ and $C^n(\{a(n_1), b(n_1)\}) = \{a(n_1)\}$. In view of (6.3) and (6.4), this implies H–consistency for naive choice. (6.5) implies that for $A(n_0) = \{a(n_0), b(n_0), c(n_0)\}$, one obtains $A(n_1) \cap C(A)(n_0) = \emptyset$, and hence, (6.7) of Definition 6.4 is irrelevant. Thus, (6.6) is sufficient to ensure H–consistency of sophisticated choice. As pointed out by Hammond (1976a), interpreting choice sets as in Definition 6.1 always yields H–consistent naive and sophisticated choices.

Now consider an alternative definition of choice sets.

Definition 6.5 *Some option $a(n_t) \in A(n_t)$ is a member of the choice set $C(A)(n_t)$ if and only if*

$$aR(n_t)b \quad \forall \quad b(n_t) \in A(n_t).$$

Here choice sets indicate currently most preferred options, that is "planned choices" in the sense of Strotz. If H–consistency is based on this notion of choice sets, then H–consistency is equivalent to the concept of dynamically consistent choices as introduced by Strotz. Recall that, according to Strotz, consistency of choice requires that "planned choices" do not change over time. To sum up, only for the special case in which choice sets are defined as in Definition 6.5, H–consistency corresponds to the notion of consistency as applied by Strotz.

The Strotz interpretation is the one usually associated with the term "dynamic consistency". We follow this convention. Whenever we use consistency in the sense of Hammond we speak of H–consistency. In the latter case it is indispensable to indicate the applied definition of choice sets.

We should mention another article by Hammond (1977), since it states a property which we denote here as H–ordinality. This property will be of particular relevance in part II of this work.[8] Using our notation, H–ordinality can be defined in the following way:

Definition 6.6 *Choice is H–ordinal if and only if for all $\tilde{A}(n_s)$ and $A(n_t)$ in $X(n_0)$, with $\tilde{A}(n_s) \subseteq A(n_t)$ and $\tilde{A}(n_s) \cap C(A)(n_t) \neq \emptyset$:*

$$C(\tilde{A})(n_s) = \tilde{A}(n_s) \cap C(A)(n_t), \qquad s \geq t. \qquad (6.8)$$

Replacing $A(n_t)$ by $A(n_0)$ and $\tilde{A}(n_s)$ by $A(n_t)$ yields the definition of H–consistency. Thus, for any concept of choice sets H–ordinality implies H–consistency.

At this point we should clarify a notational issue. As pointed out in footnote 7, $A(n_s)$ indicates subsets of $A(n_t)$, $s \geq t$, which evolve as the agent moves through the decision tree: $A(n_s) = X(n_s) \cap A(n_t)$.[9] H–consistency is based on this notion of subsets. $\tilde{A}(n_t)$, in contrast, indicates those subsets of $A(n_t)$ which were generated by excluding branches $x(n_t)$ from $A(n_t)$. This mimics a situation as if the agent disposed only of a restricted opportunity set $\tilde{A}(n_t) \subseteq A(n_t)$ at node n_t. Finally, $\tilde{A}(n_s)$ combines both cases. H–ordinality is based on this last (more general) notion of subsets. Hence, H–ordinality implies H–consistency but the reverse is in general not true.

A sophisticated agent confronted with Figure 6.2, for instance, exhibits H–consistent choices (see p.92). However, H–ordinality is violated, since for $A(n_0) = \{a(n_0), b(n_0), c(n_0)\}$ and $\tilde{A}(n_0) = \{b(n_0), c(n_0)\}$, one obtains $C(A)(n_0) = \{c(n_0)\}$ and $C(\tilde{A})(n_0) = \{b(n_0)\}$, which implies that $C(\tilde{A})(n_s) \neq \tilde{A}(n_s) \cap C(A)(n_t)$ even though $\tilde{A}(n_s) \cap C(A)(n_t) \neq \emptyset$, $s = t = 0$.

---

[8] In Hammond (1977) this property is called "ordinality". Since we use this label for a different property, we denote Hammond's ordinality as H–ordinality.

[9] Note that $A(n_s) = X(n_s) \cap A(n_0) = X(n_s) \cap X(n_t) \cap A(n_0) = X(n_s) \cap A(n_t)$.

For two–period choice problems, Hammond (1977) is able to show that if all possible decision tree configurations generate H–consistent choices,[11] then this is necessary and sufficient for H–ordinality (on the true tree structure) of this choice problem. This result is independent of the applied definition of choice sets and the applied choice mechanism.

6.3   Models with Continuous Preferences

6.3.1   Dynamic Consistency

In this section we discuss models featuring preferences which can be represented by a continuous utility function defined on the T-dimensional non-negative Euclidean orthant. All these models impose a second restriction: Options connecting to different histories are comparable. In other words, cross–history comparisons are feasible. As a consequence, related to each period exactly one intertemporal utility function exists. Then the intertemporal utility can be expressed as:

$$U_t = U_t(\bar{h}_t, x_t, x_{t+1}, \ldots, x_T),\tag{6.9}$$

where $\bar{h}_t = (x_0, \ldots, x_{t-2}, x_{t-1})$. Blackorby et $al.$ (1973) make an even more restrictive assumption. They assume that no exogenous habit formation occurs. Then, (6.9) simplifies to

$$U_t = U_t(x_t, x_{t+1}, \ldots, x_T).\tag{6.10}$$

Blackorby et $al.$ investigate the same question as Strotz (1955/56). Does the naive agent exhibit dynamically consistent choice behaviour? In section 6.3 we presented Strotz's analysis based upon the utility functional

$$U_t = \sum_{s=t}^{T} u(x_s)\theta_{s-t}.\tag{6.11}$$

---

[11] This case Hammond denotes as "metastatic consistency"

Obviously, this is a special case of (6.10).[12] Again, suppose prices are constant and equal to one and the interest rate is zero. In period t the naive individual maximizes (6.10) subject to

$$\sum_{s=t}^{T} x_s = w_t,$$

where w_t indicates wealth in period t. Suppose an optimal sequence is $(x_t^{*t}, x_{t+1}^{*t}, \ldots, x_T^{*t})$, where the superscript $*t$ indicates the period of optimization. Naive behaviour implies that in period t the agent consumes x_t^{*t}.

In period $t + 1$ the subject revises his previous plan. Now he maximizes

$$U_{t+1} = U_{t+1}(x_{t+1}, x_{t+2}, \ldots, x_T) \tag{6.12}$$

subject to

$$\sum_{s=t+1}^{T} x_s = w_t - x_t^{*t}.$$

We indicate the solution to this optimization by $(x_{t+1}^{*t+1}, x_{t+2}^{*t+1}, \ldots, x_T^{*t+1})$.

Do these optimal consumption profiles point towards dynamically consistent choices? In other words, do they satisfy $x_s^{*t} = x_s^{*t+1}$, for all s with $t + 1 \leq s \leq T$? We know from Strotz's analysis that (6.11) satisfies consistency if and only if $\theta_{s-t} = \varrho^{s-t}$. Here, however, we are concerned with the more general utility function (6.10). Backorby et al. (1973) show that for consistency of naive choice, it must be true that (6.10) can be expressed as

$$U_t = W_t[x_t, U_{t+1}(x_{t+1}, x_{t+2}, \ldots, x_T)]. \tag{6.13}$$

This says that intertemporal utility as evaluated in period t must be a recursive function of current consumption and intertemporal utility as evaluated from the perspective of $t + 1$.[13]

---

[12] Recall, however, that Strotz's result carries over to the more general case in which instantaneous utility is affected by habits.

[13] Note that (6.13) belongs to the class of recursive utility models.

6.3.2 *Indifference, Subgame Perfection, and Pareto Optimality*

Blackorby *et al.* (1973) proceed to consider an agent applying a sophisticated choice mechanism. Such a mechanism complicates matters as compared to the naive agent's simple maximization procedure described in the previous section. For the sophisticated case, future optimizing behaviour imposes additional constraints on current maximization. Blackorby *et al.* seek conditions under which the sophisticated maximization always leads to the same actual choices as naive optimization. They show that this is true if and only if the utility function is of the form (6.13).

It is furthermore pointed out that indifference may cause difficulties for current sophisticated optimization, since future optimal behaviour may not yield *unique* consumption profiles, even if U_t is strictly quasi-concave.[14] They list various escapes, most of which were pointed out to them by R. Pollak.

Pollak proposes a "type of weak precommitment". This road is taken in later work by Goldman (1979, 1980) to which we turn in due course. A rather more drastic escape is to define indifference away by positing that the agent's preferences are representable by a strong ordering. Recall that this approach is taken by Hammond (1976a). However, strong preferences do not square with consumption problems in which more than one good is available and the budget set is infinite. As an alternative route, Blackorby *et al.* point out that if U_t is homothetic for all $t > 0$, then the sophisticated consumption profile related to n_0 is unique, even in the presence of indifference.

The idea of sophisticated choice is related to game theoretic equilibrium concepts. This can be easily illustrated using the teenager example depicted in Figure 6.2. Let us interpret the agent in period 0 (the current self) as player 0 and the agent in period 1 as player 1. If, conditional on player 0 moving to n_1, it is player 1's strategy to move to terminal node a, then it is

---

[14]This will be a fundamental aspect in chapter 8, where new choice mechanisms are introduced which can incorporate indifference.

player 0's best strategy to move towards c. This pair of strategies forms a subgame perfect equilibrium. The actual choice associated with this equilibrium is $c(n_0)$.

Note that in Figure 6.2 no indifference occurs. Peleg and Yaari (1973) express their suspicion that indifference may frustrate the endeavour to identify subgame perfect equilibria. For this reason, they consider the weaker concept of Nash equilibria and show that such an equilibrium always exists.

The studies of Peleg and Yaari (1973) and Blackorby *et al.* (1973) are based on intertemporal utility function (6.10). Goldman (1980) analyses the more general function (6.9) which allows also for exogenous habit formation. He is able to prove that even in the presence of indifference a subgame perfect equilibrium always exists.[15] Hence, the same must be true for (6.10)

It is well known that Nash equilibria and subgame perfect equilibria do not necessarily imply Pareto efficient outcomes. This can be used as an objection to the game theoretic approach to dynamic utility models. Peleg and Yaari (1973) are well aware of this criticism, and defend the Nash concept on the grounds that it is a minimal property without which some given choice cannot be viewed as "a reasonable course of action for an agent with changing tastes (p.395)."

Goldman (1979) investigates the relationship between subgame perfect equilibria and Pareto efficiency in more detail. He makes four assumptions, the last of which is particularly problematic: If the agent decides to save more in period 0 than a subgame perfect equilibrium would suggest, then the new equilibrium which is subgame perfect for the game starting in period $t+1$ exhibits increased optimal consumption in all periods $t = 1, 2, \ldots, T$ as compared to the consumption profile corresponding to the original subgame perfect equilibrium.

---

[15] In section 7.4, we generalize this result to the most general universal utility function (6.1).

It is shown that, given Goldman's four assumptions, among the interior subgame perfect solutions ($x_t > 0 \ \forall t$), only those are Pareto optimal which are best in terms of U_0.[15]

6.4 Recapitulation

The models presented in this chapter abstain from any notion of instantaneous utility. We explained the relationship between preferences, choice mechanisms, choice sets, and choice functions. Building on these concepts, Hammond's (1976a) notion of H–consistency was related to Strotz's (1955/56) notion of dynamic consistency. Property α was another issue appearing in Hammond's work.

We then proceeded to more restrictive models featuring continuous intertemporal utility functions. Dynamic consistency was an issue here, too. It was furthermore illustrated how in the presence of indifference the sophisticated choice mechanism runs into difficulties and how sophisticated choice corresponds to the notion of a subgame perfect equilibrium.

This chapter completes our comprehensive survey of intertemporal choice models. The analysis in part II of this work is based on utility function (6.1). As a consequence, part II's findings can be applied to all models discussed in part I (chapters 2 to 6). Some of our results represent generalizations of findings reported in this survey.

---

[15] Recall that a related result was derived by Shefrin (1996) with respect to an additive utility model featuring hyperbolic discounting (see section 4.3).

Part II

Preferences, Choice, and Welfare in Universal Utility Models

7
Elementary Aspects of Choice in Universal Utility Models

7.1 Preliminaries

In this section we develop the universal utility model underlying the rest of this work.[1] In section 6.2.1, the model employed in Hammond (1976a) was sketched out. His analysis is restricted to strong orderings. It is not appealing to define strong orderings over *infinite* budget sets. Either one uses weak orderings over infinite sets or, if this is not possible, strong orderings over finite sets. Accordingly, in Hammond the set of terminal nodes X is assumed to be finite.

Hammond (1976a) is well aware of the fact that the restriction to strict preferences and finite sets X "... is severely limiting

---

[1] Parts of this chapter draw upon v. Auer (1998); with kind permission from Kluwer Academic Publishers.

(p.165)." He imposes it anyway, since the alternative (weak orderings defined on infinite sets) creates difficulties for the sophisticated choice mechanism. As a consequence, his results cannot be applied to the consumer problems considered in myopic, additive, and recursive models. In these models the consumer chooses from infinite budget sets and preferences are representable by a continuous utility function.

A well known result by Debreu (1954, 1959) states that if a continuous utility function represents an ordering, then this ordering must be a weak ordering. For the standard story of dynamic choice, this implies that the agent may be *indifferent* between two sequences of consumption bundles.

In this chapter we generalize Hammond's model to the case of weak preferences and compact sets.[2] That is, we develop the decision tree formulation of universal utility models. All findings of part II of this work are derived on the basis of this general framework. Hence, they are applicable to all models subsumed under the notion of universal utility models.

For most of the time, we speak of dynamic choice as the intertemporal decision problem of a single agent moving through time. Then, to a single decision maker a sequence of "selves" exists. Each self exhibits its own preferences. Our theoretical analysis, however, is also applicable to all other standard dynamic decision problems. For instance, they also cover the case of some central planner (instead of a single decision maker) who coordinates a sequence of generations (instead of a sequence of "selves"). Then a choice mechanism is to be interpreted as the decision rule of this planner for transforming the various generations' orderings into actual choice (see section 7.4). Note, however, as regards economic content, these are quite different stories. For instance, finitely lived generations may not have to bear late consequences of their decisions.

In the following section we define the framework of universal utility models in terms of decision tree notation. It is shown that,

---

[2] Compact sets are closed and bounded. They include all finite sets as well as the usual (infinite) budget sets with all prices greater than zero.

even in the presence of compact sets, graphical decision tree representations are possible. Section 7.3 reconsiders the three choice mechanisms introduced in sections 2.4 and 6.2.1 (naive, sophisticated and resolute choice) and section 7.4 relates these choice mechanisms to the game theoretic notion of subgame perfect equilibria.

7.2 The Framework

7.2.1 The Applied Decision Tree

In order to get the idea of our analysis, the concept of decision trees as introduced in section 6.2.1 is sufficient. It is for the sake of formal accuracy that in this section we provide a more formal definition of decision trees. The same notation as in section 6.2.1 is applied.

Choices can be made at discrete times $t = 0, 1, 2, \ldots$. The initial decision node is denoted as n_0. All decision nodes are members of branches. A complete branch $x(n_0)$ is a sequence of *portions* $x_0, x_1, \ldots$. Each portion x_t begins with a decision node n_t and terminates at the decision node of the next portion x_{t+1} or at some terminal node x. The set X_t indicates the set of portions x_t available in period t.[3]

The set of all possible *complete branches* is assumed to be compact and denoted by $X(n_0)$.[4] A truncated option $x(n_t)$ is the part of option $x(n_0)$ which is still open to the agent located at decision node n_t. The set of all truncated options connecting to decision node n_t is denoted as $X(n_t)$ and $A(n_t) \subseteq X(n_t)$ is the agent's opportunity set at n_t.

X is the set of terminal nodes. Let N_t denote the set of decision nodes n_t related to period t and $N = \bigcup_{0 \leq t \leq T} N_t$ the set of all possible decision nodes. For present and later purposes, the following definition is useful:

---

[3] In Example 2.1, for instance, X_t was {coffee with milk, black coffee}.

[4] In order to avoid sequences $x_0, x_1, \ldots$ converging to zero, one may impose a finite time horizon T.

Definition 7.1 *Decision node n_s^{ab} is the discrimination node of options $a(n_0)$ and $b(n_0)$. It indicates the last node n_t at which both options are identical.*

In decision trees, two compact sets $X(n_s)$ and $X(n_r)$ are disjoint if and only if for all $a(n_0)$ and $b(n_0)$ with $a(n_s) \in X(n_s)$ and $b(n_r) \in X(n_r)$, n_t^{ab} is such that $t < s$ and $t < r$. Otherwise, $X(n_s) \subseteq X(n_r)$ for $s \geq r$ and $X(n_r) \subseteq X(n_s)$ for $r \geq s$. This also implies that in decision trees branches do not rejoin. The union $\bigcup_{n_t \in N} X(n_t)$ determines the complete decision tree.

Recall from section 6.1, that in universal utility models associated with each decision node n_t is a weak ordering $R(n_t)$. For instance, $bR(n_0)a$ would say that at the initial node the complete option $b(n_0)$ is weakly preferred to the complete option $a(n_0)$. In all universal utility models the orderings $R(n_t)$ are defined exclusively on those options available at the respective node n_t. Specifically, no retrospective preferences are formed, that is preferences over past options which are no longer available at n_t. Furthermore, each preference $aR(n_t)b$ remains unaltered as some option $c(n_s)$ is added or excluded from the decision tree (independence of irrelevant alternatives). We should stress, however, that, even though *preferences* remain unaltered as the opportunity set is varied, the resulting *actual choices* may change (as was illustrated in Example 6.1).

7.2.2   Graphical Representations of Universal Utility Models

In the preceding section it was argued that every universal utility model can be equally formalized in terms of decision tree notation. Even in the presence of infinite compact sets X_t, the theoretical concept of decision trees remains valid and there is no need to modify previously employed notation. Infinite compact sets, though, complicate the *graphical* exposition of decision trees. For choice problems with more than two periods it is no longer possible to find a graphical representation.

We illustrate how a decision tree, depicting a single two–period choice problem defined on *finite* sets X_t, can be modified to depict the case in which this choice problem is based on *in-*

finite compact sets X_t. For this purpose, we return to the short lived broker of Example 2.1.

Example 7.1 *At each of the two evenings of his short life the broker sits in his favourite pub. At both nights he allows himself one drink. The pub's drinks variety, though, is extremely limited. They only have sparkling water or pure apple juice.*

The associated decision tree is depicted in Figure 7.1. This

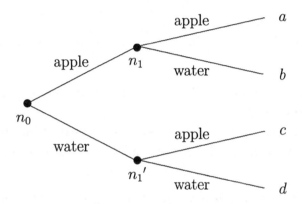

FIGURE 7.1. The Broker's Night Drink Problem – Finite X_t.

choice problem can be generalized to infinite compact sets.

Example 7.2 *Alternatively to apple juice and sparkling water, the broker may order any mixture of the two components.*

This choice problem is depicted in Figure 7.2. Now the tree rather looks like a "wrapped" decision tree. The set of decision nodes N_1 is given by the line connecting n_1 and n_1'. The set of terminal nodes X is represented by the surface $abcd$. Drinking pure apple juice in period 0, brings the broker to decision node n_1. Terminal node a represents the case in which the broker also in period 1 drinks pure apple juice, whereas terminal node b says that the broker has switched to pure water. More generally, the line connecting terminal nodes a and b indicates all possible drink profiles in which the period 0 drink was pure apple juice. Obviously, if the broker lives longer than two periods than the

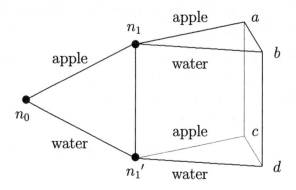

FIGURE 7.2. The Broker's Night Drink Problem – Infinite Compact X_t.

set of terminal nodes is no longer a plane but must be imagined as a hyperplane.

Similarly, one may depict a simple consumption problem where the inidividual's choice possibilities are restricted by some budget set:

Example 7.3 *At the beginning of the choice problem an individual is given a cake which she may or may not finish during the two–period horizon.*

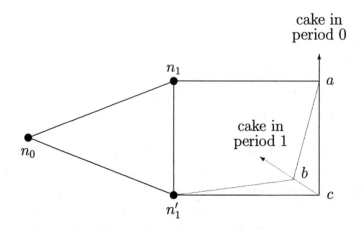

FIGURE 7.3. The Two–Period Cake Problem.

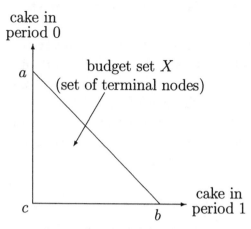

FIGURE 7.4. The Cake Problem's Budget Set.

The associated decision tree is depicted in Figure 7.3. At decision node n_1 she has eaten up the complete cake in period 0. There is no longer a choice to make for period 1. Accordingly, she must move along the only branch available at n_1 which brings her to terminal node a. This terminal node indicates the consumption profile: "complete cake in period 0, no cake in period 1". Conversely, if in period 0 she has not touched the cake at all, she finds herself in n_1'. For period 1 she can choose between the full range of options. She may continue to abstain from sweet stuff altogether, c, or she may eat the complete cake in period 1, b, or she may eat any fraction of the cake which would bring her to some terminal node indicated by the straight line connecting b and c.

If we rotate this "wrapped decision tree" such that the triangular abc becomes the front side, one obtains Figure 7.4. This is the ordinary textbook representation of two–period consumer problems. Figure 7.3 illustrates which decision tree lies behind the usual budget set representation depicted in Figure 7.4. Points a, b, and c of Figure 7.4 correspond to the terminal nodes in Figure 7.3. Point c, for instance, indicates the case in which the cake is not touched during both periods, whereas the budget line ab corresponds to the cases in which the cake is eaten up in the course of the two periods, with a and b indicating the extreme cases in which the complete cake is consumed in a single period.

The purpose of this section was to illustrate that all universal utility models, including those based upon infinite compact sets X, can be thought of and analysed in terms of decision trees. As a consequence, *all* findings of part II of this work can be applied to myopic, additive, and recursive utility models. In fact, some of our findings are generalizations of results which were derived for more restricted models.

7.2.3   Choice Sets Re–Considered

In Definition 6.1, choice sets were specified in the following way:

Definition 6.1 *Imagine an agent located at n_t who faces the opportunity set $A(n_t)$. $C(A)(n_t)$ denotes the set of options this agent may find himself choosing.*

Recall that a choice set *is not* necessarily the set of options an agent willingly chooses. It is the set of options the agent ends up with! $C(A)(n_t)$ describes the entire sequence of decisions taken by an agent *who starts his decision process at node n_t*.

For an agent located at node n_0, no *past* preferences exist. Hence, past preferences are irrelevant for $C(A)(n_0)$. The choice sets associated with subsequent nodes are defined analogously. Preferences of the past are not considered. $C(A)(n_1)$, for instance, is unaffected by $R(n_0)$. This is not to say, however, that we exclude any sort of habit formation. For instance, the *portion* x_0 leading to node n_1 may well be relevant for the following preferences $R(n_1)$, and thus for $C(A)(n_1)$. Only past *preferences* are irrelevant. In other words, $C(A)(n_t)$ is a choice set of an agent located at n_t who has no recall of past *preferences* but possibly of past consumption. We will see in section 7.4 that this specification of choice sets allows also for a straightforward application of game theoretic equilibrium concepts.

That this is a sensible way of defining choice sets might be even easier to accept once one interprets the dynamic decision problem as that of a sequence of generations. In this interpretation $C(A)(n_t)$ is the choice set of generation t (the options generation t ends up with) given that generation $t - 1$ has decided to move to node n_t. For generation t it is a *fait accompli* that generation $t - 1$ has decided to move to n_t, and the underlying *preferences* responsible for this move are of no concern to generation t. However, the move itself may well be crucial since it may shape generation t's preferences.

7.3   Choice Mechanisms

7.3.1   Trivial Choice

As we described in part I of this thesis, a standard story in the literature on dynamic choice runs as follows: An agent has to decide on the sequence of consumption bundles he wants to consume, the agent's choices being restricted by his life time wealth (some infinite compact budget set).[5]

Since the tastes of the consumer may change over time, the crucial question is how to select a particular consumption path. The agent has to apply some choice mechanism which transforms the sequence of orderings (or utility functions) into actual choices. The most simple mechanism one can think of is adopted from static choice problems:

Trivial Choice:

Trivial choice postulates that, for an option $a(n_t)$ to be in the choice set of some set $A(n_t)$, it must be weakly preferred to each option in $A(n_t)$, and this preference must extend also to each subsequent node along path $a(n_t)$.

Definition 7.2 *For an option $a(n_t) \in A(n_t)$ to be a member of a trivial agent's choice set $C(A)(n_t)$, it must be true that at all nodes $n_s \in a(n_t)$, $s \geq t$:*

$$aR(n_s)b \quad \forall \quad b(n_s) \in A(n_s). \tag{7.1}$$

---

[5] Recall that "infinite" indicates that life time wealth is infinitely divisible between the various periods. For consumption problems with infinitely many periods, a compact opportunity set (e.g. due to bounded life time wealth) must lead to a consumption profile which in some periods exhibits consumption levels arbitrarily close or equal to zero.

Though uncontroversial for a static choice context, the trivial choice function seems too trivial for the dynamic case, since it may lead to empty choice sets which contradicts the definition of a choice function. This will become clearer in the following example:[6]

Example 7.4 *Imagine the Pope who faces a two–period choice problem. Of course, the Pope has got full information and no uncertainty is involved. Suppose there are only three options:*
   a) watching TV for both periods,
   b) watching TV during the first period and reading the Koran during
       the second,
   c) reading the Koran during both periods.

Suppose that the Pope's preferences at n_0 are $bP(n_0)cP(n_0)a$. It is assumed, however, that watching TV is habit–forming – even for the Pope. Having seen the first episode of a soap opera he wants to watch more episodes, in short $aP(n_1)b$. Figure 7.5 represents this simple choice problem in a decision tree.[7]

Clearly, the Pope located at n_0 and adhering to the trivial choice function cannot find any option satisfying (7.1), and thus $C(A)(n_0) = \emptyset$. Hence, one has to look for more elaborate mechanisms. Such mechanisms were introduced in section 2.4 (naive and sophisticated choice) and 6.2.1 (resolute choice).

Before we proceed to re–consider these mechanisms, it is worth emphasizing again the strict distinction between preferences and choice behaviour. There is no *a priori* compulsion

---

[6] Hammond (1976a) uses an equivalent example featuring "drugs" instead of "TV" and "abstaining from drugs" instead of "reading a book". Correspondingly, at n_1, the choice maker prefers drugs to abstention. The snag with this example is that it suggests an *a priori* relationship between preferences and choices, even though no choice mechanism has yet been specified. The impression is that at n_1 the drug addict must choose according to her addiction expressed in her preferences at n_1. However, there is no reason why we should restrict our attention only to those choice mechanisms in which choices at final nodes are executed in compliance with this node's preferences.

[7] In decision trees we simply write aRb instead of $aR(n_0)b$ or $aR(n_1)b$. No confusion should arise, since in the trees preferences are stated right at the respective decision node.

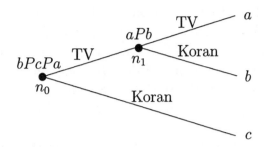

FIGURE 7.5. The Pope's Choice Problem.

that the Pope's decision at node n_1, say, is such that he moves along the option which at n_1 he likes best. The relationship between choices and preferences is exclusively determined by the Pope's *choice mechanism*.

7.3.2 Naive and Resolute Choice

In this section we briefly compare naive and resolute choice and provide formal definitions of these two choice mechanisms. Both mechanisms can be viewed as "short–sighted". To "forward–looking" (or sophisticated) choice mechanisms we turn in section 7.3.3.

Naive Choice:

This mechanism was introduced by Strotz (1955/56), though under the label of "myopic" choice. At each decision node a naive agent embarks on the option that currently seems best. In our example depicted in Figure 7.5, the Pope does not care about the fact that once he starts watching TV, at n_1, he will prefer to follow up $a(n_1)$ rather than $b(n_1)$. His naivity leads him into a situation in which his initial preference $bP(n_0)a$ gets reversed, and he ends up on a path he initially did not wish to follow. In the simple example depicted in Figure 7.5 the naive choice set associated with node n_0 therefore yields $C(A)(n_0) = \{a(n_0)\}$, with $A(n_0) = \{a(n_0), b(n_0), c(n_0)\}$.

Imagine that at n_0 the Pope is told that the TV-set will be confiscated after the first period. In other words, path $a(n_0)$ is not feasible. Then, at n_0, the Pope plans to choose $b(n_0)$.

Let us derive the complete naive choice function (see Definition 6.2). In the absence of option $a(n_0)$, at n_1 there is no longer an alternative. He has to do without soap operas. So following portion $b(n_1)$ he puts into effect his initial plan. Thus, $C(\{b(n_0), c(n_0)\}) = \{b(n_0)\}$.

Next, assume that $b(n_0)$ is eliminated from the decision tree. That is, the naive Pope is given the choice between watching TV the entire time, $a(n_0)$, and no TV at all, $c(n_0)$. We said that the Pope does not like to get used to watching TV, and therefore prefers $c(n_0)$: $C(\{a(n_0), c(n_0)\}) = \{c(n_0)\}$. Finally, if the Koran is not available at n_0, then the agent follows option $a(n_0)$ to the end: $C(\{a(n_0), b(n_0)\}) = \{a(n_0)\}$.

To summarize, the choice function associated with n_0 is characterized by $C(\{a(n_0), b(n_0), c(n_0)\}) = \{a(n_0)\}$, $C(\{a(n_0), b(n_0)\}) = \{a(n_0)\}$, $C(\{a(n_0), c(n_0)\}) = \{c(n_0)\}$, and $C(\{b(n_0), c(n_0)\}) = \{b(n_0)\}$. Of course, also a choice function exists related to node n_1 of Figure 7.5. Obviously, we obtain $C(\{a(n_1), b(n_1)\}) = \{a(n_1)\}$ The notion of naive choice is formalized in the following definition:

Definition 7.3 *For option $a(n_t) \in A(n_t)$ to be a member of a* **naive** *agent's choice set $C(A)(n_t)$, some option $d(n_t) \in A(n_t)$ must exist, with $a_t = d_t$ (possibly $d(n_t) = a(n_t)$), such that*

$$dR(n_t)b \quad \forall \quad b(n_t) \in A(n_t).$$

Furthermore, it must hold that if $a(n_{t+1})$ exists,[8] then $a(n_{t+1}) \in C(A)(n_{t+1})$.

For illustrative purpose, we apply this definition to the choice problem depicted in Figure 7.6.[9] For $e(n_2) \in C(A)(n_2)$, Definition 7.3 demands two things. Firstly, if $e(n_3)$ exists, then it

---

[8] That is $a(n_t)$ is not the last decision node along $a(n_0)$.

[9] We use e, f, g, and h instead of a, b, c, and d, in order to avoid confusion with the options' labels used in Definition 7.3.

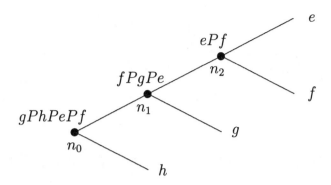

FIGURE 7.6. An Illustration of the Definition of Naive Choice.

must be a member of $C(A)(n_3)$. Since, $e(n_3)$ does not exist, this requirement is trivially satisfied. Secondly, $e(n_2)$, or some alternative option $x(n_2)$ with $x_2 = e_2$, must be weakly preferred to all other options available at n_2. In Figure 7.6, option $e(n_2)$ itself is preferred to all options: $eP(n_2)f$. We can conclude that $e(n_2) \in C(A)(n_2)$.

Analogously, for $e(n_1) \in C(A)(n_1)$ Definition 7.3 demands that $e(n_2) \in C(A)(n_2)$, which it is. Furthermore it is required that $e(n_1)$, or some alternative option $x(n_1)$ with $x_1 = e_1$, must be weakly preferred to all other options available at n_1. Now $e(n_1)$ is not weakly preferred to all other available options. In fact, $e(n_1)$ is the worst option. However, an alternative option exists, namely $f(n_1)$, which is weakly preferred to all options available at n_1 and $f_1 = e_1$. Thus, the requirements for $e(n_1) \in C(A)(n_1)$ are satisfied.

Finally, for $e(n_0) \in C(A)(n_0)$ it is required that $e(n_1) \in C(A)(n_1)$ and that $e(n_0)$, or some alternative option $x(n_0)$ with $x_0 = e_0$, must be weakly preferred to all other options available at n_0. Both conditions are satisfied, since such an alternative option exists: $g(n_0)$, $g_0 = e_0$. Hence, we obtain $e(n_0) \in C(A)(n_0)$.

This illustration demonstrates that Definition 7.3 covers also decision trees with more than two periods. In fact, it applies to all general decision trees as specified in 7.2.1.

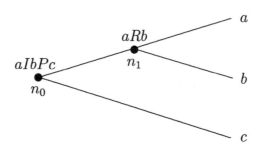

FIGURE 7.7. An Illustration of Resolute Choice.

Next, we turn to the short–sighted choice mechanism which was introduced by McClennen (1990), though the basic idea is also due to Strotz (1955/56).

Resolute Choice:

At n_0 an agent embarks on the option that currently seems best and also sticks to this decision at each subsequent decision node. In Figure 7.5 we obtain $C(A)(n_0) = \{b(n_0)\}$, with $A(n_0) = \{a(n_0), b(n_0), c(n_0)\}$. This implies that at n_1 the agent moves towards b even though his preference suggests otherwise.

It is important to realize that these considerations are related to the initial node's choice set. In particular, we do not say that $b(n_1)$ is necessarily a member of the choice set related to node n_1. In fact, we obtain $C(\{a(n_1), b(n_1)\}) = \{a(n_1)\}$. In seeing this recall that the choice set $C(\{a(n_1), b(n_1)\})$ is the set of options an agent located at n_1, *who is unaware of past preferences*, may find himself choosing. Such an agent finds himself opting for $a(n_1)$.

Note also that if the decision problem was given by Figure 7.7, then applying a resolute choice mechanism, would lead to $C(A)(n_0) = \{a(n_0), b(n_0)\}$, even though at n_1 option $a(n_1)$ is preferred to option $b(n_1)$. Therefore, in a sensible variation of resolute choice, $b(n_0)$ would not appear in the choice set $C(A)(n_0)$. We may denote this mechanism as *steadfast choice*. In Figure 7.7 steadfast choice differs from resolute choice since, at n_0, there exist more than one best option, namely $a(n_0)$

and $b(n_0)$. Now, for the "best option" $b(n_0)$ being a member of $C(A)(n_0)$ it is also required that at n_1 it is not worse than the other "best option" (option $a(n_0)$). In the following we do not consider this variation any further.

The formal definition of *resolute* choice is as follows:

Definition 7.4 *For some option $a(n_t) \in A(n_t)$ to be a member of a **resolute** agent's choice set $C(A)(n_t)$, it must hold that $aR(n_t)b \,\forall b(n_t) \in A(n_t)$.*

One might be inclined to regard Strotz's (1955/56) precommitment and McClennen's resolute choice as the same thing. In fact, Strotz remains rather vague about what he actually means by precommitment. Is it some "external" or "internal precommitment"? In order to support the novelty of his resolute choice mechanism, McClennen favours the view that precommitment indicates some external force. Recall, for instance, the Pope's decision problem depicted in Figure 7.5. The naive Pope can not reach b, since at n_1 he moves to a. External precommitment, according to McClennen and Hammond (1976a), merely says that if some option exists which is identical to b but features no additional choice possibilities, then the Pope should choose this option. Then, however, the *true* underlying decision tree is not Figure 7.5 but Figure 7.8. Option b' represents the case in

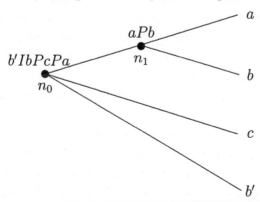

FIGURE 7.8. An Illustration of Precommitment.

which the TV–set disintegrates after period 0 and the Pope has simply no choice but to read the Koran during period 1. The classic example is Ulysses who is given the option to be tied to the mast of his ship as it passes the Sirens. In this interpretation precommitment is not a choice mechanism, but involves a change of the underlying decision context.

Resolute choice, in contrast, does not invoke new options. The decision problem remains that of Figure 7.5. The resolute choice mechanism simply says that at n_1 the decision maker overrules his preferences at n_1 and sticks to those of node n_0. Analogously, Ulysses passes the Sirens without giving in to his currently valid preference when he hears the Sirens singing. He is resolute enough to stick to his former preferences and to overrule later preferences. This could be called internal precommitment.

We emphasize again, that the applied choice mechanism, and only the choice mechanism, determines which preferences are decisive and which are not. In resolute choice the decisive preferences are those at the beginning. The converse is true in sophisticated choice to which we turn next.

7.3.3   Sophisticated Choice

The sophisticated choice mechanism, too, was introduced by Strotz (1955/56). It applies the idea of folding back and assumes a finite time horizon T. In the event of indifference, a simple folding back mechanism runs into difficulties. In other words, it is not possible to apply the sophisticated choice mechanism to the standard story of dynamic choice in which agents choose from infinite compact budget sets. The widespread use of continuous utility functions necessitates a re–examination of sophisticated choice.

In this section we introduce a number of new choice mechanisms which are refined versions of sophisticated choice. They can be applied even in the presence of indifference. This section provides also formal definitions of all these mechanisms. For the illustration of the new choice mechanisms, we return to Example 7.4.

In a first step, a *sophisticated* Pope eliminates all those options which he regards as being *irrelevant* for his decision at

n_0. Whether he regards an option at n_0 as relevant or not depends on the preferences at future nodes. In Figure 7.5, option $b(n_0)$ is deemed irrelevant for the decision at n_0, since at n_1 an option exists – option $a(n_1)$ – which is strictly preferred to $b(n_1)$. Hence, $b(n_0)$ is "mentally erased" and the preference at n_0 between $b(n_0)$ and any other option is meaningless. More formally, an option $a(n_t)$ is *relevant* at node n_t if $a(n_{t+1})$ is a member of $C(A)(n_{t+1})$, provided $a(n_{t+1})$ exists.[10] Besides option $c(n_0)$, only option $a(n_0)$ is relevant for the decision at node n_0. Of those two relevant options the Pope prefers $c(n_0)$. Thus, far–sightedness gives rise to the choice set $C(A)(n_0) = \{c(n_0)\}$, with $A(n_0) = \{a(n_0), b(n_0), c(n_0)\}$.

In order to derive the complete choice function $C(n_0)$, suppose the TV set is known to be confiscated at n_1. The opportunity set shrinks to $\{b(n_0), c(n_0)\}$. In this case, option $b(n_0)$ is a relevant option at n_0, since upon arriving at n_1 the agent will indeed follow through path $b(n_0)$. Because at n_0, $b(n_0)$ is the best relevant option, we obtain $C(\{b(n_0), c(n_0)\}) = \{b(n_0)\}$. Finally, we get $C(\{a(n_0), b(n_0)\}) = \{a(n_0)\}$ and $C(\{a(n_0), c(n_0)\}) = \{c(n_0)\}$.

The same simple procedure of folding back can be applied to the three–period example depicted in Figure 7.9. Since

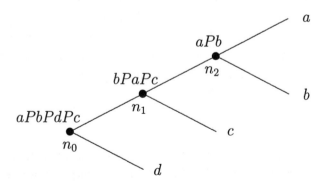

FIGURE 7.9. Sophisticated Choice in a Three–Period Example.

$aP(n_2)b$, option $b(n_0)$ is eliminated and at n_0 and n_1 the pref-

---

[10] The notion of relevant options makes sense only for sophisticated choice mechanisms.

erence between options $b(n_1)$ or $b(n_0)$ and any other options
is meaningless. Hence, at n_1, only options $a(n_1)$ and $c(n_1)$
are relevant. Since $aP(n_1)c$, $c(n_0)$ is erased and at n_0 only
options $a(n_0)$ and $d(n_0)$ are relevant. Due to $aP(n_0)d$, $a(n_0)$
is the only member of the agent's sophisticated choice set:
$C(\{a(n_0), b(n_0), c(n_0), d(n_0)\}) = \{a(n_0)\}$.

However, the case of sophisticated choice is more subtle than
the existing literature appears to have noticed. Once we allow
for *weak preferences* we have to be very careful about the exact
definition of sophisticated choice. In fact, we have to discriminate between a number of sophisticated choice mechanisms.

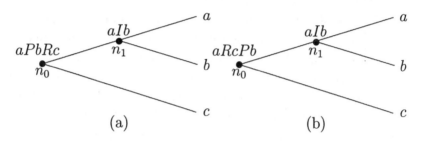

FIGURE 7.10. Sophisticated Choice Re-Considered.

In Figure 7.10a the Pope located at n_0 takes into account
that at n_1 he will be indifferent between options $a(n_1)$ and $b(n_1)$.
Here, in contrast to the decision problem depicted in Figure 7.5,
both options $a(n_0)$ and $b(n_0)$ are relevant for the decision at n_0.
Obviously, option $c(n_0)$ is a third relevant option. The question
now arises as to which of the relevant options form the choice
set $C(A)(n_0)$?

Dogmatic Choice:

Intuitively, one might postulate that a relevant option is a member of $C(A)(n_0)$ if and only if at n_0 it is weakly preferred to *all
relevant options*. We label this type of forward–looking choice as
dogmatic choice. In our example depicted in Figure 7.10a only
option $a(n_0)$ satisfies this postulate. For the sake of legibility,
formal definitions of the various types of sophisticated choice
are deferred to the end of this section.

Recall that a choice set is the set of options an agent may end up with. Hence, saying that only option $a(n_0)$ is in $C(A)(n_0)$ calls upon the Pope to show some sense of "resolution" once he arrives at n_1. Contrary to his indifference, at n_1 he has to move towards a, rejecting option $b(n_1)$. In other words, the decision at node n_1 is in compliance with past preferences. It is in this sense that dogmatic choice sets $C(A)(n_0)$ feature resolution.[11]

Sagacious Choice:

Alternatively, we could accept some relevant option $a(n_0)$ as a member of $C(A)(n_0)$, if and only if at n_0 it is weakly preferred to all *relevant options splitting from $a(n_0)$ at n_0*. In Figure 7.10a this would yield $C(A)(n_0) = \{a(n_0), b(n_0)\}$, since $aP(n_0)b$ is no longer a cause for $b(n_0)$ to be excluded from $C(A)(n_0)$. We have chosen to denote this mechanism as *sagacious choice*.

The example highlights that, compared to dogmatic choice, sagacious choice is less restrictive, in the sense that the conditions for $b(n_0)$ to be a member of the choice set $C(A)(n_0)$ are weakened. Yet, the decision at n_1 is still affected by past preferences. To understand this, consider a slightly modified example depicted in Figure 7.10b. Here we get $C(A)(n_0) = \{a(n_0)\}$, since only $a(n_0)$ is weakly preferred to the relevant option $c(n_0)$. This again implies that at n_1 the Pope is resolute enough to reject $b(n_1)$.

Lenient Choice:

Yet, we could imagine an even less restrictive variety of choice behaviour: For a relevant option $a(n_0)$, to be a member of $C(A)(n_0)$, it is merely required that *some* relevant option exists which at n_0 is identical to $a(n_0)$ and weakly preferred to all relevant options. For Figure 7.10b, this type of choice would yield $C(A)(n_0) = \{a(n_0), b(n_0)\}$. Even though, at n_0, option $b(n_0)$ is strictly less preferred to option $c(n_0)$ it is in the choice set. This

---

[11]Recall that the decision at n_1 is part of a sequence of decisions which finally lead to the choice set $C(A)(n_0)$. $C(A)(n_1)$, in contrast, indicates the choice set of an agent who *starts* his decision process at node n_1 and *who has got no recall of past preferences* (see section 7.2.3). We get $C(A)(n_1) = \{a(n_0), b(n_0)\}$.

is due to option $a(n_0)$, which, at n_0, is identical to $b(n_0)$ and weakly preferred to $c(n_0)$. Loosely speaking, option $a(n_0)$ serves as a "vehicle" for option $b(n_0)$ to become a member of $C(A)(n_0)$.

This third type of anticipatory decision making is labelled as *lenient choice*. It is a characteristic of lenient choice that past preferences no longer bear any weight on present decisions. No trace of resolution remains.

Cautious choice:[12]

Finally, one could imagine some kind of *cautious choice* featuring the maximin–principle. In Figure 7.10b, for instance, cautious choice would yield $C(A)(n_0) = \{c(n_0)\}$. The agent avoids to move to n_1 since the worst of those options available at n_1 and relevant at n_0 – option $b(n_0)$ – is worse than option $c(n_0)$: $cP(n_0)b$.[13]

We now provide formal definitions of the various sophisticated choice mechanism. We state the conditions for some option $a(n_t)$ to be in the choice set $C(A)(n_t)$. We repeatedly refer to options $b(n_t)$, $c(n_t)$, and $d(n_t)$ which are defined in the following way:

Definition 7.5
$b(n_t) \in A(n_t)$ *denotes an option, such that, if* $b(n_{t+1})$ *exists, then* $b(n_{t+1}) \in C(A)(n_{t+1})$.[14]
$c(n_t) \in A(n_t)$ *denotes an option, such that, if* $c(n_{t+1})$ *exists, then* $c(n_{t+1}) \in C(A)(n_{t+1})$ *and* $a_t \neq c_t$.
$d(n_t) \in A(n_t)$ *denotes an option, such that, if* $d(n_{t+1})$ *exists, then* $d(n_{t+1}) \in C(A)(n_{t+1})$ *and* $a_t = d_t$.

We then obtain:

---

[12] This mechanism I owe to a suggestion by U. Schmidt.

[13] An interesting alternative was pointed out to me by Prof. Seidl. He proposes a *sanguine choice mechanism*. In Figure 7.10(b), for instance, the individual moves towards n_1, since the best of those options available at n_1 and relevant at n_0 – option $a(n_0)$ – is better than option $c(n_0)$: $aR(n_0)c$. This mechanism shows some similarity to the notion of "optimistic behaviour" as used by Greenberg (1990, p.18). Greenberg's notion of "conservative behaviour" is linked to the idea of cautious choice. However, he is not concerned with dynamic choice of a single agent but with *social* situations. He studies formal models of social behaviour in the spirit of game theory.

[14] If $b(n_{t+1})$ does not exist, then $b(n_t)$ is the last decision node along $b(n_0)$.

Definition 7.6 *For some option $a(n_t) \in A(n_t)$ to be a member of a **dogmatic** agent's choice set $C(A)(n_t)$, it must hold that*

$$aR(n_t)b \quad \forall \quad b(n_t) \in A(n_t), \tag{7.2}$$

and if $a(n_{t+1})$ exists, then it is also required that $a(n_{t+1}) \in C(A)(n_{t+1})$.

Definition 7.7 *For some option $a(n_t) \in A(n_t)$ to be a member of a **sagacious** agent's choice set $C(A)(n_t)$, it must hold that*

$$aR(n_t)c \quad \forall \quad c(n_t) \in A(n_t), \tag{7.3}$$

and if $a(n_{t+1})$ exists, then it is also required that $a(n_{t+1}) \in C(A)(n_{t+1})$.

Definition 7.8 *For some option $a(n_t) \in A(n_t)$ to be a member of a **lenient** agent's choice set $C(A)(n_t)$, some option $d(n_t)$ must exist (possibly $d(n_t) = a(n_t)$), such that*

$$dR(n_t)b \quad \forall \quad b(n_t) \in A(n_t),$$

and if $a(n_{t+1})$ exists, then it is also required that $a(n_{t+1}) \in C(A)(n_{t+1})$.

Definition 7.9 *Let $c'(n_t)$ indicate particular options $c(n_t)$ for which it is true that $cR(n_t)c'$ for all $c(n_t)$ which share their decision node n_{t+1} with $c'(n_t)$. Furthermore, let $d'(n_t)$ indicate a particular option $d(n_t)$, for which it is true that $dR(n_t)d'$ for all $d(n_t) \in A(n_t)$.*

*For some option $a(n_t) \in A(n_t)$ to be a member of a **cautious** agent's choice set $C(A)(n_t)$, it must hold that*

$$d'R(n_t)c' \quad \forall \quad c'(n_t) \in A(n_t), \tag{7.4}$$

and if $a(n_{t+1})$ exists, then it is also required that $a(n_{t+1}) \in C(A)(n_{t+1})$.

On first sight, one might be tempted to read into these definitions that the agent anticipates only one period. This is not true. Definitions 7.6 to 7.9 exploit the fact that all sophisticated choice mechanisms employ a simple folding back procedure. This allows us to express the sophisticated choice mechanisms' definitions, too, in terms of a two–period choice problem with periods t and $t + 1$. As was true for naive choice, these definitions are equally applicable to multi–period decision problems. Without such a move it would hardly be possible to provide definitions at all. This scepticism is supported by the fact that in the literature on universal utility models no formal definitions of different choice mechanisms exist.

It is now illustrated how these definitions can be applied to a specific decision problem. As an example, consider a dogmatic agent (Definition 7.6) confronted with the decision problem depicted in Figure 7.11, with $A(n_0) = \{e(n_0), f(n_0), g(n_0), h(n_0)\}$.[15]

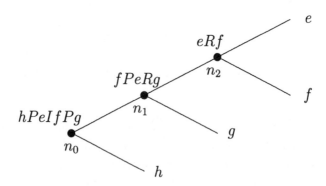

FIGURE 7.11. An Illustration of the Definition of Dogmatic Choice.

Since only for $e(n_2)$ condition (7.2) of Definition 7.6 is satisfied, one obtains $C(A)(n_2) = \{e(n_2)\}$. For $e(n_1)$ to be a member of $C(A)(n_1)$, two requirements must be satisfied. Firstly, it must be true that $e(n_2) \in C(A)(n_2)$, which it is. Secondly, (7.2) postulates that, at n_1, $e(n_1)$ must be weakly preferred to all other options "relevant" at n_1 (that is, to all options which are in

---

[15] As in Figure 7.6, we use e, f, g, and h instead of a, b, c, and d, in order to avoid confusion with the options' labels used in Definition 7.6.

the consecutive node's choice set $C(A)(n_2)$ and to all options for which n_1 represents the last decision node). Since only $e(n_1)$ and $g(n_1)$ are relevant at node n_1, and since $eP(n_1)g$, we obtain $C(A)(n_1) = \{e(n_1)\}$.

Note that encoded in this choice set is the application of Definition 7.6 to the last two periods. It remains to apply Definition 7.6 to the first period. Again, for $e(n_0) \in C(A)(n_0)$ two conditions must be satisfied: $e(n_1) \in C(A)(n_1)$ and, at n_0, $e(n_0)$ weakly preferred to all options relevant at n_0. The former requirement is satisfied but the latter is not. An alternative option exists, namely $h(n_0)$, which is relevant at n_0 but weakly (and strictly) preferred to all other relevant options. At n_0, $h(n_0)$ is relevant simply because the next node along $h(n_0)$ is the terminal node. For $h(n_0)$ (7.2) is satisfied, since $hP(n_0)e$. As a result, $C(A)(n_0) = \{h(n_0)\}$. Definitions 7.7 to 7.9 work analogously.

Note also that Definitions 7.6 to 7.9 imply that choice sets derived by a dogmatic, sagacious, lenient, or cautious choice mechanism are never empty. At each node n_t, associated with each departing branch a relevant option exists. The ordering at n_t selects the best among these relevant options. This best option, in turn, is relevant at the preceding node n_{t-1}, and so forth. This aspect is particularly important for the game theoretic analysis of section 7.4.

Our list of sophisticated choice mechanisms is certainly not complete. Other varieties, however, are either less "plausible" or more complex or both. In the absence of any indifference, dogmatic, sagacious, lenient, and cautious choice coincide and are equivalent to the simpler notion of sophisticated choice. Differences can only arise from the fact that choice sets $C(A)(n_t)$ are not necessarily singletons. Without indifference, however, they are singletons.

Reading through the literature one gets the impression that sophisticated choice is regarded as a superior way of intertemporal decision making. In section 2.4, for instance, we illustrated Yaari's (1977) view on this issue. We should emphasize, however, that a choice mechanism always carries with it an *ad hoc* assumption on the agent's freedom to act. A sophisticated agent acts on the presumption that he is not able to overrule the preferences associated with final decision nodes, but initial preferences can be revoked. A resolute agent, in contrast, feels bound by initial preferences, but preferences at final decision nodes may be overruled. For a naive agent, it is never possible to revoke any preferences.[16]

7.4 Sophisticated Choice and Subgame Perfection

As described in section 6.3.2, Peleg and Yaari (1973) point out that indifference may cause ambiguous choice behaviour. Instead of a single agent moving through time, they consider a sequence of generations. Then, a choice mechanism could be interpreted as the decision rule of an independent central planner for transforming the various generations' orderings into actual choice. The basic idea of Peleg and Yaari can be easily illustrated in Figure 7.12.

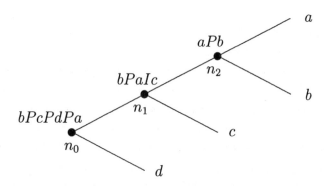

FIGURE 7.12. Ambiguities Arising from Indifferences.

---

[16] For an interesting alternative based upon the psychological notion of self–control see Thaler and Shefrin (1981). In their model the choice mechanism is endogenously determined. They formalize this idea by distinguishing between a doer's and a planner's utility function. Broadly speaking, the more resolute (the less naive) the mechanism, that is the more the planner interferes with the doer's planned choices, the higher the costs. Such an approach requires some *ad–hoc* utility function of the planner which weighs the gains from more resolution (they speak of self–control or control over the doer) against the costs of implementing it.

Suppose the central planner applies some sophisticated choice mechanism. Since at n_2, $a(n_2)$ is preferred to $b(n_2)$, the latter option is irrelevant for generation 1, and hence, $a(n_0)$ and $c(n_0)$ are *relevant* for generation 0. This generation prefers $c(n_0)$ to $d(n_0)$, the third relevant option. However, $d(n_0)$ is preferred to $a(n_0)$.

It should be emphasized that all orderings in Figure 7.12 are single–peaked. Nevertheless, the ambiguity arises: Depending on whether the central planner applies a lenient or dogmatic (sagacious) choice mechanism, option $a(n_0)$ is a member of $C(A)(n_0)$, with $A(n_0) = \{a(n_0), b(n_0), c(n_0), d(n_0)\}$.

Peleg and Yaari express their suspicion that indifference implies that, in general, no pure subgame–perfect equilibrium exists.[17] Goldman (1980) refutes this view (they all speak of "Strotz–Pollak equilibria" rather than subgame–perfect equilibria). He shows that in the Peleg and Yaari framework a (pure) subgame–perfect equilibrium always exists. Note, however, that the Peleg and Yaari framework is a very special case of the framework underlying our own work. In their work it is assumed that preference orderings are representable by continuous utility functions defined on infinite compact opportunity sets. Furthermore, preferences can be formed across different decision nodes of the same period (cross–history comparisons). In our own analysis it is sufficient that the opportunity set is compact. Moreover, preference orderings may or may not be representable by a continuous utility function and cross–history comparisons may or may not be feasible.

The strategy profiles proposed by Goldman turn out to be an analogue of what we denoted in our study as a dogmatic choice mechanism. More generally, a choice mechanism can be interpreted as a set of possible pure strategies which the central planner prescribes for each generation. Obviously, every subgame–perfect equilibrium results in the actual choice of some option $x(n_t)$. We denote such an option as *subgame–perfect* with re-

---

[17]The idea of subgame–perfection is formalized in Selten's classic paper (1965).

spect to $A(n_t)$. Transformed in our notation, one can formalize the notion of subgame perfection in the following way:

Definition 7.10 *Let $e(n_t) \in A(n_t)$ denote an option, such that either $e(n_{t+1})$ is subgame perfect with respect to $A(n_{t+1})$ or $e(n_{t+1})$ does not exist. Let $e'(n_t)$ indicate particular options $e(n_t)$ for which it is true that $eR(n_t)e'$ for all $e(n_t)$ which share their decision node n_{t+1} with $e'(n_t)$.*

For some option $f(n_t) \in A(n_t)$ to be subgame perfect with respect to $A(n_t)$, it must hold that

$$fR(n_t)e' \quad \forall \quad e'(n_t) \in A(n_t),$$

and if $f(n_{t+1})$ exists, then $f(n_{t+1})$ also must be subgame perfect with respect to $A(n_{t+1})$.

In Figure 7.13, for instance, $a(n_1)$ and $b(n_1)$ are subgame perfect with respect to $A(n_1^{ab}) = \{a(n_1^{ab}), b(n_1^{ab})\}$, and $c(n_1)$ and $d(n_1)$ are subgame perfect with respect to $A(n_1^{cd}) = \{c(n_1^{cd}), d(n_1^{cd})\}$. Now consider the opportunity set $A(n_0) = \{a(n_0), b(n_0), c(n_0), d(n_0)\}$. The two options $b(n_0)$ and $c(n_0)$ are of the type "$e'(n_t)$" of Definition 7.10. Option $a(n_0)$ is subgame perfect with respect to $A(n_0)$, since, firstly, it is weakly preferred to $b(n_0)$ and $c(n_0)$, the options of type "$e'(n_t)$", and secondly, it is subgame perfect with respect to $A(n_{t+1})$. The same is true for $d(n_0)$.

We now investigate which sophisticated choice mechanism prescribes (pure) strategy profiles which form a *subgame–perfect equilibrium*.

Theorem 7.1 *All members of $C(A)(n_t)$ generated by a dogmatic, sagacious, or cautious choice mechanism, are subgame–perfect with respect to $A(n_t)$.*

PROOF:

[3] Suppose that, for all $n_{t+1} \in A(n_t)$, all members of $C(A)(n_{t+1})$ are subgame–perfect.

[4] Let $c(n_t) \in A(n_t)$ denote an option with $c_t \neq a_t$ and $c(n_{t+1}) \in C(A)(n_{t+1})$. Let $c'(n_t)$ indicate particular options

$c(n_t)$, for which it is true that $cR(n_t)c'$ for all $c(n_t)$ which share their decision node n_{t+1} with $c'(n_t)$.

[5] We know from Definitions 7.6, 7.7, and 7.9 that $a(n_t) \in C(A)(n_t)$ implies that $a(n_{t+1}) \in C(A)(n_{t+1})$. Then, for each $a(n_t) \in C(A)(n_t)$ to be subgame–perfect it is sufficient that $aR(n_t)c' \lor c'(n_t) \in A(n_t)$. (7.2), (7.3), and (7.4) ensure that this is satisfied for dogmatic, sagacious, and cautious choice.

[6] Since for dogmatic, sagacious, and cautious choice all members of $C(A)(n_T)$ are subgame–perfect, one can recursively apply [3] to [5], beginning with $t = T - 1$.   ‖

In contrast, members of a lenient choice set are not necessarily subgame–perfect. In Figure 7.10b lenient choice yields $C(A)(n_0) = \{a(n_0), b(n_0)\}$. Due to $cP(n_0)b$, however, $b(n_0)$ is not subgame–perfect with respect to $A(n_0)$.

Since Definitions 7.6, 7.7, and 7.9 imply that $C(A)(n_t)$ is never empty, we can conclude:

Corollary 7.1 *All choice problems possess at least one option which is subgame–perfect.*

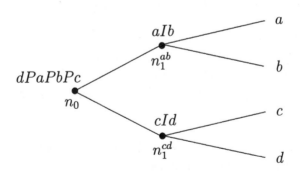

FIGURE 7.13. Subgame–Perfection of Sophisticated Choice.

Notice that the reverse of Theorem 7.1 is not true. Not all subgame–perfect options appear in a dogmatic, sagacious, or cautious choice set. Consider Figure 7.13, where, for $A(n_0) = \{a(n_0), b(n_0), c(n_0), d(n_0)\}$, we have three subgame–perfect options, namely $a(n_0)$, $b(n_0)$, and $d(n_0)$. None of our choice mechanisms, however, exhibits a choice set $C(A)(n_0)$ with $b(n_0)$ as its member.

Is it possible to define a choice mechanism which generates exactly those actual choices which are subgame–perfect? In other words, is it possible to define subgame perfect solutions in terms of dynamic choice mechanisms? Making use of Definition 7.5, we introduce the following choice mechanism:

Definition 7.11 *Let $b'(n_t)$ indicate particular options $b(n_t)$ for which it is true that $bR(n_t)b'$ for all $b(n_t)$ which share their decision node n_{t+1} with $b'(n_t)$.*

*For some option $a(n_t) \in A(n_t)$ to be a member of a **perfect** agent's choice set $C(A)(n_t)$, it must hold that*

$$aR(n_t)b' \quad \forall \quad b'(n_t) \in A(n_t),$$

and if $a(n_{t+1})$ exists, then it is also required that $a(n_{t+1}) \in C(A)(n_{t+1})$.

This mechanism leads to the following result:

Theorem 7.2 *An option is subgame–perfect with respect to $A(n_t)$, if and only if it is a member of the choice set $C(A)(n_t)$ generated by the perfect choice mechanism.*

PROOF: The proof is trivial, since Definition 7.10 can be easily transformed into Definition 7.11: Simply replace $e(n_t)$, $e'(n_t)$, and $f(n_t)$ by $b(n_t)$, $b'(n_t)$, and $a(n_t)$ and substitute "subgame perfect with respect to $A(n_t)$" by "a member of choice set $C(A)(n_t)$". ‖

It is well known that subgame–perfect solutions are not necessarily Pareto–efficient (see section 6.3.2). Our own choice framework is no exception. Recall that at each decision node preferences are formed only with respect to the options available at this node. A discussion of Pareto–efficiency requires cross–history comparisons. That is, we need to know preferences across decision nodes of the same period. In Figure 7.13, for instance, replace $cI(n_1^{cd})d$ by $cP(n_1^{cd})d$ and assume that generation 1 prefers both $c(n_1)$ and $d(n_1)$ to $a(n_1)$ and $b(n_1)$. The only Pareto–efficient options would be $c(n_0)$ and $d(n_0)$. These two options, however, appear in none of the sophisticated choice sets $C(A)(n_0)$, with $A(n_0) = \{a(n_0), b(n_0), c(n_0), d(n_0)\}$.

7.5   Recapitulation

Most dynamic frameworks to be found in the literature are based on weak preferences defined on infinite compact sets. In contrast, contributions to the analysis of choice mechanisms usually assume strict preferences defined on finite sets. It was the purpose of this chapter to bridge this gap. The decision tree formulation of the universal utility model allows also for the analysis of weak preferences defined on the general class of compact sets. It contains as special cases all standard models of dynamic choice.

We introduced a number of new forward–looking choice mechanisms (dogmatic, sagacious, lenient, cautious, and perfect choice) which can cope also with indifference. These refined versions of sophisticated choice were compared to naive and resolute choice. Furthermore, formal definitions were provided for all these choice mechanisms. Finally, we showed that each finite choice problem possesses at least one subgame–perfect equilibrium and that the notion of subgame perfection can be formalized in terms of choice mechanisms. More specifically, an actual choice is generated by a subgame perfect equilibrium if and only if it is a member of the choice set generated by the perfect choice mechanism.

In the following chapter we develop some properties characterizing the agent's choice behaviour.

8
Properties of Dynamic Choice Functions

8.1 Preliminaries

In the previous chapter we primarily discussed six choice mechanisms: naive, resolute, dogmatic, sagacious, lenient and cautious choice.[1] These choice mechanisms specify the rule according to which preferences are transformed into choice sets. The present chapter is concerned with the choice sets themselves, and not with the mechanism they are generated from. Specifically, we describe in which way the choice sets vary as we change the opportunity sets, that is we analyse a choice function (see Definition 6.2). Depending on the way the choice sets vary, we say that the choice function exhibits a certain *property*.

---

[1]In the context of subgame perfection (section 7.4), we also introduced the perfect choice mechanism. We do not consider this last choice mechanism any further.

Various properties can be thought of for the characterization of choice functions. In section 6.2.3 we described three such properties, namely property α, H–consistency, and H–ordinality. In the present chapter we are primarily concerned with two properties labelled as *stability* and *ordinality*.

In section 8.2 we explain what is meant by the property of ordinality, and we relate ordinality to the well–known properties usually referred to as property α and property β. Furthermore, the property of stability is introduced. Choices which satisfy both ordinality and stability are denoted as *contractible*. Here, we demonstrate the relationship between H–ordinality (as introduced in section 6.2.3) and contractibility.

A driving force behind the debate on dynamically changing preferences is the endeavour to reduce dynamic choice problems to static ones, in order to apply the powerful tools of static optimization. Such a simplification is acceptable if the actual choices generated in the dynamic setup are identical to those one would obtain from the corresponding static formulation of the decision problem. Contractibility ensures that this requirement is satisfied.

Finally, we should stress that the satisfaction of some property of choice may depend on the applied choice mechanism. For a given decision problem, it is quite possible that a naive choice mechanism generates choice sets satisfying the property of stability, say, whereas a sagacious mechanism does not lead to stability. We turn to these aspects in chapter 10 and section 11.8.

8.2   Contractible Choice Functions

8.2.1   Ordinality of Choice

Ordinal choice can be decomposed into two properties known as property α and property β. In order to understand the meaning of these two properties, let us imagine a simple essentially static choice problem with n_0 being the only decision node.

Example 8.1 *An individual has three options concerning his life-time nutrition. He may live either on*

    a) apple pie,

    b) beerwurst (an odd German meat product), or

    c) chewing gum.

We define the opportunity set $A(n_0)$ as $A(n_0) = \{a(n_0), b(n_0), c(n_0)\}$, and the opportunity set $\tilde{A}(n_0)$ as $\tilde{A}(n_0) = \{b(n_0), c(n_0)\}$. Apparently $\tilde{A}(n_0) \subset A(n_0) \subseteq X(n_0)$. When confronted with set $\tilde{A}(n_0)$, suppose the agent, quite understandably, chooses chewing gum, $c(n_0)$ and rejects beerwurst, $b(n_0)$.

Now, property α requires that confronting the agent with $A(n_0)$, that is extending the opportunity set to include apple pie, $a(n_0)$, he still rejects beerwurst. In other words, adding new options to an opportunity set should not have the effect that a previously rejected option (a member of $\tilde{A}(n_t) \setminus C(\tilde{A})(n_t)$) suddenly becomes favourable (a member of $C(A)(n_t)$). In a dynamic choice context, this was expressed in Definition 6.3:

Definition 6.3 *Choices satisfies property α if and only if for all $A(n_t)$ and $\tilde{A}(n_t)$ in $X(n_0)$, with $\tilde{A}(n_t) \subseteq A(n_t)$:*

$$C(A)(n_t) \cap [\tilde{A}(n_t) \setminus C(\tilde{A})(n_t)] = \emptyset.$$

It is generally accepted that for choice behaviour to be "rational" in a *static set–up*, it must satisfy property α. In Lemma 2, Sen (1969), p.384, has shown, however, that every static choice function that is generated by a binary relation satisfies property α.[2] In Corollary 1, p.385, he proves that, if and only if C satisfies property β, the underlying binary relation is an *ordering*.

To understand this property suppose the individual's choices related to Example 8.1 are as follows: Confronted with $\tilde{A}(n_0)$ the indidividual would in principle accept both choices chewing gum and beerwurst. Property β then requires that the agent

---

[2] This may become clearer from the following *static* example: Suppose a binary relation with aRb, aRc, bRa, cRa, cPb. Then static choice (that is trivial choice as specified in Definition 7.2) generates the following choice function: $C(\{a,b,c\}) = \{a,c\}$, $C(\{a,b\}) = \{a,b\}$, $C(\{a,c\}) = \{a,c\}$, $C(\{b,c\}) = \{c\}$. So despite intransitivity (bRa, aRc, and not$\{bRc\}$) choice satisfies property α.

confronted with $A(n_0)$ either keeps accepting both chewing gum and beerwurst or neither of them. In other words, property β excludes the possibility that one option previously in the choice set is rejected from it as new options are added, while simultaneously another option remains in the choice set. Again, we state the dynamic version of this property's definition:

Definition 8.1 *Choice satisfies property β if and only if for all $A(n_t)$, $\tilde{A}(n_t)$ in $X(n_0)$, with $\tilde{A}(n_t) \subseteq A(n_t)$, either*

$$C(\tilde{A})(n_t) \subseteq C(A)(n_t) \tag{8.1}$$

or

$$C(\tilde{A})(n_t) \cap C(A)(n_t) = \emptyset. \tag{8.2}$$

Sen's results lead directly to a finding which is applicable only to *static* decision problems: If a static choice function C is generated by some ordering R then it satisfies properties α and β.[3]

In a dynamic context, however, things become more confusing by the fact that there are orderings and choices at several points in time and it is now much harder to satisfy properties α and β. Regardless of whether a static or dynamic decision problem is considered, *preferences* are exogenously given and remain unaltered as options are added or excluded from the opportunity set. Dynamic *choices*, in contrast, are not invariant to changes in the opportunity set.

This may become clearer once we consider the naive choice function related to node n_0 of Figure 8.1. Adding option $b(n_0)$ to the set $\{a(n_0), c(n_0)\}$ yields $C(\{a(n_0), b(n_0), c(n_0)\}) = \{a(n_0)\}$. Option $a(n_0)$, however, was previously rejected: $C(\{a(n_0), c(n_0)\}) = \{c(n_0)\}$. Therefore, the naive agent exhibits choices that violate property α, even though at each node the agent's preferences over options can be represented by an ordering.

---

[3] Moreover, Sen's (1971, p.310) Theorem 3 shows that a choice function satisfying properties α and β generates an ordering R, which in turn, generates a choice function $\tilde{C}$ such that $\tilde{C} = C$. If also $R = \tilde{R}$, then a perfect correspondence exists between choice and preference.

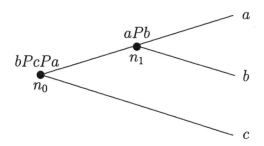

FIGURE 8.1. A Simple Choice Problem Violating Ordinality.

Choice which satisfies both property α and property β we denote as *ordinal*.[4] More formally we obtain:

Definition 8.2 *Choice is ordinal if and only if for all $A(n_t)$ and $\tilde{A}(n_t)$ in $X(n_0)$, with $\tilde{A}(n_t) \subseteq A(n_t)$ and $\tilde{A}(n_t) \cap C(A)(n_t) \neq \emptyset$:*

$$C(\tilde{A})(n_t) = \tilde{A}(n_t) \cap C(A)(n_t). \tag{8.3}$$

The term "ordinal" indicates that an agent's choice function related to node n_t, say, can be thought of as the result of *static choice* based on some *shadow ordering* $\mathsf{R}(\mathsf{n_t})$, even though they actually were the product of a complicated dynamic decision process. It is important to note that this shadow ordering is not necessarily identical to $R(n_t)$.

Consider Figure 8.2. For the purpose of illustration, we now derive a shadow ordering corresponding to a sagacious agent's choice function related to node n_0. Recall that a sagacious agent accepts some relevant option in the choice set $C(A)(n_0)$ if it is weakly preferred to all splitting relevant options. In Figure 8.2 with $A(n_0) = \{a(n_0), b(n_0), c(n_0)\}$, only options $a(n_0)$ and $c(n_0)$ are relevant at n_0. Of these two options $a(n_0)$ is preferred: $C(\{a(n_0), b(n_0), c(n_0)\}) = \{a(n_0)\}$. The choice function's various choice sets are listed to the left of Table 8.1, and the shadow preferences required to generate just these choice sets are listed to the right. The sagacious agent located at n_0 would, there-

---

[4]This is Arrow's (1959) property $C4$, p.123 stated in a dynamic terminology.

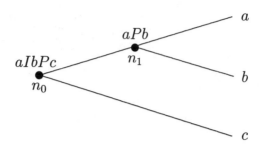

FIGURE 8.2. A Sagacious Agent's Choice Problem.

$$C(\{a(n_0), b(n_0), c(n_0)\}) = \{a(n_0)\} \iff a\mathsf{P}(n_0)b, a\mathsf{P}(n_0)c,$$
$$C(\{a(n_0), b(n_0)\}) = \{a(n_0)\} \iff a\mathsf{P}(n_0)b,$$
$$C(\{a(n_0), c(n_0)\}) = \{a(n_0)\} \iff a\mathsf{P}(n_0)c,$$
$$C(\{b(n_0), c(n_0)\}) = \{b(n_0)\} \iff b\mathsf{P}(n_0)c,$$

$\ldots$

TABLE 8.1. Ordinal Sagacious Choices and Shadow Preferences.

fore, arrive at the same choice sets as if static choice were applied based on the shadow ordering $a\mathsf{P}(n_0)b\mathsf{P}(n_0)c$. Table 8.1 shows that the agent's choices exhibit ordinality. Note that $\mathsf{R}(n_0) \neq R(n_0)$. At this point we should stress that ordinality merely says that some shadow ordering exists at each node. Note, however, that these shadow orderings may change between different nodes.

8.2.2 Stability of Choice

The second property to be discussed here is denoted as *stability*. Whereas ordinality captures the behaviour of a single choice function as options are added, stability is a constraint on the logical relationship between choice functions related to consecutive nodes.

Definition 8.3 *Choice is stable if and only if for all $A(n_s)$ and $A(n_t)$ in $X(n_0)$, with $A(n_s) \subseteq A(n_t)$ and $A(n_s) \cap C(A)(n_t) \neq \emptyset$:*

$$C(A)(n_s) = A(n_s) \cap C(A)(n_t). \tag{8.4}$$

This says that if some option $a(n_t)$ is in the choice set of node n_t, and a truncated part $a(n_s)$ $(s \geq t)$ is still available at decision node n_s, then stability requires two things: Firstly, $a(n_s)$ must also be in the choice set at n_s, and secondly, available truncated options $b(n_s)$ of options $b(n_t)$ which were rejected at n_t should not appear in the choice set related to node n_s.

How does stability relate to Hammond's (1976a) concept of H–consistency, which we introduced in section 6.2.3? There, H–consistency was defined in the following way:

Definition 6.4 *Choice is H–consistent if and only if for all $A(n_t)$ and $A(n_0)$ in $X(n_0)$, with $A(n_t) \subseteq A(n_0)$ and $A(n_t) \cap C(A)(n_0) \neq \emptyset$:*

$$C(A)(n_t) = A(n_t) \cap C(A)(n_0).$$

It is easy to prove the following finding:

Theorem 8.1 *Stability and H–consistency coincide.*

PROOF:

[7] Stability implies H–consistency, since, for $n_s = n_t$ and $n_t = n_0$, Definition 8.3 yields Definition 6.4.

[8] H–consistency implies stability since H–consistency postulates that, for $s \geq t$, $C(A)(n_s) = A(n_s) \cap C(A)(n_0) = A(n_s) \cap A(n_t) \cap C(A)(n_0) = A(n_s) \cap C(A)(n_t)$, which is Definition 8.3. ‖

8.2.3   Contractibility of Choice

Contractibility postulates that the dynamic choice problem is representable by a static decision problem. More specifically, it must be possible that actual choices out of any opportunity set $A(n_t)$ can be derived from the shadow ordering $R(n_0) = R$.

In Figure 8.2, for instance, sagacious choices at n_0 as well as choices at n_1 can be directly derived from the same shadow ordering R. The shadow ordering related to n_0 is $aP(n_0)bP(n_0)c$ (see Table 8.1). The dynamic choice problem yields $C(\{a(n_1), b(n_1)\}) = \{a(n_1)\}$. Hence, we obtain $aP(n_1)b$ which is identical to the shadow preference expressed in $R(n_0)$.

In other words, contractibility implies that the dynamic choice problem depicted in Figure 8.2 can be transformed into a static one depicted in Figure 8.3. The label *contractibility* is designed to reflect the contracted form of Figure 8.3 as compared to the original tree Figure 8.2. Contractibility is defined in the follow-

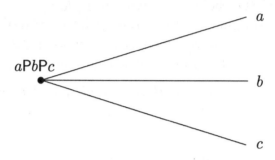

FIGURE 8.3. A Contracted Choice Problem.

ing way:

Definition 8.4 *Choice is contractible, if and only if a shadow ordering* R *exists, such that for all* $A(n_t)$ *in* $X(n_0)$:

$$a(n_t) \in C(A)(n_t) \quad \Longleftrightarrow \quad aRb \,\forall\, b(n_t) \in A(n_t).$$

Combining ordinality and stability (Definitions 8.2 and 8.3) leads to the following finding:

Theorem 8.2 *Choice is stable and ordinal if and only if for all* $\tilde{A}(n_s)$ *and* $A(n_t)$ *in* $X(n_0)$, *with* $\tilde{A}(n_s) \subseteq A(n_t)$ *and* $\tilde{A}(n_s) \cap C(A)(n_t) \neq \emptyset$:

$$C(\tilde{A})(n_s) = \tilde{A}(n_s) \cap C(A)(n_t).$$

PROOF: See the proof of Theorem 11.3.

In order to emphasize the different meanings of Definitions 8.2, 8.3, and Theorem 8.2, we repeat a notational aspect which was pointed out in section 6.2.3. $A(n_s)$ indicates subsets of $A(n_t)$, $s \geq t$, which evolve as the agent moves through the decision tree: $A(n_s) = X(n_s) \cap A(n_t)$. These are the subsets employed by the property of stability. $\tilde{A}(n_t)$, in contrast, indicates those subsets of $A(n_t)$ which are generated by excluding options $x(n_t)$ from $A(n_t)$. Ordinality corresponds to this latter type of subsets. Finally, $\tilde{A}(n_s)$ combines both cases. Theorem 8.2 applies this last notion of subsets.

We saw that ordinality implies that to each node a shadow ordering $R(n_t)$ exists, but recall that these shadow orderings may well differ from node to node. It is this last aspect which makes the joint satisfaction of ordinality and stability so interesting. Stability ensures that the shadow ordering $R(n_0)$ is valid also at each subsequent node. It is therefore straightforward to arrive at the following finding:

Theorem 8.3 *Choice is contractible if and only if it is stable and ordinal.*

PROOF: See the proof of Theorem 11.4.

Note that Theorem 8.2 corresponds exactly to the definition of H–ordinality (Definition 6.6) as introduced in section 6.2.3.[5] In view of Theorem 8.3, one can conclude that contractibility and H–ordinality are equivalent properties. The relationship between the various properties is summarized in Figure 8.4.

An important question to ask is whether and how a shadow ordering R can be directly deduced from a decision tree. The answer is surprisingly simple.

Theorem 8.4 *If choice is contractible, then the shadow preference between each pair of options $a(n_t)$ and $b(n_t)$ can be read off the dynamic decision tree. It is the preference related to their discrimination node n_s^{ab}, $s \geq t$.*

PROOF: See the proof of Theorem 11.5.

Is it possible to proclaim contractibility, if combining the discrimination nodes' respective preferences yields an ordering? In

---

[5] The property in its dynamic application goes back to Hammond (1977), though he appears unaware of its far–reaching implications. In Hammond's study, H–ordinality is labelled as ordinality.

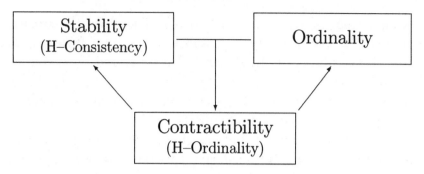

FIGURE 8.4. A Synopsis of Properties of Dynamic Choice Functions

other words, does the *existence* of a shadow ordering R (which is generated by the discrimination nodes' preferences) imply that contractibility is satisfied? We will see in chapter 10 that this is true only for some of our choice mechanisms.

We conclude this chapter with an important finding which directly follows from Definition 8.4 and Theorem 8.4:

Corollary 8.1 *For a given decision tree, if, out of the types of choice mechanisms presented in this study, any types exhibit contractibility, then the choice sets generated by these types are identical.*

8.3   Recapitulation

The link between preferences and actual choices is the applied choice mechanism. The various choice mechanisms were discussed in chapter 7. In the present chapter we looked at the resulting choices. Specifically, properties were investigated which characterize an agent's actual choices.

Two properties were introduced which we labelled as stability and ordinality. We proved that choices which satisfy both are contractible. The term is designed to reflect the fact that all dynamic choices can be equally generated by a static decision model which is based on a shadow ordering.

In the following chapter we discuss the question of whether this shadow ordering can be used as a valid yardstick for an agent's "overall preferences".

9
Welfare Judgements

9.1 Preliminaries

In this chapter it is argued that, given contractibility, the shadow ordering R can be viewed as a valid construct revealing an agent's *overall preferences*. This is an extremely valuable property of shadow preferences, since it allows us to make welfare judgements even in the presence of changing preferences!

To make the point more sharply, let us consider the simple example depicted in Figure 9.1:

Example 9.1 *A representative citizen may choose between a number of proposals for modifying the existing tax system. Terminal node a represents a fundamental tax reform and terminal node d indicates that taxes remain as they are. Options b and c* *represent minor reforms. The citizen's changing preferences are depicted in Figure 9.1.*

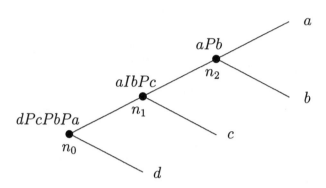

FIGURE 9.1. Changing Preferences on a Tax Reform.

Figure 9.1 illustrates why dynamic choice problems usually do not square with welfare judgements. Let us consider the preferences between options $a(n_t)$ and $b(n_t)$. Viewed from node n_0, the minor reform, $b(n_0)$, appears as the better option, viewed from node n_1, the citizen is undecided, but from the perspective of n_2 she strictly supports the fundamental tax reform, $a(n_2)$. This discrepancy is ususally taken as a reason to abstain from any judgement as to whether the individual is better off with the fundamental or with the limited tax reform. That is, one avoids claiming that the sequence of truncated branches $a(n_0), a(n_1), a(n_2)$ is revealed preferred to the sequence $b(n_0), b(n_1), b(n_0)$. Or to put it more simply, terminal node a is not necessarily overall preferred to terminal node b.

We take a different view. More specifically, we take a revealed preference view. The idea of using a revealed preference argument is not completely new. In section 3.3, we briefly discussed a similar idea put forward in v. Weizsäcker's (1971) classic paper. In section 9.2, v. Weizsäcker's argument is illustrated in decision tree notation. It is pointed out where and why we do not agree with his line of reasoning. In section 9.3 we propose an alternative approach which can be viewed as the offspring of our criticism expressed in section 9.2. The fundamental finding of this alternative approach is that contractibility, and only contractibility, allows for welfare judgements in the presence of changing preferences.

9.2   The Revealed Preference Approach of v. Weizsäcker

In this section we investigate v. Weizsäcker's (1971) claim that under certain conditions choice behaviour reveals "overall preferences". He is concerned with a myopic utility model, though, featuring a naive agent. As a side effect, we illustrate how a myopic utility problem looks like in decision tree terminology.

Example 9.2 *In each of two consecutive periods, an agent may choose between three consumption bundles $x_t = (x_t^1, x_t^2)$ each featuring different quantities of the two goods x_t^1 and x_t^2. The three bundles are (12,8), (11,9), and (10,10). Suppose that preferences at each decision node are determined by*

$$U = \frac{1}{2}\ln(x_t^1 - \frac{2}{3}x_{t-1}^1) + \frac{1}{2}\ln(x_t^2 - \frac{2}{3}x_{t-1}^2). \qquad (9.1)$$

and that in period -1 the agent consumed bundle (12,8).[1] The decision problem is depicted in Figure 9.2.

First of all notice that (9.1) is a myopic utility function. Given past consumption, the preferences at n_0 exclusively depend on consumption during period 0. The bundle of period 1 is completely irrelevant for the preference at n_0. Hence, $aI(n_0)bI(n_0)c$, $dI(n_0)eI(n_0)f$, and $gI(n_0)hI(n_0)i$. It is easy to compute that $dP(n_0)aP(n_0)g$ and $bP(n_1)aP(n_1)c$. Furthermore, $fP(n_1')eP(n_1')d$ and $iP(n_1'')hP(n_1'')g$.

In the introduction to this chapter we considered the overall preference between two *truncated branches* (or options) $a(n_t)$

---

[1]This utility function falls into the class of utility functions considered by v. Weizsäcker.

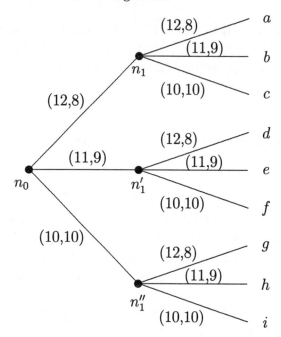

FIGURE 9.2. An Illustration of v. Weizsäcker's Argument.

and $b(n_t)$. It is important to realize that v. Weizsäcker does not
consider *branches* (e.g. sequences of consumption bundles) but
single consumption bundles, that is *portions* (see page 103). In
Figure 9.2, he does not evaluate $a(n_0) = (a_1, a_2)$ versus $i(n_0) = (i_1, i_2)$, say, but bundle (12,8) versus bundle (10,10), that is a_0
versus i_0.

The ranking of some given bundles may well depend on past
consumption. At n_0 and n_1, (12,8) is preferred to (10,10) but
at n_1' and n_1'' the preference is reversed.[2] It is claimed by v.
Weizsäcker that in spite of these different preferences a "welfare
statement" is admissable ranking the two *bundles* (12,8) and
(10,10). Specifically, bundle (10,10) is deemed (revealed) overall
preferred to (12,8).

What justification is given for this judgement? He puts forward the argument that it is possible to move to bundle (12,8)

---

[2] Only in so–called atemporal dynamic models, that is models in which time is not
real time but "computing" time, the ranking between two bundles can be taken as
independent of the past.

in a finite number of steps such that in each period the move to the new bundle is regarded as an improvement. Specifically, at n_0 the naive agent moves to n_1' which implies consumption of (11,9) instead of (12,8). This change is considered as beneficial, since $dP(n_0)a$. In a second step the agent moves from n_1' towards f. Again, the change is regarded as an improvement: $fP(n_1')e$.

Is the existence of this sequence of moves sufficient to justify a welfare statement which takes bundle (10,10) as (revealed) overall preferred to bundle (12,8)? We object that the voluntary moves leading to the adoption of bundle (10,10) crucially depend on the underlying set of bundles, and hence on the opportunity set $A(n_0)$. More specifically, if (11,9) was not available, that is, if only $a(n_0)$, $c(n_0)$, $g(n_0)$, and $i(n_0)$ existed, then the agent would have sticked to bundle (12,8). It were no longer possible to claim that the agent's actual choices reveal an overall preference for bundle (10,10).

Our point is that only if the agent would end up with bundle (10,10) in *all* feasible choice situations, will a revealed preference argument judging (10,10) as superior be convincing. This aspect is taken up in the following section.

9.3 A Revealed Preference Approach Based on Contractibility

Let us return to the introductory Example 9.1 and consider the pair of terminal nodes a and b. Under which conditions is it justified to regard a as (revealed) overall preferred to b? Or analogously, which property ensures that the sequence of truncated branches $a(n_0)$, $a(n_1)$, and $a(n_2)$, is preferred to the sequence $b(n_0)$, $b(n_1)$, and $b(n_2)$? As alluded to in the previous section, in contrast to v. Weizsäcker, we intend to establish overall preferences on sequences of *branches* and not on *bundles*.

In making a revealed preference argument, we have to investigate the various choice sets reflecting the citizen's actual choices. Obviously, if neither $a(n_t)$ nor $b(n_t)$ appear in the opportunity set $A(n_t)$, then $C(A)(n_t)$ gives us no clue about the overall preference between a and b. The same is true if neither $a(n_t)$ nor $b(n_t)$ appear in the choice set $C(A)(n_t)$ even though $\{a(n_t), b(n_t)\} \subseteq A(n_t)$. In the latter case preferences over $a(n_t)$ and $b(n_t)$ are formed but they are not *revealed*. Only if both options are in $A(n_t)$ and at least one of them is a member of $C(A)(n_t)$, some information is revealed about the ranking of these two options. We therefore confine our interest to those opportunity sets $A(n_t)$ for which it is true that $\{a(n_t), b(n_t)\} \subseteq A(n_t)$ and that $\{a(n_t), b(n_t)\} \cap C(A)(n_t) \neq \emptyset$. Let us indicate such an opportunity set as $\hat{A}(n_t)$. Note that for all $\hat{A}(n_t)$ one has $t \leq s$, where s indicates the period of discrimination node n_s^{ab}.

If for some opportunity set $\hat{A}(n_t)$ it is true that $a(n_t) \in C(\hat{A})(n_t)$ and $b(n_t) \notin C(\hat{A})(n_t)$, but for some alternative opportunity set $\hat{A}'(n_r)$, we observe that $a(n_r) \notin C(\hat{A}')(n_r)$ and $b(n_r) \in C(\hat{A}')(n_r)$, then no welfare judgement can be made. Even if for *all* $\hat{A}(n_t)$ it is true that $a(n_t) \in C(\hat{A})(n_t)$ and if some opportunity set $\hat{A}'(n_r)$ leads to $b(n_r) \in C(\hat{A}')(n_r)$, it is debatable whether a welfare judgement can be justified. After all, for opportunity set $\hat{A}'(n_r)$ both options $a(n_r)$ and $b(n_r)$ appear indifferent. If, however, for all $\hat{A}(n_t)$ one observes $a(n_t) \in C(\hat{A})(n_t)$ and $b(n_t) \notin C(\hat{A})(n_t)$, then there is no reason left to question a's welfare superiority over b. Only for this last case a welfare statement appears admissable. These considerations are formalized in the following definition:

Definition 9.1 *Terminal node a is (revealed) overall preferred to terminal node b if and only if for all opportunity sets $\hat{A}(n_t)$, that is, for all opportunity sets with $\{a(n_t), b(n_t)\} \subseteq \hat{A}(n_t)$ and $\{a(n_t), b(n_t)\} \cap C(\hat{A})(n_t) \neq \emptyset$, one has*

$$\{a(n_t), b(n_t)\} \cap C(\hat{A})(n_t) = \{a(n_t)\},$$

and it is (revealed) overall indifferent to terminal node b if and only if for all opportunity sets $\hat{A}(n_t)$, that is, for all opportunity sets with $\{a(n_t), b(n_t)\} \subseteq \hat{A}(n_t)$ and $\{a(n_t), b(n_t)\} \cap C(\hat{A})(n_t) \neq \emptyset$, one has

$$\{a(n_t), b(n_t)\} \cap C(\hat{A})(n_t) = \{a(n_t), b(n_t)\}.$$

As a result of this postulate, for many pairs of terminal nodes no overall preference may exist. For terminal nodes a and b of Figure 9.1, however, an overall preference exists. In order to see this, we list all opportunity sets $\hat{A}(n_t)$, that is, all opportunity sets $A(n_t)$ for which it is true that $\{a(n_t), b(n_t)\} \subseteq A(n_t)$ and that $\{a(n_t), b(n_t)\} \cap C(A)(n_t) \neq \emptyset$:

$$\begin{aligned}
\hat{A}(n_0) &= \{a(n_0), b(n_0), c(n_0)\}, \\
\hat{A}(n_0) &= \{a(n_0), b(n_0)\}, \\
\hat{A}(n_1) &= \{a(n_1), b(n_1), c(n_1)\}, \\
\hat{A}(n_1) &= \{a(n_1), b(n_1)\}, \\
\hat{A}(n_2) &= \{a(n_2), b(n_2)\}.
\end{aligned}$$

For each of these opportunity sets, option $a(n_t)$ is the agent's actual choice and $b(n_t)$ is not chosen, and hence, Definition 9.1 is satisfied. One can conclude that for the citizen the fundamental tax reform, a, represents an overall improvement as compared to the minor reform, b.

How is Definition 9.1 related to the property of contractibility? Recall that contractibility implies that a shadow ordering R exists such that choices from *any opportunity set* can be directly derived from R.[3] It is easy to prove the following finding:

---

[3] See the illustrative example on page 138.

Theorem 9.1 *For all pairs of terminal nodes, a (revealed) overall preference (in the sense of Definition 9.1) exists, if and only if choices are contractible. Overall preferences then correspond to the shadow ordering* R.

PROOF: See the proof of Theorem 11.6.

In Figure 9.1, for instance, the naive citizen's choices are contractible.[4] The corresponding shadow ordering can be directly read off the decision tree: $dPaPbPc$. According to this shadow ordering, a is overall preferred to b.

9.4   Recapitulation

In this chapter we related the property of contractibility to the question of whether, in the presence of changing preferences, one can judge an agents "overall preferences". It was pointed out that a revealed preference approach can be taken which under certain conditions allows for such welfare statements. More specifically, we argued that if an agent's choices are contractible, then the shadow ordering R represents the agent's overall preferences. However, if contractibility is not satisfied, then no welfare statement is admissable.

This directly leads to the next question. What do the underlying preferences have to look like in order to generate contractible choices? This is the object of the following chapter.

---

[4] The proof is provided in Theorem 10.3.

10
Conditions for Stability, Ordinality, and Contractibility

10.1 Preliminaries

In the preceding two chapters we investigated the far reaching implications of contractibility. It was pointed out that contractibility ensures that the dynamic choice problem collapses into an essentially static one generating the same choice sets as its dynamic counterpart. Furthermore, the shadow ordering associated with the static representation can be used to make judgements on the agent's welfare.

In the present chapter we analyse which decision trees together with which preference orderings lead to contractibility. Notice that the findings depend on the applied choice mechanism. Hence, each mechanism must be treated separately.

First of all, one may ask whether constant preferences are necessary for contractibility. In order to avoid any misunderstandings, we should state a formal definition of constant preferences (Definition 2.1) in terms of decision tree terminology:

Definition 10.1 *Preferences are constant if and only if for any pair of options* $a(n_0)$, $b(n_0)$:

$$aR(n_s^{ab})b \qquad \Longleftrightarrow \qquad aR(n_t)b \quad \forall\, t \leq s.^1 \qquad (10.1)$$

Equation (10.1) simply says that the preference between a pair of options at the node where these two options split (their discrimination node), is identical to the preference at all preceding nodes.

To motivate the following analysis, we begin with the following finding:

Theorem 10.1 *For naive, dogmatic, sagacious, lenient, and cautious choice to be contractible, constant preferences are a sufficient but not necessary condition. For resolute choice, it is a necessary and sufficient condition.*

PROOF:

[9] For the sufficiency part, refer to Definition 10.1. All choice sets $C(A)(n_t)$ can be derived from $R(n_0) = R(n_0)$.

[10] That constant preferences are not a necessary condition can be seen in Figure 10.1. Though not constant, the preferences assumed in Figure 10.1 lead to naive, dogmatic, sagacious, lenient, and cautious choice functions which are contractible.

[11] Resolute choice is stable (if and) only if the preferences are constant (see Theorem 10.5).   ‖

If constant preferences are not necessary for contractibility, then one may attempt to derive necessary conditions. This task is pursued in the following section. In section 10.3 we look separately at the properties of stability and ordinality.

---

[1] In models which allow for retrospective preferences, that is preferences over options which are no longer available, it would be necessary to modify this definition accordingly (see also section 2.3.2). Recall, however, that such models do not fall into the class of universal utility models.

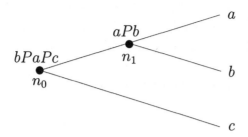

FIGURE 10.1. Contractible Choices in the Presence of Changing Preferences.

10.2 Necessary and Sufficient Conditions for Contractibility

Before we proceed, we should recall that actual choices depend on the applied choice mechanism. Hence, it may well happen that applying a naive choice mechanism, say, induces the satisfaction of contractibility, whereas a dogmatic choice mechanism does not.

For each of our choice mechanisms, we derive necessary and sufficient conditions on the underlying preference structure, such that a given dynamic choice problem exhibits contractibility. It is straightforward to derive the following finding:

Theorem 10.2 *Resolute choice is contractible if and only if preferences are constant.*

PROOF: See the proof of Theorem 11.7.

Theorem 10.3 *Naive, sagacious, lenient, and cautious choice are contractible if and only if no triple of options* $\{a(n_0), b(n_0), c(n_0)\}$ *exists, such that*

(i) $aR(n_t^{ac})cR(n_t^{ac})b$,
(ii) $bR(n_s^{ab})a$, $s > t$,

and at least one preference strict.

PROOF: See the proof of Theorem 11.8.

It appears rather surprising that, despite its different definitions, three of the sophisticated choice mechanisms exhibit identical conditions for contractibility. What is even more remarkable, the conditions are identical to those of naive choice. It remains to look at dogmatic choice.

Theorem 10.4 *Dogmatic choice is contractible if and only if no triple of options $\{a(n_0), b(n_0), c(n_0)\}$ exists, such that either*

  (i) $aR(n_t^{ac})cR(n_t^{ac})b$,
  (ii) $bP(n_s^{ab})a$,

or

  (iii) $aP(n_t^{ac})b$,
  (iv) $aI(n_s^{ab})b$, $s > t$.

PROOF: See the proof of Theorem 11.9.

Now it is possible to answer a question we asked in chapter 7. Is the mere *existence* of a shadow ordering R (which is formed by the discrimination nodes) sufficient for contractibility? Theorem 10.3 lists exactly those triples of options which generate intransitive shadow preferences. Only in the absence of these triples the shadow preferences induced by the respective discrimination nodes form an ordering. We conclude that for naive, sagacious, lenient, and cautious choice the existence of such a shadow ordering is a (necessary and) sufficient condition for contractibility. For contractibility of resolute and dogmatic choice, it is not sufficient.

Suppose we do not know an agent's underlying preferences, but we know all his choices, the underlying choice mechanism and the dynamic structure of the choice problem. How much does contractibility reveal about the underlying preferences?

Theorem 10.1 reminds us that, except for resolute choice, contractibility of the agent's choices does not necessarily imply that the underlying preferences are constant with $R(n_0) = \mathsf{R}(n_0)$. In view of Theorem 8.4, however, we can conclude that the underlying preferences *at the respective discrimination nodes* are those of the shadow ordering $\mathsf{R}(n_0)$. Depending on the applied choice mechanism, we furthermore can assert that no underlying preferences exist as listed in Theorem 10.3, and 10.4 respectively.

Combining this section's theorems, we can summarize the relationship between the six choice mechanisms in a single corollary:

Corollary 10.1 *For naive, sagacious, lenient, and cautious choice, the necessary and sufficient conditions for contractibility are identical. These conditions are necessary though not sufficient for contractibility of dogmatic choice. The conditions for contractible dogmatic choice, in turn, are necessary though not sufficient for contractibility of resolute choice.*

If, as in Hammond (1976a), the analysis is confined to strict preferences, the choice sets obtained by dogmatic, sagacious, lenient and cautious choice are identical. From Theorems 10.2 to 10.4, it is easy to obtain the following finding:

Corollary 10.2 *If an agent's underlying preferences at each node n_t can be represented by a strict ordering $P(n_t)$, then naive, sagacious, dogmatic, lenient, and cautious choice are contractible if and only if no triple of options $\{a(n_0), b(n_0), c(n_0)\}$ exists, such that:*

(i) $aP(n_t^{ac})cP(n_t^{ac})b$,
(ii) $bP(n_s^{ab})a, \quad s > t$.

Resolute choice is contractible if and only if preferences are constant.

Contractibility can be decomposed into stability and ordinality. In the following section we separately investigate the conditions for these two properties.

10.3   Necessary and Sufficient Conditions for Stability and Ordinality

10.3.1   Stability

In section 8.2.2 we explained that stability is concerned with the logical relationship between choice functions related to consecutive nodes. Stability postulates that if some option $a(n_t) \in C(A)(n_t)$ and if $a(n_s) \in A(n_s)$, $s \geq t$, then $a(n_s)$ must also be in $C(A)(n_s)$ and no option rejected at n_t should be in $C(A)(n_s)$.

For the proofs of the following Theorems 10.6 to 10.8, we have to draw upon the formal definitions of the various types of choice (see chapter 7.3.2 and 7.3.3). It is convenient to reformulate the definition of stability (Definition 8.3). We simply replace (8.4) by

$$C(A)(n_{t+1}) = A(n_{t+1}) \cap C(A)(n_t),$$

where $A(n_{t+1}) \cap C(A)(n_t) \neq \emptyset$. For each type of choice, we derive necessary and sufficient conditions for stability. First we examine the two short–sighted varieties of choice, that is naive and resolute choice. We will show that instability can arise only for resolute but not for naive choice. We then proceed to the varieties of sophisticated choice. It will turn out that only dogmatic and sagacious choice may exhibit instability, whereas lenient and cautious choice are always stable. Finally, a brief comparison of all six types of choice is provided.

Theorem 10.5 *Resolute choice is stable if and only if preferences are constant.*

PROOF: It is trivial that constant preferences are sufficient for stability. To see that constant preferences are also necessary imagine a change of preference for options $a(n_0)$ and $b(n_0)$ between nodes n_t and n_{t+1}. Let $A(n_0) = \{a(n_0), b(n_0)\}$. Then $C(A)(n_t) \cap A(n_{t+1}) \neq C(A)(n_{t+1})$ and $C(A)(n_t) \cap A(n_{t+1}) \neq \emptyset$.
$\parallel$

Next, we look at naive choice.

Theorem 10.6 *Regardless of the underlying orderings, naive choice is stable.*

PROOF:

[12] Definition 7.3 states that all members of $C(A)(n_t)$ must be in the consecutive choice set(s) $C(A)(n_{t+1})$. Hence, also all members of $C(A)(n_t) \cap A(n_{t+1})$ are in $C(A)(n_{t+1})$: $C(A)(n_{t+1}) \supseteq A(n_{t+1}) \cap C(A)(n_t)$.

[13] In order to generate instability we, therefore, have to derive necessary conditions for $C(A)(n_{t+1}) \supset A(n_{t+1}) \cap C(A)(n_t)$, with $A(n_{t+1}) \cap C(A)(n_t) \neq \emptyset$.

[14] Thus, a pair of options $a(n_t)$ and $b(n_t)$ must exist, such that $b(n_t) \notin C(A)(n_t)$, $a(n_t) \in C(A)(n_t)$, and $\{a(n_{t+1}), b(n_{t+1})\} \subseteq C(A)(n_{t+1})$. This implies that $a_t = b_t$.

[15] $b \notin C(A)(n_t)$ requires some option $c(n_t)$ splitting from $a(n_t)$ and $b(n_t)$ at node $n_t(= n_t^{bc} = n_t^{ac})$ such that $cP(n_t)\bar{b} \vee \bar{b}(n_t) : \bar{b}_t = b_t(= a_t)$. Then, however, it can never be true that $a(n_t) \in C(A)(n_t)$.   ‖

We now turn to the sophisticated varieties of choice. It is easy to see that Figure 10.2a, for instance, leads to unstable dogmatic choices: $C(A)(n_0) = \{b(n_0)\}$ and $C(A)(n_1) = \{a(n_1), b(n_1)\}$. The natural question to ask then is under which restrictions on the preference structure is dogmatic choice stable?

Theorem 10.7 *Dogmatic choice is stable if and only if no pair of options $\{a(n_0), b(n_0)\}$, exists such that*

    (i) $aP(n_t)b$,
    (ii) $aI(n_s^{ab})b$, $s > t$.

PROOF:

[16] For $A(n_0) = \{a(n_0), b(n_0)\}$, conditions (i) and (ii) imply instability. Hence, they are sufficient for generating instability.

[17] Definition 7.6 directly implies that $C(A)(n_{t+1}) \supseteq A(n_{t+1}) \cap C(A)(n_t)$.

[18] See [13] and [14].

[19] Let options $a(n_t)$ and $b(n_t)$ split in period s: n_s^{ab}, $s > t$. For $\{a(n_{t+1}), b(n_{t+1})\} \subseteq C(A)(n_{t+1})$, we need that $aI(n_s^{ab})b$ [$\Longrightarrow$ (ii)].

[20] $a(n_t) \in C(A)(n_t)$ together with $b(n_t) \notin C(A)(n_t)$ and $b(n_{t+1}) \in C(A)(n_{t+1})$ implies that $aP(n_t)b$ [$\Longrightarrow$ (i)].

[21] Hence, (i) and (ii) are also necessary conditions for unstable dogmatic choice. $\|$

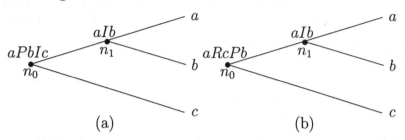

FIGURE 10.2. Unstable Dogmatic (a) and Sagacious (b) Choice.

Instability of sagacious choice occurs in Figure 10.2b: $C(A)(n_0) = \{a(n_0)\}$ and $C(A)(n_1) = \{a(n_1), b(n_1)\}$. Again, it is possible to derive necessary and sufficient conditions for stability.

Theorem 10.8 *Sagacious choice is stable if and only if no triple of options $\{a(n_0), b(n_0), c(n_0)\}$ exists, such that*

(i) $aR(n_t^{ac})cP(n_t^{ac})b$,
(ii) $aI(n_s^{ab})b, \quad s > t$.

PROOF:

[22] For $A = \{a(n_0), b(n_0), c(n_0)\}$, conditions (i) and (ii) imply instability. Hence, they are sufficient for generating instability.

[23] Definition 7.7 directly implies that $C(A)(n_{t+1}) \supseteq A(n_{t+1}) \cap C(A)(n_t)$.

[24] See [13], [14], and [19].

[25] $b \notin C(A)(n_t)$ together with $b \in C(A)(n_{t+1})$ stipulates that some option $c(n_t)$ splits from $a(n_t)$ and $b(n_t)$ in period t: $n_t = n_t^{ac}$, and that $cP(n_t)b$ [$\Longrightarrow$ second relation of (i)]. $a \in C(A)(n_t)$ requires that $aR(n_t)c$ [$\Longrightarrow$ first relation of (i)].

[26] Hence, (i) and (ii) are also necessary conditions for unstable sagacious choice. $\|$

For lenient and cautious choice we obtain a different result:

Theorem 10.9 *Regardless of the underlying orderings, lenient and cautious choice are stable.*

PROOF:

[27] Definitions 7.8 and 7.9 directly imply that $C(A)(n_{t+1}) \supseteq A(n_{t+1}) \cap C(A)(n_t)$.

[28] See [13] and [14].

[29] Definition 7.9 (cautious choice) implies that if $\{a(n_{t+1}, b(n_{t+1})\} \subseteq C(A)(n_{t+1})$ and $a(n_t) \in C(A)(n_t)$, then $b(n_t) \in C(A)(n_t)$, which contradicts [14]. [30] By Definition 7.8 (lenient choice), $b \notin C(A)(n_t)$ together with $b(n_{t+1}) \in C(A)(n_{t+1})$ implies that some option $c(n_t)$ must split from $a(n_t)$ and $b(n_t)$ in period t $(n_t = n_t^{ac})$, such that $cP(n_t)\bar{b} \vee \bar{b}(n_t) : \{\bar{b}_t = b_t$ and $\bar{b}(n_t) \in C(A)(n_{t+1})\}$, and hence $cP(n_t)a$. However, this contradicts $a(n_t) \in C(A)(n_t)$.   ∥

Finally, we combine Theorems 10.6 to 10.9 in the following corollary:

Corollary 10.3 *If resolute choice is stable, then dogmatic choice is stable which in turn implies stability of sagacious choice. Lenient, cautious, and naive choice are always stable.*

We know that if a choice problem features only strict preferences, then dogmatic, sagacious, lenient, and cautious choice coincide. This directly leads to the following finding:

Corollary 10.4 *If an agent's underlying preferences at each node n_t can be represented by a strict ordering $P(n_t)$, naive, sagacious, dogmatic, lenient, and cautious choice are always stable. Resolute choice is stable if and only if preferences are constant.*

10.3.2 Ordinality

The present section derives conditions on the underlying preference structure which guarantee that choice is ordinal. Recall that ordinality captures the behaviour of a single choice function as options are added. Ordinality can be decomposed into property α and property β (see section 8.2.1).

The following lemma is of interest in its own right, but also helps to keep some of this section's proofs manageable:

Lemma 10.1 *If a decision tree is such that by adding some set $A^2(n_t)$ to some set $A^1(n_t)$ ($A^1(n_t) \cup A^2(n_t) = A(n_t)$) we can generate a violation of ordinality, then we can do this by choosing an appropriate subset $\tilde{A}^1(n_t) \subset A(n_t)$ and adding a single option $x \in A(n_t) \backslash \tilde{A}^1(n_t)$.*

PROOF:

[31] Suppose we have generated a violation of ordinality by adding to the original subset $A^1(n_t)$ a set of options $\{a(n_t), b(n_t), \ldots\}$, with $A^1(n_t) \cup \{a(n_t), b(n_t), \ldots\} = A(n_t)$. Thus, $C(A^1)(n_t) \neq A^1(n_t) \cap C(A)(n_t)$.

[32] Adding to $A^1(n_t)$ only option $a(n_t)$ ($a(n_t) \cup A^1(n_t) = A^2(n_t)$) either directly leads to a violation of ordinality (then this was generated by adding to subset $A^1(n_t)$ a *single* option $a(n_t)$), or $C(A^1)(n_t) = A^1(n_t) \cap C(A^2)(n_t)$.

[33] If the latter is true, then adding to $A^2(n_t)$ option $b(n_t)$ ($b(n_t) \cup A^2(n_t) = A^3(n_t)$) either leads to a violation of ordinality (generated by adding to subset $A^2(n_t)$ a *single* option $b(n_t)$), or $C(A^2)(n_t) = A^2(n_t) \cap C(A^3)(n_t)$, which implies that $C(A^1)(n_t) = A^1(n_t) \cap A^2(n_t) \cap C(A^3)(n_t) = A^1(n_t) \cap C(A^3)(n_t)$.

[34] Analogous reasoning finally leads to $C(A^1)(n_t) = A^1(n_t) \cap C(A)(n_t)$ which contradicts [31].   ‖

Again, the analysis of resolute choice is straightforward.

Theorem 10.10 *Resolute choice is ordinal regardless of the underlying ordering.*

PROOF:

Property α:

[35] According to Definition 7.4, $a(n_t) \notin C(\tilde{A})(n_t)$ if and only if an option $b(n_t) \in \tilde{A}(n_t)$ exists, with $bP(n_t)a$. Yet, adding any new options to $\tilde{A}(n_t)$ cannot affect this preference. Hence, $a(n_t)$ will never become a member of $C(A)(n_t)$ with $\tilde{A}(n_t) \subseteq A(n_t)$.

Property β:

[36] Let the pair of options $a(n_t)$ and $b(n_t)$ be any members of $C(\tilde{A})(n_t)$. Then $bR(n_t)d \,\forall d(n_t) \in \tilde{A}(n_t)$ and $aR(n_t)d \,\forall d(n_t) \in \tilde{A}(n_t)$. Thus, $aI(n_t)b$.

[37] Then adding a new option $c(n_t)$ to $\tilde{A}(n_t)$, it either holds that $cP(n_t)a$ and $cP(n_t)b$ (then $\{a(n_t), b(n_t)\} \cap C(A)(n_t) = \emptyset$), or $bR(n_t)$ and $aR(n_t)$ (then $\{a(n_t), b(n_t)\} \subseteq C(A)(n_t)$). $\parallel$

Next, we consider naive, sagacious, lenient, and cautious choice.

Theorem 10.11 *Naive, sagacious, lenient, and cautious choice are ordinal if and only if no triple of options $\{a(n_0), b(n_0), c(n_0)\}$ exists, such that*

> (i) $aR(n_t^{ac})cR(n_t^{ac})b$,
> (ii) $bR(n_s^{ab})a, \quad s > t$,

and at least one preference strict.

PROOF:

[38] The proof for sagacious choice is provided in Appendix A.

[39] In Theorems 10.6 and 10.9 we showed that naive, lenient, and cautious choice generate stable choices regardless of the underlying preferences. Hence, the conditions for ordinality coincide with those for contractibility as stated in Theorem 10.3.

$\parallel$

Remarkably, also for sagacious choice the above conditions are the same as for contractibility, even though sagacious choice is not always stable. Hence, ordinality of sagacious choice implies stability. The converse, though, is not true.

Dogmatic choice is the last choice mechanism to be examined in this section. It turns out that the conditions for ordinality are more complex, than those for contractibility.

Theorem 10.12 *Dogmatic choice is ordinal if and only if no set of options $\{a(n_0), b(n_0), \ldots\}$ exists, such that either*

> (i) $aR(n_t^{ac})cR(n_t^{ac})b$,
> (ii) $bP(n_s^{ab})a$,

or

(iii) $aR(n_t^{ac})cR(n_t^{ac})b$,
(iv) $bP(n_r)a$,
(v) $aI(n_s^{ab})b$, $s > r > t$.

PROOF: The proof is provided in Appendix B.

Now we have the ingredients necessary for presenting the relationship between all six varieties of choice in a single corollary:

Corollary 10.5 *For naive, sagacious, lenient, and cautious choice, the necessary and sufficient conditions for ordinality are identical. They are neither sufficient nor necessary for ordinal dogmatic choice.[2] Resolute choice is always ordinal.*

Finally, one should mention the case of strict preferences. Recall that for strict preferences the four forward–looking choice mechanisms coincide. Thus, Theorems 10.10 and 10.11 lead to the following result:

Corollary 10.6 *If an agent's preferences at each node n_t can be represented by a strict ordering $P(n_t)$, then naive, dogmatic, sagacious, lenient and cautious choice are ordinal, if and only if no triple of options $\{a(n_0), b(n_0), c(n_0)\}$ exists, such that:*
(i) $aP(n_t^{ac})cP(n_t^{ac})b$,
(ii) $bP(n_s^{ab})a$, $s > t$.
Resolute choice is always ordinal.

10.4   Recapitulation

Stability together with ordinality ensures that choices are contractible. For all three properties, the present chapter derived necessary and sufficient conditions. That is, those preference configurations were identified which lead to a violation of stability or ordinality (or both).

---

[2]Note that for (i) $aI(n_t^{ac})cI(n_t^{ac})b$, (ii) $bP(n_r)a$, (iii) $aI(n_s^{ab})b$, $s > r > t$, naive (sagacious, lenient, and cautious) choice is ordinal, but dogmatic choice is not. Conversely, for (i) $aP(n_t^{ac})cP(n_t^{ac})b$, (ii) $aI(n_s^{ab})b$, $s > t$, dogmatic choice is ordinal, but naive (sagacious, lenient, and cautious) choice is not.

We were able to prove that contractibility of naive, sagacious, lenient, and cautious choice is necessary but not sufficient for contractibility of dogmatic choice. Contractible resolute choice requires that preferences are constant.

Do the various concepts and findings of chapter 7 to 10 carry over to the case of uncertainty? The answer to this question is provided in the following chapter.

11
An Extension to Uncertainty

11.1 Preliminaries

Hitherto, the analysis was confined to deterministic choice problems with full information. The individual confronted with the decision tree of Figure 11.1, for instance, is completely informed about future preferences and all future subtrees. From a descriptive point of view this is a highly unrealistic assumption. One may whish to accomodate uncertainty with respect to future preferences and subtrees. Both can be easily accomodated by incorporating *chance nodes* into the decision tree framework. One should point out that uncertainty does not change the basic undercurrents. If in the preceding chapters we had allowed for uncertainty, some of the essential aspects might have been

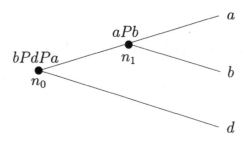

FIGURE 11.1. A Simple Deterministic Decision Problem.

obscured. It is primarily for this reason, that the inclusion of uncertainty has been deferred until now.

The plan of this chapter is as follows. In section 11.2 the basic framework is developed. Then some comments on the Independence Axiom are provided. Section 11.4 discusses the various choice mechanisms. The notion of subgame perfection is analyzed in section 11.5, and the concepts of stability, ordinality, and contractibility in section 11.6. Section 11.7 generalizes the welfare discussion of chapter 9 to the case of uncertainty. Section 11.8 is in the spirit of chapter 10. It presents necessary and sufficient conditions for contractibility.

11.2 The Framework

First, one has to generalize the notion of decision trees in order to include chance nodes. Again, each portion x_t begins with a (possibly trivial) decision node n_t and terminates in the consecutive *decision node* n_{t+1}. A decision node n_t (indicated by filled circles) may or may not be followed by a chance node l_t (indicated by empty circles). In Figure 11.2, for instance, portion a_0 connects the decision nodes n_0 and n_1, and n_0 is followed by the chance node l_0. As in the deterministic case, at each decision node, the agent is assumed to possess a preference ordering. Note, however, that these orderings are defined on lotteries, rather than on single branches. Associated with each subtree $X(n_t)$ is the set of all underlying lotteries

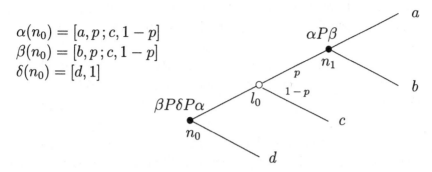

$$\alpha(n_0) = [a, p\,; c, 1 - p]$$
$$\beta(n_0) = [b, p\,; c, 1 - p]$$
$$\delta(n_0) = [d, 1]$$

FIGURE 11.2. A Simple Decision Problem under Uncertainty.

$L(n_t) = \{\alpha(n_t), \beta(n_t), \gamma(n_t), \ldots\}$ in $X(n_t)$. In Figure 11.2, $L(n_0)$ consists of the three lotteries listed at the left hand side. More generally, lotteries are specified in the following way:

Definition 11.1 *All lotteries $\xi(n_t)$ in $L(n_t)$ satisfy the following two properties:*

1. *They all share n_t as their initial decision node,*

2. *they are subtrees of $X(n_t)$ such that*

   - *at each of the lottery's decision nodes n_s, $s \geq t$, only a single branch is available and*

   - *the characteristics of all chance nodes $l(n_s) \in \xi(n_t)$ do not differ from those these nodes exhibit in $X(n_t)$.[1]*

Truncating $\xi(n_t)$ at some node n_s, $s \geq t$, yields the sublottery $\xi(n_s)$.

In other words, in order to "reduce" $X(n_0)$ to a lottery $\xi(n_0)$, one starts at n_0 cutting off all except one of the available subtrees. Then one follows the remaining subtree to the next period's decision nodes. Again, at each of these nodes one cuts off all subtrees except for one. Repeating this process to the end of

---

[1] That is, the number of departing branches and the associated propabilities are unaffected as one "reduces" $X(n_t)$ to some lottery $\xi(n_t)$.

the tree finally yields a lottery $\xi(n_0)$ which itself is a subtree. Cutting off the subtree (or lottery) $\xi(n_0)$ at decision node n_t yields the (sub)lottery $\xi(n_t)$, which, again, can be viewed as a subtree.

Of course, the probability of reaching a specific terminal node changes as one moves from decision node n_t to node n_{t+1}, say. However, the probabilities assigned to the branches departing from some chance node are given and do not change.

In the decision tree depicted in Figure 11.2, it is assumed that $\alpha P(n_1)\beta$ and $\beta P(n_0)\delta P(n_0)\alpha$. That is, from the vantage point of n_1, the agent prefers to end up in a rather than in b. At n_0 the lottery of reaching b with probability p and reaching c with probability $1 - p$ is preferred to the lottery of reaching d with certainty. The latter, in turn, is preferred to the lottery of ending up in a with probability p and ending up in c with probability $1 - p$. Note that for $p = 1$ one exactly obtains the decision problem depicted in Figure 11.1.

Figure 11.2 depicts uncertainty with respect to the *subtrees* available to the agent if he decides to reject option d. One may just as well depict the case in which uncertainty exists with respect to *future preferences*. Suppose, for instance, that the individual is not sure about his preference in period 1. This kind of uncertainty is depicted in Figure 11.3, where the subtrees available at nodes n_1 and n_1' are assumed to be identical. The only aspect which is different are the preferences over the sublotteries (or truncated lotteries) available at the respective nodes: $\alpha P(n_1)\beta$ and $\beta P(n_1')\alpha$. That is, with probability p the preferences are as in Figure 11.1 and with probability $1 - p$ they are the other way round. For $p = 1$ one obtains the same decision problem as depicted in Figure 11.1.

To begin with, one has to adopt the notion of discrimination nodes (Definition 7.1) to the case of uncertainty.

Definition 11.2 *Decision node $n_s^{\alpha\beta}$, $s \geq 0$, is the discrimination node of lotteries $\alpha(n_0)$ and $\beta(n_0)$. It indicates the last node n_t at which it is true that $\alpha(n_0)\backslash\alpha(n_t) = \beta(n_0)\backslash\beta(n_t)$.*

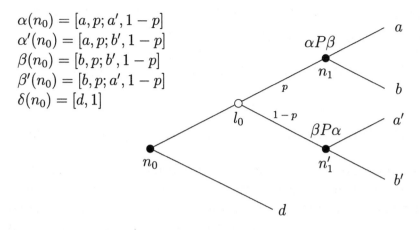

$$\alpha(n_0) = [a, p; a', 1 - p]$$
$$\alpha'(n_0) = [a, p; b', 1 - p]$$
$$\beta(n_0) = [b, p; b', 1 - p]$$
$$\beta'(n_0) = [b, p; a', 1 - p]$$
$$\delta(n_0) = [d, 1]$$

FIGURE 11.3. Uncertainty over Preferences.

To put it somewhat losely, the discrimination node $n_s^{\alpha\beta}$ indicates the decision node at which lotteries $\alpha(n_0)$ and $\beta(n_0)$ begin to differ. In Figure 11.2, we observe that $n_s^{\alpha\beta} = n_1$. In Figure 11.4, the discrimination nodes are $n_s^{\alpha\beta} = n_1$, $n_s^{\alpha\alpha'} = n_1'$, $n_s^{\beta\beta'} = n_1'$, $n_s^{\alpha'\beta'} = n_1$, $n_s^{\alpha\beta'} = n_0$, and $n_s^{\alpha'\beta} = n_0$. In the following sections discrimination nodes will play a prominent role.

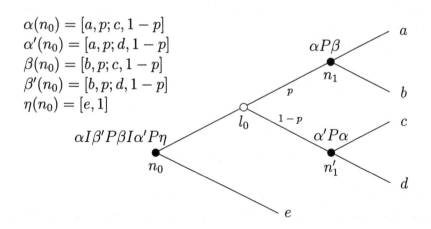

$$\alpha(n_0) = [a, p; c, 1 - p]$$
$$\alpha'(n_0) = [a, p; d, 1 - p]$$
$$\beta(n_0) = [b, p; c, 1 - p]$$
$$\beta'(n_0) = [b, p; d, 1 - p]$$
$$\eta(n_0) = [e, 1]$$

FIGURE 11.4. Changing Preferences.

The preferences in Figure 11.4 are not constant, since at n_0 lottery $\alpha(n_0)$ is preferred to $\alpha'(n_0)$, but at n_1' sublottery $\alpha'(n_1') = d(n_1')$ is preferred to sublottery $\alpha(n_1') = c(n_1')$.

Definition 11.3 *Preferences are constant if and only if for each pair of lotteries* $\alpha(n_s^{\alpha\beta})$ *and* $\beta(n_s^{\alpha\beta})$, $s \geq t$:

$$\alpha R(n_s^{\alpha\beta})\beta \quad \Longleftrightarrow \quad \alpha R(n_t)\beta, \quad 0 \leq t \leq s.^2$$

11.3   Some Remarks on the Independence Axiom

Since chapter 11 is concerned with choice under uncertainty, one may wonder whether the Independence Axiom, as used in expected utility theory, is of any significance for the questions we deal with in this work. In this section, it is demonstrated that under a certain assumption it is possible to establish a correspondence between the Independence Axiom and the notion of *constant* preferences (Definition 11.3). The primary concern of this work, however, is *changing* preferences. Hence, for our analysis, the Independence Axiom is of minor interest.

Originally, the Independence Axiom was formulated for *static* decision problems. In such models, at n_0, choices have to be made once and for all. No later decision nodes exist at which the individual could deviate from original decisions. Such a decision problem is depicted in Figure 11.5. Four lotteries form the set of all underlying lotteries:

$$
\begin{aligned}
L(n_0) \;=\; & \{(a, q; d, 1-q), \\
& [(b, p; c, 1-p), q\,; d, 1-q], \\
& (a', 1), \\
& (b', p; c', 1-p)\}.
\end{aligned}
$$

In this set, we have one degenerate lottery, two one–stage lotteries, and one two–stage lottery. Suppose that all terminal nodes in this decision tree represent payoffs and that utility from the various branches depends only on these payoffs and the associated probabilities. Let $a = a'$, $b = b'$, and $c = c'$. Then, the

---

[2] This definition is equivalent to the notion of "dynamically consistent" preferences as used by Machina (1989) and McClennen (1988, 1990).

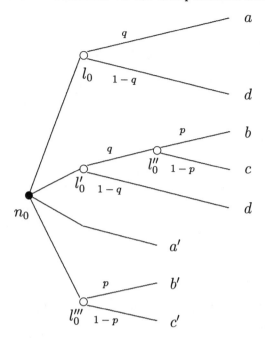

FIGURE 11.5. An Illustration of the Independence Axiom.

Independence Axiom postulates that

$$\text{if} \quad (a', 1)\, P(n_0)\, (b', p; c', 1 - p), \qquad\qquad (11.1)$$

$$\text{then} \quad (a, q; d, 1 - q)\, P(n_0)\, [(b, p; c, 1 - p), q\, ; d, 1 - q]. \ (11.2)$$

Note that the lotteries in (11.2) differ from those in (11.1) only with respect to the sublotteries associated with probability q, namely $(a, 1)$ and $(b, p; c, 1 - p)$. Since $a = a'$, $b = b'$, and $c = c'$, these two sublotteries are identical to $(a', 1)$ and $(b', p\, ; c', 1 - p)$ which are related to each other in (11.1).[3]

The questions this work deals with are rooted in a *dynamic* decision context. This raises the question of whether the Independence Axiom can be applied to dynamic choice situations. We demonstrate that a connection exists between the Independence Axiom and the notion of constant preferences (Definition 11.3). Consider Figure 11.6 which can be regarded as a dynamic

---

[3] Abundant evidence exists on people violating the Independence Axiom. For a recent review of this literature see Seidl (1996b).

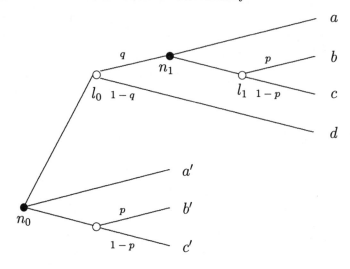

FIGURE 11.6. The Independence Axiom's Implications in a Dynamic Setting.

version of Figure 11.5. Notice that the set of all underlying lotteries $L(n_0)$ is identical in both decision trees.[4] Suppose Independence applies as specified in (11.1) and (11.2). So far, this tells us nothing about the preference at node n_1 of Figure 11.6. However, if we invoke another postulate, known as "consequentialism", then the preference at n_0 of Figure 11.6 determines the preference at n_1.

Consequentialism says that at each node preferences are independent of the past. Then, both past consumption and uncertainty experienced during previous periods exert no impact on current preferences.[5] Thus, if the agent at n_0 prefers $(a', 1)$ to $(b', p; c', 1 - p)$, then the same must be true at n_1:

$$(a, 1)\ P(n_1)\ (b, p; c, 1 - p). \tag{11.3}$$

---

[4]LaValle and Fishburn (1987) denote trees with identical opportunity sets as strategically equivalent.

[5]A number of studies of dynamic choice under uncertainty are concerned with the timing of resolution of uncertainty. Examples are Chew and Epstein (1989), Epstein and Zin (1989), Johnsen and Donaldson (1985), Kreps and Porteus (1978), and Selden (1978).

If (11.3) is true, however, then, in view of (11.2), preferences satisfy the notion of constant preferences as expressed in Definition 11.3. One may argue also the other way round. If the preferences in Figure 11.6 are constant, then preferences at n_0 satisfy the Independence Axiom, provided consequentialism is invoked. In short, given consequentialism, the Independence Axiom and the notion of constant preferences do correspond to each other.

The preceding paragraphs were merely an illustration of the relationship between the Independence Axiom and our own framework. These matters are formally elaborated in Karni and Schmeidler (1991).[6]

As is obvious from the preceding chapters, this work is not interested in the case of constant preferences. It examines the consequences of *changing* preferences. Hence, for our purpose, the Independence Axiom is of peripheral interest, and throughout this chapter (and work) it is neither invoked nor required.

Finally, one should again point out that the correspondence between the Independence Axiom and the notion of constant preferences can only be established under the premise of consequentialism. Consequentialism postulates that the past is irrelevant for the evaluation of options. In other words, no habit formation takes place. However, it is then necessary to give up the generality of universal utility models. Recall that, out of the four classes of utility models surveyed in part I of this work, only the recursive class excludes habit formation. The other classes allow for habit formation, and hence, cannot be reconciled with consequentialism.

11.4 From Preferences to Choices

11.4.1 *Opportunity Sets and Choice Sets*

Since orderings are defined on lotteries, we have to re-consider the notion of opportunity sets and choice sets. Let $G(n_t) \subseteq$

---

[6]Other important contributions to the discussion on dynamic consistency and consequentialism are Hammond (1988, 1989), Machina (1989), McClennen (1990), and Weller (1978).

$L(n_t)$ indicate an opportunity set of lotteries. Notice that *not all* subsets of $L(n_t)$ are opportunity sets! Specifically, for any pair of lotteries $\alpha(n_t)$ and $\beta(n_t)$, with $n_s^{\alpha\beta} = n_t$, either $\{\alpha(n_t), \beta(n_t)\} \subseteq G(n_t)$ or $\{\alpha(n_t), \beta(n_t)\} \cap G(n_t) = \emptyset$. In Figure 11.4, for instance, the sets $\{\alpha(n_0), \beta'(n_0)\}$ and $\{\alpha'(n_0), \beta(n_0)\}$ are no opportunity sets even though they are in $L(n_t)$.

Of course, if all lotteries are degenerate lotteries, then $L(n_t) = X(n_t)$ and $G(n_t) = A(n_t)$. In the presence of non–degenerate lotteries we have to generalize our definition of choice sets (Definition 6.1).

Definition 11.4 *Imagine an agent located at n_t who faces the opportunity set of lotteries $G(n_t)$. The choice set $C(G)(n_t)$ is the set of lotteries this agent may find himself choosing.*

One may wonder why it is justified to continue to use set notation. In Figure 11.4, for instance, the largest opportunity set is $G(n_0) = \{\alpha(n_0), \alpha'(n_0), \beta(n_0), \beta'(n_0), \eta(n_0)\}$. It is crucial to realize that each of these lotteries is a *subtree* of $X(n_0)$. That is, $G(n_0)$ is formed by five subtrees. Now consider some alternative opportunity set $\tilde{G}(n_0) = \{\alpha(n_0), \beta(n_0), \eta(n_0)\}$. Here, the opportunity set is formed by three subtrees. Since each of these subtrees is also a member of $G(n_0)$, it is prefectly accurate to write $\tilde{G}(n_0) \subset G(n_0)$. This appears uncontroversial.

Now consider the opportunity set $G(n_1) = \{\alpha(n_1), \beta(n_1)\} = \{a_1, b_1\}$. Is it true that this opportunity set, too, is a subset of $G(n_0)$? After all, this would require that sublotteries $\alpha(n_1)$ and $\beta(n_1)$ can be viewed as subsets of lotteries $\alpha(n_0)$ and $\beta(n_0)$. In view of Definition 11.1, sublotteries are nothing else but subtrees, and since $\alpha(n_1)$ and $\beta(n_1)$ are subtrees of (subtrees) $\alpha(n_0)$ and $\beta(n_0)$, it is correct to write $\alpha(n_1) \subset \alpha(n_0)$ and $\beta(n_1) \subset \beta(n_0)$. As a consequence, $G(n_1)$ is a subset of $G(n_0)$.

Before we proceed, one should point out a notational issue which arose also in section 8.2.3, p.138. There, we explained different types of subsets of opportunity set $A(n_t)$. For the subsets of some opportunity set $G(n_t)$, analogous notation is used. That is, $G(n_s)$ denotes a subset of $G(n_t)$ evolving as one moves through the decision tree: $G(n_s) = X(n_s) \cap G(n_t)$, $s \geq t$. $\tilde{G}(n_t)$, in contrast, indicates subsets of $G(n_t)$ generated by excluding lotteries $\xi(n_t)$ from $G(n_t)$. This notational aspect is important in order to understand the properties of stability and ordinality, which will be discussed in section 11.6.

11.4.2 Choice Mechanisms and Choice Functions

The sequence of orderings induces a sequence of decisions which eventually result in actual choices (of lotteries). The rule for transforming orderings into actual choices was denoted as *choice mechanism*. All of the choice mechanisms introduced in chapter 7 can be adopted to the case of uncertainty.

A *naive* choice mechanism, for instance, postulates that at each decision node the agent embarks on the lottery which currently seems best. In Figure 11.2, the agent initially likes best lottery $\beta(n_0)$. Accordingly, he moves towards l_0 on the presumption that he will move to node b should the state of nature be up. However, if, in fact, the state of nature is up, he follows "lottery" $\alpha(n_1)$, the lottery most preferred at n_1. Hence, the lottery he actually ends up playing is $\alpha(n_0)$, that is $C(G)(n_0) = \{\alpha(n_0)\}$.

This highlights again that a choice set is not necessarily the set of lotteries an agent willingly chooses. It is rather the set of lotteries the agent ends up with. Even though initially the agent liked lottery $\beta(n_0)$ best, we observe in Figure 11.2 the naive choice set $C(G)(n_0) = \{\alpha(n_0)\}$, with $G(n_0) = \{\alpha(n_0), \beta(n_0), \delta(n_0)\}$. More formally we obtain:

Definition 11.5 *Let $\delta(n_t) \in G(n_t)$ denote a lottery which shares all its decision nodes n_{t+1} with lottery $\alpha(n_t)$.*

*For lottery $\alpha(n_t) \in G(n_t)$ to be a member of a **naive** agent's choice set $C(G)(n_t)$, some lottery $\delta(n_t)$ must exist (possibly $\delta(n_t) = \alpha(n_t)$), such that*

$$\delta R(n_t)\beta \quad \forall \quad \beta(n_t) \in G(n_t).$$

Furthermore, all sublotteries $\alpha(n_{t+1})$ must be members of $C(G)(n_{t+1})$.

In Figure 11.7, for instance, for $\gamma(n_1)$ to be a member of $C(G)(n_1)$, it must be true, firstly, that all its sublotteries $\gamma(n_2)$

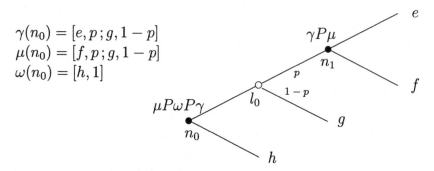

FIGURE 11.7. An Illustration of the Definition of Naive Choice under Uncertainty).

are members of $C(G)(n_2)$. Since no such sublotteries exist, this requirement is trivially satisfied. Secondly, it must be true that $\gamma(n_1)$, or some lottery which shares all its decision nodes n_2 with $\gamma(n_1)$ (again, no such lottery exists), is weakly preferred to $\mu(n_1)$. Since $\gamma P(n_1)\mu$, this condition is satisfied, too. Hence, one obtains $\gamma(n_1) \in C(G)(n_1)$.

For $\gamma(n_0)$ to be a member of $C(G)(n_0)$, Definition 11.5 again puts forward two conditions. Firstly, all sublotteries $\gamma(n_1)$ must be in $C(G)(n_1)$. In Figure 11.7, only one sublottery $\gamma(n_1)$ exists and, as was demonstrated above, this sublottery is in $C(G)(n_1)$. Secondly, $\gamma(n_0)$, or a lottery which shares all its decision nodes n_1 with $\gamma(n_0)$, must be weakly preferred to all lotteries available at (n_0). Lottery $\gamma(n_0)$ is not weakly preferred to all lotteries available at n_0, but lottery $\mu(n_0)$ is, and it shares all its decision nodes with $\gamma(n_0)$. Since both conditions are met, we obtain $\gamma(n_0) \in C(G)(n_0)$.

Note that Definiton 11.5 is cast in terms of a two–period problem. As was illustrated in section 7.2, p.112, its repeated application shows that it equally covers any multi–period decision problem. The same is true for the definitions of all following choice mechanisms (resolute, dogmatic, sagacious, lenient, and cautious choice).

As an alternative to the naive choice mechanisms, an agent could apply a *resolute* choice mechanism. Then, at n_0 the agent embarks on the lottery which currently seems best and sticks to this decision also at each subsequent node. In Figure 11.2, we obtain the resolute choice set $C(G)(n_0) = \{\beta(n_0)\}$. The resolute choice mechanism is formalized in the following definition:

Definition 11.6 *For some lottery $\alpha(n_t) \in G(n_t)$ to be a member of a **resolute** agent's choice set $C(G)(n_t)$, it must hold that*

$$\alpha R(n_t)\beta \quad \forall \quad \beta(n_t) \in G(n_t).$$

Next, we turn to the sophisticated varieties of choice. What is the choice set of a *dogmatic* agent faced with the decision problem depicted in Figure 11.2? If $G(n_0) = \{\alpha(n_0), \beta(n_0), \delta(n_0)\}$, then for a dogmatic agent lottery $\beta(n_0)$ is deemed irrelevant at node n_0. Of the remaining two lotteries he prefers $\delta(n_0)$. Thus, the choice set's only member is $\delta(n_0)$.

If the choice problem was as depicted in Figure 11.8, then

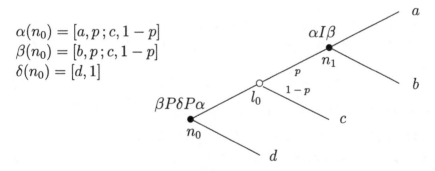

$$\alpha(n_0) = [a, p\,;c, 1 - p]$$
$$\beta(n_0) = [b, p\,;c, 1 - p]$$
$$\delta(n_0) = [d, 1]$$

FIGURE 11.8. An Illustration of Sophisticated Choice Mechanisms.

for the dogmatic agent located at n_0 all three lotteries would be relevant. Since only $\beta(n_0)$ is weakly preferred to all other relevant lotteries, it would be the only member of the dogmatic agent's choice set related to node n_0. The same would be true for the *sagacious* agent, since only $\beta(n_0)$ is weakly preferred to all other *splitting* relevant lotteries. The lenient choice set in contrast would contain both $\alpha(n_0)$ and $\beta(n_0)$. The cautious agent, finally, would opt for $\delta(n_0)$.

The following formal definitions may remove any vagueness remaining from our preceding description of the various sophisticated choice mechanisms. In these definitions we state the conditions for some lottery $\alpha(n_t)$ to be in the choice set $C(G)(n_t)$. We repeatedly refer to lotteries $\beta(n_t)$, $\gamma(n_t)$, and $\delta(n_t)$, which are defined in the following way:

Definition 7.7

$\beta(n_t) \in G(n_t)$ *denotes a lottery, such that all its sublotteries $\beta(n_{t+1})$ are members of $C(G)(n_{t+1})$.*

$\gamma(n_t) \in G(n_t)$ *denotes a lottery, such that all its sublotteries $\gamma(n_{t+1})$ are members of $C(G)(n_{t+1})$. Furthermore, all its decision nodes n_{t+1} are different from nodes n_{t+1} in $\alpha(n_t)$.*

$\delta(n_t) \in G(n_t)$ *denotes a lottery, such that all its sublotteries $\delta(n_{t+1})$ are members of $C(G)(n_{t+1})$. In addition, it shares all its decision nodes n_{t+1} with $\alpha(n_t)$.*

We now can state the formal definitions of dogmatic, sagacious, lenient, and cautious choice.

Definition 11.8 *For some lottery $\alpha(n_t) \in G(n_t)$ to be a member of a **dogmatic** agent's choice set $C(G)(n_t)$, it must hold that*

$$\alpha R(n_t)\beta \quad \forall \quad \beta(n_t) \in G(n_t), \tag{11.4}$$

and all sublotteries $\alpha(n_{t+1})$ must be members of $C(G)(n_{t+1})$.

Definition 11.9 *For some lottery $\alpha(n_t) \in G(n_t)$ to be a member of a **sagacious** agent's choice set $C(G)(n_t)$, it must hold that*

$$\alpha R(n_t)\gamma \quad \forall \quad \gamma(n_t) \in G(n_t), \tag{11.5}$$

and all sublotteries $\alpha(n_{t+1})$ must be members of $C(G)(n_{t+1})$.

Definition 11.10 *For some lottery $\alpha(n_t) \in G(n_t)$ to be a member of a **lenient** agent's choice set $C(G)(n_t)$, some lottery $\delta(n_t)$ must exist (possibly $\delta(n_t) = \alpha(n_t)$), such that*

$$\delta R(n_t)\beta \quad \forall \quad \beta(n_t) \in G(n_t),$$

and all sublotteries $\alpha(n_{t+1})$ must be members of $C(G)(n_{t+1})$.

Definition 11.11 *Let* $\gamma'(n_t)$ *indicate a particular lottery* $\gamma(n_t)$ *for which it is true that* $\gamma R(n_t)\gamma'$ *for all* $\gamma(n_t)$ *which share all their decision nodes* n_{t+1} *with* $\gamma'(n_t)$. *Furthermore, let* $\delta'(n_t)$ *indicate a particular lottery* $\delta(n_t)$ *for which it is true that* $\delta R(n_t)\delta'$ *for all* $\delta(n_t) \in G(n_t)$.

For some lottery $\alpha(n_t) \in G(n_t)$ *to be a member of a* **cautious** *agent's choice set* $C(G)(n_t)$, *it must hold that*

$$\delta' R(n_t)\gamma' \quad \forall \quad \gamma'(n_t) \in G(n_t), \tag{11.6}$$

and all sublotteries $\alpha(n_{t+1})$ *must be members of* $C(G)(n_{t+1})$.

The last ingredient we need for the following analysis is the concept of *choice functions*:

Definition 11.12 *A choice function* $C(n_t)$ *maps each non–empty opportunity set* $G(n_t) \subseteq L(n_t)$ *into a non–empty choice set* $C(G)(n_t)$.

In Figure 11.8, for instance, the choice function of a sagacious agent starting his decision process at n_0 is given by

$$
\begin{aligned}
C(\{\alpha(n_0), \beta(n_0), \delta(n_0)\}) &= \{\beta(n_0)\}, \\
C(\{\alpha(n_0), \beta(n_0)\}) &= \{\alpha(n_0), \beta(n_0)\}, \\
C(\{\alpha(n_0), \delta(n_0)\}) &= \{\delta(n_0)\}, \\
C(\{\beta(n_0), \delta(n_0)\}) &= \{\beta(n_0)\}, \\
&\cdots
\end{aligned}
$$

Since choice sets are based on some choice mechanism, choice functions, too, depend on the applied choice mechanism.

11.5 Subgame Perfection

We are now in the position to generalize the definitions and findings of section 7.4 to the case of uncertainty:

Definition 11.13 *Let* $\eta(n_t) \in G(n_t)$ *denote a lottery, such that all sublotteries* $\eta(n_{t+1})$ *are subgame perfect with respect to*

$G(n_{t+1})$. Let $\eta'(n_t)$ indicate particular lotteries $\eta(n_t)$ for which it is true that $\eta R(n_t)\eta'$ for all $\eta(n_t)$ which share all their decision nodes n_{t+1} with $\eta'(n_t)$.

For some lottery $\nu(n_t) \in G(n_t)$ to be subgame perfect with respect to $G(n_t)$, it must hold that

$$\nu R(n_t)\eta' \quad \forall \quad \eta'(n_t) \in G(n_t),$$

and all sublotteries $\nu(n_{t+1})$ must be subgame perfect with respect to $G(n_{t+1})$.

Theorem 11.1 *All members of $C(G)(n_t)$ generated by a dogmatic, sagacious, or cautious choice mechanism, are subgame–perfect with respect to $G(n_t)$.*

PROOF: The proof is completely analogous to the proof of Theorem 7.1.

Members of a lenient choice set are not necessarily subgame–perfect. According to Definitions 11.8, 11.9, and 11.11 choice sets are never empty. This directly leads to the following finding:

Corollary 11.1 *All choice problems possess at least one lottery which is subgame–perfect.*

In section 7.4, we defined a fifth variety of sophisticated choice which we denoted as perfect choice. It is straightforward to extend this mechanism to frameworks featuring uncertainty. Making use of Definition 11.7, perfect choice is defined in the following way:

Definition 11.14 *Let $\beta'(n_t)$ indicate a particular lottery $\beta(n_t)$ for which it is true that $\beta R(n_t)\beta'$ for all $\beta(n_t)$ which share all their decision nodes n_{t+1} with $\beta'(n_t)$.*

*For some lottery $\alpha(n_t) \in G(n_t)$ to be a member of a **perfect** agent's choice set $C(G)(n_t)$, it must hold that*

$$\alpha R(n_t)\beta' \quad \forall \quad \beta'(n_t) \in G(n_t), \tag{11.7}$$

and all sublotteries $\alpha(n_{t+1})$ must be members of $C(G)(n_{t+1})$.

Also the last finding of section 7.4 carries over to the case of uncertainty:

Theorem 11.2 *A lottery is subgame perfect with respect to $G(n_t)$ if and only if it is a member of the choice set $C(G)(n_t)$ generated by the perfect choice mechanism.*

PROOF: The proof is completely analogous to the proof of Theorem 7.2.

11.6   Properties of Choice

11.6.1   Ordinality and Stability

In section 8.2.1, we were concerned with the consequences of changing the opportunity set $A(n_t)$ by adding or excluding *branches* $x(n_t)$. The property of stability was related to these modifications of $A(n_t)$. Analogously, in the present section we look at the consequences of adding (or excluding) *lotteries* $\xi(n_t)$ to (or from) the opportunity set $G(n_t)$. Obviously, adding or excluding any branch $x(n_t)$ does not change the characteristics of the other branches. Recall from page 168, that changing the opportunity set $G(n_t)$ does not change the other lotteries either! For instance, a two stage lottery remains a two stage lottery and the probabilities of reaching some particular terminal node are not affected. As in the deterministic case, *preferences* are exogenously given and remain unaltered as lotteries are added to or excluded from the opportunity set.

Choices, in contrast, are not invariant to changes in the opportunity set. Imagine an opportunity set to which we add new lotteries. Recall that *ordinality* postulates two things. Firstly, a previously rejected lottery should not suddenly become favourable. Secondly, it should not happen that from a pair of lotteries previously in the choice set, one lottery is rejected from the new choice set while simultaneously the other lottery remains in the new choice set. These two requirements were coined by Sen (1969) as property α and property β. More formally, we obtain:

Definition 11.15 *Choice is ordinal if and only if for all* $G(n_t)$ *and* $\tilde{G}(n_t)$ *in* $X(n_0)$, *with* $\tilde{G}(n_t) \subseteq G(n_t)$ *and* $\tilde{G}(n_t) \cap C(G)(n_t) \neq \emptyset$:

$$C(\tilde{G})(n_t) = \tilde{G}(n_t) \cap C(G)(n_t). \tag{11.8}$$

The second property to be discussed here is *stability*. Stability is a constraint on the logical relationship between choice functions related to consecutive nodes.

Definition 11.16 *Choice is stable if and only if for all* $G(n_s)$ *and* $G(n_t)$ *in* $X(n_0)$, *with* $G(n_s) \subseteq G(n_t)$ *and* $G(n_s) \cap C(G)(n_t) \neq \emptyset$:

$$C(G)(n_s) = G(n_s) \cap C(G)(n_t). \tag{11.9}$$

This says that if some lottery $\alpha(n_t)$ is in the choice set of node n_t, and a sublottery $\alpha(n_s)$ of $\alpha(n_t)$ is still available at decision node n_s, then stability requires two things: Firstly, $\alpha(n_s)$ must also be in the choice set at n_s, and secondly, available sublotteries $\beta(n_s)$ of lotteries $\beta(n_t)$ which were rejected at n_t should not appear in the choice set related to node n_s.

11.6.2 Contractibility

Uncertainty makes it more difficult to contract a dynamic decision problem into a static one. Accordingly, one has to generalize the definition of contractibility.

Definition 11.17 *Choice is contractible, if and only if a shadow quasi–ordering*[7] R *exists, such that for all* $G(n_t) \in X(n_0)$:

$$\alpha(n_t) \in C(G)(n_t) \quad \Longleftrightarrow \quad \hat{\alpha}R\hat{\beta}, \tag{11.10}$$

---

[7] A quasi–ordering is a binary relation which is reflexive and transitive but not necessarily complete. Recall that not all sets in $L(n_t)$ necessarily represent opportunity sets. For this reason, in contractible models featuring uncertainty, the shadow preferences form a quasi–ordering but not necessarily an ordering.

for all pairs of options $\hat{\alpha}(n_0)$, $\hat{\beta}(n_0)$, such that $\hat{\alpha}(n_0) \supseteq \alpha(n_t)$
and $\hat{\beta}(n_0) \supseteq \beta(n_t)$, with $\beta(n_t) \in G(n_t)$, and $\hat{\alpha}(n_0) \setminus \hat{\alpha}(n_t) =$
$\hat{\beta}(n_0) \setminus \hat{\beta}(n_t)$.[8]

This says that actual choices out of any opportunity set $G(n_t)$ can be derived from the shadow quasi–ordering R defined on $L(n_0)$. In Figure 11.9, for instance, the

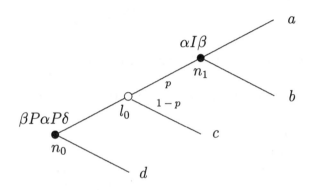

FIGURE 11.9. Shadow Preferences Derived from Sagacious Choice.

sagacious choice function $C(n_0)$ yields the shadow (quasi–) ordering $\alpha\mathsf{I}(n_0)\beta\mathsf{P}(n_0)\delta$. If we apply this shadow ordering to the sublotteries $\{\alpha(n_1), \beta(n_1)\}$, then this yields $C(G)(n_1) = \{\alpha(n_1), \beta(n_1)\}$. We conclude that the shadow ordering $\mathsf{R}(n_0)$ generates the same choice set $C(G)(n_1)$ as the sagacious choice mechanism applied to node n_1, since the latter yields $C(G)(n_1) = \{\alpha(n_1), \beta(n_1)\}$, too. In other words, the dynamic decision problem depicted in Figure 11.9 can be represented by Figure 11.10.

In Figure 11.11 things are slightly more complex. For $\alpha(n_1) \in C(G)(n_1)$, Definition 11.17 postulates both $\alpha\mathsf{R}\beta$ and $\alpha'\mathsf{R}\beta'$.[9] Otherwise, the shadow preference would not necessarily indicate

---

[8] Note that for the case of certainty $\hat{\alpha}(n_0) = \alpha(n_0)$, and *to each* option $\hat{\beta}(n_0)$ only one option $\beta(n_0)$ exists, and thus, only one truncated option $\beta(n_t) \in G(n_t)$. Hence, Definition 11.17 simplifies to Definition 8.4.

[9] Note that $\alpha(n_1) = \alpha'(n_1) = a(n_1)$.

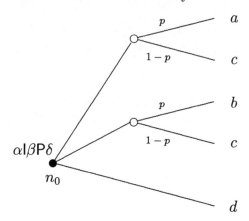

FIGURE 11.10. The Static Representation.

$\alpha(n_1) \in C(G)(n_1)$. Combining stability and ordinality yields the

$$\alpha(n_0) = [a, p; c, 1 - p]$$
$$\alpha'(n_0) = [a, p; d, 1 - p]$$
$$\beta(n_0) = [b, p; c, 1 - p]$$
$$\beta'(n_0) = [b, p; d, 1 - p]$$
$$\eta(n_0) = [e, 1]$$

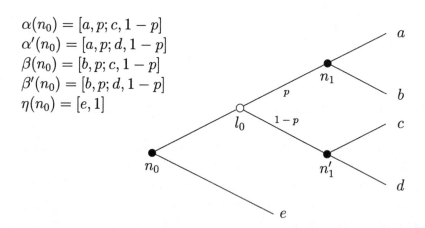

FIGURE 11.11. Contractibility of More Complex Decision Trees.

following result:

Theorem 11.3 *Choice is stable and ordinal if and only if for all $\tilde{G}(n_s)$ and $G(n_t)$ in $X(n_0)$, with $\tilde{G}(n_s) \subseteq G(n_t)$ and $\tilde{G}(n_s) \cap C(G)(n_t) \neq \emptyset$:*

$$C(\tilde{G})(n_s) = \tilde{G}(n_s) \cap C(G)(n_t).$$

PROOF: (11.8) and (11.9) imply that $C(\tilde{G})(n_s) = \tilde{G}(n_s) \cap C(G)(n_s) = \tilde{G}(n_s) \cap G(n_s) \cap C(G)(n_t) = \tilde{G}(n_s) \cap C(G)(n_t)$.

‖

For the deterministic case, Theorem 8.3 stated that stability together with ordinality is equivalent to contractibility. This result carries over to the case of uncertainty.

Theorem 11.4 *Choice is contractible if and only if it is ordinal and stable.*

PROOF:

[40] In [41] to [43] it is proved that Definition 11.17 implies Theorem 11.3, and the converse is shown in [45] to [51].

[41] It is shown that a violation of Theorem 11.3 is impossible, if Definition 11.17 is satisfied. Suppose $\tilde{G}(n_s) \subseteq G(n_t)$, $\tilde{G}(n_s) \cap C(G)(n_t) \neq \emptyset$, and $C(\tilde{G})(n_s) \neq \tilde{G}(n_s) \cap C(G)(n_t)$. Two cases arise.

[42] Case 1: Some option $\delta(n_s) \in [\tilde{G}(n_s) \cap C(G)(n_t)]$ is not in $C(\tilde{G})(n_s)$. Definition 11.17 implies $\hat{\delta} R \hat{\beta}$ for all $\hat{\delta}(n_0)$, $\hat{\beta}(n_0)$, such that $\hat{\delta}(n_0) \supseteq \delta(n_t)$ and $\hat{\beta}(n_0) \supseteq \beta(n_t)$, with $\beta(n_t) \in G(n_t)$. Hence, $\hat{\delta} R \hat{\beta}$ also for all $\hat{\beta}(n_0) \supseteq \beta(n_s)$, with $\beta(n_s) \in \tilde{G}(n_s)$. For the latter, however, Definition 11.17 implies that $\delta(n_s) \in C(\tilde{G})(n_s)$ which contradicts the starting assumption of Case 1.

[43] Case 2: Some option $\alpha \in C(\tilde{G})(n_s)$ is not in $[\tilde{G}(n_s) \cap C(G)(n_t)]$. Since $\tilde{G}(n_s) \cap C(G)(n_t) \neq \emptyset$, some lottery $\gamma(n_s) \in [\tilde{G}(n_s) \cap C(G)(n_t)]$ exists for which Definition 11.17 implies $\hat{\gamma} R \hat{\beta}$ for all $\hat{\gamma}(n_0)$, $\hat{\beta}(n_0)$, such that $\hat{\gamma}(n_0) \supseteq \gamma(n_t)$ and $\hat{\beta}(n_0) \supseteq \beta(n_t)$, with $\beta(n_t) \in G(n_t)$. Hence, $\hat{\gamma} R \hat{\beta}$ also for all $\hat{\beta}(n_0) \supseteq \beta(n_s)$, with $\beta(n_s) \in \tilde{G}(n_s)$. This implies $\hat{\gamma} R \hat{\alpha}$. If $\hat{\gamma} P \hat{\alpha}$, then Definition 11.17 implies that $\alpha \notin C(\tilde{G})(n_s)$ and if $\hat{\gamma} I \hat{\alpha}$ then $\alpha(n_s) \in [\tilde{G}(n_s) \cap C(G)(n_t)]$. Both contradicts the starting assumption of Case 2.

[44] A violation of Definition 11.17 requires that (11.10) leads to intransitive shadow preferences $\alpha R \beta R \gamma P \alpha$, with $\{\alpha(n_r), \beta(n_r)\} \subseteq G(n_r)$, $\{\beta(n_s), \gamma(n_s)\} \subseteq G'(n_s)$, and $\{\alpha(n_t), \gamma(n_t)\} \subseteq G''(n_t)$. It is shown that if Theorem 11.3 is satisfied, no such intransitivity can arise.

[45] Due to stability, $\alpha(n_0) \in C(G)(n_0)$, $\beta(n_0) \in C(G')(n_0)$, $\gamma(n_0) \in C(G'')(n_0)$, and $\alpha(n_0) \notin C(G'')(n_0)$.

[46] Due to ordinality, $\alpha(n_0) \notin C(G'')(n_0)$ implies $\alpha(n_0) \notin C(G \cup G'')(n_0)$. Since $\alpha(n_0) \in C(G)(n_0)$, ordinality postulates that $G(n_0) \cap C(G \cup G'')(n_0) = \emptyset$. Hence, all members of $C(G \cup$

$G'')(n_0)$ are members of $G''(n_0) \setminus G(n_0)$ and $G''(n_0) \cap C(G \cup G'')(n_0) \neq \emptyset$.

[47] Since $\gamma(n_0) \in C(G'')(n_0)$, $C(G'')(n_0) = G''(n_0) \cap C(G \cup G'')(n_0)$ implies that $\gamma(n_0) \in C(G \cup G'')(n_0)$.

[48] In view of [46], $\beta(n_0) \notin C(G \cup G'')(n_0)$, and hence, $\beta(n_0) / \in C(G \cup G' \cup G'')(n_0)$.

[49] Since $\beta(n_0) \in C(G')(n_0)$, ordinality requires that $G'(n_0) \cap C(G \cup G' \cup G'')(n_0) = \emptyset$. Thus, $C(G \cup G' \cup G'')(n_0) \subseteq [G(n_0) \cup G''(n_0)] \setminus G'(n_0)$.

[50] $\gamma(n_0) \in G'(n_0)$ implies that $\gamma(n_0) \notin [G(n_0) \cup G''(n_0)] \setminus G'(n_0)$. From [49], $\gamma(n_0) \notin C(G \cup G' \cup G'')(n_0)$.

[51] From [47], however, $\gamma(n_0) \in C(G \cup G'')(n_0)$. Due to ordinality, either $\gamma(n_0) \in C(G \cup G' \cup G'')(n_0)$, which contradicts [50], or $[G(n_0) \cup G''(n_0)] \cap C(G \cup G' \cup G'')(n_0) = \emptyset$. If the latter applies, then it must be true that $C(G \cup G' \cup G'')(n_0) \subseteq G'(n_0) \setminus [G(n_0) \cup G''(n_0)]$, which contradicts [49]. $\|$

If a shadow quasi–ordering exists, then it can be directly deduced from the underlying decision tree.

Theorem 11.5 *If choice is contractible, then the shadow preference between each pair of lotteries $\alpha(n_t)$ and $\beta(n_t)$ which form an opportunity set $G(n_t)$, can be read off the dynamic decision tree. It is the preference related to their discrimination node $n_s^{\alpha\beta}$, $s \geq t$ (see Definition 11.2).*

PROOF: Imagine the contrary: $\alpha R(n_0)\beta$, but $\beta R(n_s^{\alpha\beta})\alpha$. For all of our choice mechanisms, restricting the opportunity set to $G(n_s^{\alpha\beta}) = \{\alpha(n_s^{\alpha\beta}), \beta(n_s^{\alpha\beta})\}$ would yield $C(G)(n_s^{\alpha\beta}) = \{\beta(n_s^{\alpha\beta})\}$, whereas $\alpha R(n_0)\beta$ implies that $\alpha(n_s^{\alpha\beta}) \in C(G)(n_s^{\alpha\beta})$. $\|$

11.7 Shadow Quasi–Orderings and Welfare Judgements

In chapter 9, we pointed out that a shadow ordering R can be viewed as a valid construct revealing an agent's *overall prefer-*

ences. The same reasoning can be applied to the case of uncertainty:

Definition 11.18 *Consider some pair of lotteries $\alpha(n_0)$ and $\beta(n_0)$ which form some opportunity set $G(n_0)$. Lottery $\alpha(n_0)$ is (revealed) overall preferred to lottery $\beta(n_0)$ if and only if for all opportunity sets $\hat{G}(n_t)$, that is, for all opportunity sets with $\{\alpha(n_t), \beta(n_t)\} \subseteq \hat{G}(n_t)$ and $\{\alpha(n_t), \beta(n_t)\} \cap C(\hat{G})(n_t) \neq \emptyset$, one has*

$$\{\alpha(n_t), \beta(n_t)\} \cap C(\hat{G})(n_t) = \{\alpha(n_t)\}, \qquad (11.11)$$

and it is (revealed) overall indifferent to lottery $\beta(n_0)$ if and only if for all opportunity sets $\hat{G}(n_t)$, that is, for all opportunity sets with $\{\alpha(n_t), \beta(n_t)\} \subseteq \hat{G}(n_t)$ and $\{\alpha(n_t), \beta(n_t)\} \cap C(\hat{G})(n_t) \neq \emptyset$, one has

$$\{\alpha(n_t), \beta(n_t)\} \cap C(\hat{G})(n_t) = \{\alpha(n_t), \beta(n_t)\}. \qquad (11.12)$$

Recall that contractibility implies that a shadow quasi–ordering R exists and that this ordering indicates choices from any opportunity set of lotteries. This leads to the following finding:

Theorem 11.6 *Given Definition 11.18, for any pair of lotteries $\alpha(n_0)$ and $\beta(n_0)$ which form an opportunity set $G(n_t)$, a (revealed) overall preference exists, if and only if choices are contractible. Overall preferences are then identical to the shadow preferences* R.

PROOF:

[52] Suppose choice is not contractible. Then we know from Theorems 11.3 and 11.4 that for some sets $G(n_t)$ and $\tilde{G}(n_s)$ it is true that $C(\tilde{G})(n_s) \neq \tilde{G}(n_s) \cap C(G)(n_t)$, where $\tilde{G}(n_s) \subseteq G(n_t)$ and $\tilde{G}(n_s) \cap C(G)(n_t) \neq \emptyset$. Two cases arise.

[53] Case 1: Some option $\delta(n_s) \in [\tilde{G}(n_s) \cap C(G)(n_t)]$ is not in $C(\tilde{G})(n_s)$. Then, some lottery $\beta(n_t) \in G(n_t)$ exists, such that $\beta(n_s) \in C(\tilde{G})(n_s)$. Obviously, $\{\beta(n_t), \delta(n_t)\} \subseteq G(n_t)$ and $\{\beta(n_s), \delta(n_s)\} \subseteq \tilde{G}(n_s)$. Since $\{\beta(n_s), \delta(n_s)\} \cap C(\tilde{G})(n_s) = \{\beta(n_s)\}$ and $\{\beta(n_t), \delta(n_t)\} \cap C(G)(n_t) \supseteq \{\delta(n_t)\}$, (11.11) and (11.12) are violated.

[54] Case 2: Some option $\alpha(n_s) \in C(\tilde{G})(n_s)$ is not in $[\tilde{G}(n_s) \cap C(G)(n_t)]$. Since $\tilde{G}(n_s) \cap C(G)(n_t) \neq \emptyset$, some lottery $\gamma(n_s) \in [\tilde{G}(n_s) \cap C(G)(n_t)]$ exists. Obviously, $\{\alpha(n_t), \gamma(n_t)\} \subseteq G(n_t)$ and $\{\alpha(n_s), \gamma(n_s)\} \subseteq \tilde{G}(n_s)$. Since $\{\alpha(n_s), \gamma(n_s)\} \cap C(\tilde{G})(n_s) \supseteq \{\alpha(n_s)\}$ and $\{\alpha(n_t), \gamma(n_t)\} \cap C(G)(n_t) = \{\gamma(n_t)\}$, (11.11) and (11.12) are violated.

[55] It remains to show that, if Theorem 11.3 is true, then it is impossible that Definition 11.18 is violated. Suppose for some pair of lotteries $\alpha(n_0)$ and $\beta(n_0)$, Definition 11.18 is violated. A violation requires a pair of sets $\hat{G}(n_t)$ and $\hat{G}'(n_s)$, such that $\{\alpha(n_t), \beta(n_t)\} \cap C(\hat{G})(n_t) = \{\beta(n_t)\}$ and $\{\alpha(n_s), \beta(n_s)\} \cap C(\hat{G}')(n_s) \supseteq \{\alpha(n_s)\}$. Due to ordinality, the former implies that $C\{\alpha(n_t), \beta(n_t)\}) = \{\beta(n_t)\}$, and thus $\beta P \alpha$, whereas the latter implies that $C(\{\alpha(n_s), \beta(n_s)\}) \supseteq \{\alpha(n_s)\}$, and thus $\alpha R \beta$. Contradictory shadow preferences, however, do not square with contractibility (Theorems 11.3 and 11.4).   ‖

11.8 Necessary and Sufficient Conditions for Contractibility

In this section we derive necessary and sufficient conditions on the underlying preference structure, such that a given dynamic choice problem exhibits contractibility. First, we look at resolute choice.

Theorem 11.7 *Resolute choice is contractible if and only if preferences are constant.*

PROOF: It is trivial that constant preferences are sufficient for contractibility. To see that constant preferences are also necessary imagine a change of preference for lotteries $\alpha(n_0)$ and $\beta(n_0)$ between nodes n_t and n_{t+1}. Let $G(n_0) = \{\alpha(n_0), \beta(n_0)\}$. Then $C(G)(n_t) \cap G(n_{t+1}) \neq C(G)(n_{t+1})$ and $C(G)(n_t) \cap G(n_{t+1}) \neq \emptyset$. This constitutes a violation of stability, and hence of contractibility.   ‖

Theorem 11.8 *Naive, sagacious, lenient, and cautious choice are contractible if and only if no triple of lotteries* $\{\alpha(n_0), \beta(n_0), \gamma(n_0)\}$ *exists, such that*

(i) $\alpha R(n_t^{\alpha\gamma})\gamma R(n_t^{\alpha\gamma})\beta,$
(ii) $\beta R(n_s^{\alpha\beta})\alpha,$ $s > t,$

and at least one preference strict.

PROOF:

[56] From Definition 11.17 and Theorem 11.5 we know that the existence of a shadow quasi–ordering R which is generated by the discrimination nodes' respective preferences, is a necessary condition for contractibility. Such a shadow ordering can always be constructed as long as no triple of lotteries exists with discrimination nodes exhibiting preferences which produce intransitive shadow preferences. All possible triples which generate intransitive preferences are listed in Theorem 11.8.

[57] It remains to be shown that the members of $C(G)(n_t)$ are exactly those lotteries one would obtain if one applied R to $G(n_t)$, where R is in accordance with Theorem 11.5.

[58] Consider some lottery $\alpha(n_t) \in G(n_t)$ such that $\alpha R\beta \,\forall\, \beta(n_t) \in G(n_t)$ and some lottery $\gamma(n_t) \in G(n_t)$ exists such that $\alpha P\gamma$. [57] postulates that $\alpha(n_t) \in C(G)(n_t)$ and $\gamma(n_t) \notin C(G)(n_t)$.

[59] $\alpha R\beta \,\forall\, \beta(n_t) \in G(n_t)$ implies that for all discrimination nodes $n_s^{\alpha\beta}$, $s \geq t$, lottery $\alpha(n_s^{\alpha\beta})$ is weakly preferred to each splitting lottery. Hence, for naive, sagacious, lenient, and cautious choice, $\alpha(n_s^{\alpha\beta}) \in C(G)(n_s^{\alpha\beta}) \,\forall s > t$ and $\alpha(n_t) \in C(G)(n_t)$.

[60] $\alpha P\gamma$ implies that $\alpha P(n_s^{\alpha\gamma})\gamma$, $s \geq t$. Thus, for sagacious and cautious choice $\gamma(n_s^{\alpha\gamma}) \notin C(G)(n_t^{\alpha\gamma})$, and hence $\gamma(n_t) \notin C(G)(n_t)$.

[61] For naive and lenient choice, $\gamma(n_t) \in C(G)(n_t)$ would require some option $\delta(n_t) \in G(n_t)$, such $\delta I(n_s^{\alpha\gamma})\alpha$ with $n_r^{\gamma\delta}$, $r > s$. The existence of R, however, implies that if $\delta I(n_s^{\alpha\gamma})\alpha$, then $\delta P(n_r^{\gamma\delta})\gamma$. Repeating this argument finally implies that also for naive and lenient choice $\gamma(n_t) \notin C(G)(n_t)$. ∥

Theorem 11.9 *Dogmatic choice is contractible if and only if no triple of lotteries $\{\alpha(n_0), \beta(n_0), \gamma(n_0)\}$ exists, such that either*

$\quad$ (i) $\alpha R(n_t^{\alpha\gamma})\gamma R(n_t^{\alpha\gamma})\beta,$
$\quad$ (ii) $\beta P(n_s^{\alpha\beta})\alpha,$

or

$\quad$ (iii) $\alpha P(n_t)\beta,$
$\quad$ (iv) $\alpha I(n_s^{\alpha\beta})\beta, \quad s > t.$

PROOF:

[62] See [56] and [58]. Note that Theorem 11.8 lists special cases of Theorem 11.9. [63] If $\alpha P\beta \vee \beta(n_t) \in G(n_t)$, then also for dogmatic choice $\alpha(n_t) \in C(G)(n_t)$ and all $\beta(n_t) \notin C(G)(n_t)$.

[64] Alternatively, suppose that $\alpha R\beta \vee \beta(n_t) \in G(n_t)$ and some lottery $\beta'(n_t) \in G(n_t)$ exists such that $\alpha I\beta'$. Thus, $\alpha I(n_s^{\alpha\beta'})\beta'$ [$\implies$ (vi)] . If dogmatic choice is applied, then for $\{\alpha(n_t), \beta'(n_t)\} \subseteq C(G)(n_t)$, it also must be true, that $\alpha I(n_v)\beta'$, for all v, with $t \le v < s$ [$\implies$ (iii)]. Otherwise, for some v and $G(n_v) = \{\alpha(n_v), \beta'(n_v)\}$ we would either get $\alpha(n_v) \notin C(G)(n_v)$ or $\beta'(n_v) \notin C(G)(n_v)$, and hence $\{\alpha(n_t), \beta'(n_t)\} \subset C(G)(n_t)$. $\|$

The relationship between the six choice mechanisms is summarized in the following corollary:

Corollary 11.2 *For naive, sagacious, lenient, and cautious choice, the necessary and sufficient conditions for contractibility are identical. These conditions are necessary though not sufficient for contractibility of dogmatic choice. The conditions for contractible dogmatic choice, in turn, are necessary though not sufficient for contractibility of resolute choice.*

For strict preferences one obtains the following finding:

Corollary 11.3 *If an agent's underlying preferences at each node n_t can be represented by a strict ordering $P(n_t)$, then naive, sagacious, dogmatic, lenient, and cautious choice are contractible if and only if no triple of lotteries $\{\alpha(n_0), \beta(n_0), \gamma(n_0)\}$ exists, such that:*

$\quad$ (i) $\alpha P(n_t^{\alpha\gamma})\gamma P(n_t^{\alpha\gamma})\beta,$
$\quad$ (ii) $\beta P(n_s^{\alpha\beta})\alpha, \quad s > t.$

Resolute choice is contractible if and only if preferences are constant.

11.9   Recapitulation

In this chapter we extended the dynamic decision framework to allow for uncertainty. This involved a re–examination of the notions of discrimination nodes, opportunity sets, choice sets, and choice mechanisms.

The basic findings, though, remained unaffected. We showed that for any choice problem at least one subgame–perfect solution exists. The property of contractibility ensures that the dynamic choice problem collapses into an essentially static one based on shadow preferences. Note, however, that these shadow–preferences form a quasi–ordering and not necessarily an ordering.

As in deterministic frameworks, the shadow preferences are formed by the dynamic model's preferences related to the respective discrimination nodes. Furthermore, the shadow quasi–ordering can be interpreted as a yardstick for an agent's overall welfare.

If all lotteries are degenerate, that is representable by a single branch, then the present chapter's results (and proofs) simplify to those stated in chapters 7 to 10.

12
Concluding Remarks

In part I of this work we reviewed the literature on dynamic utility. It was demonstrated that all models are special cases of the universal utility framework. Part II was dedicated to a thorough analysis of this general framework.

The rule for transforming sequences of orderings into actual choices was denoted as a choice mechanism. We distinguished between the naive and resolute choice mechanism, and introduced a number of refinements of the sophisticated choice mechanism. These refinements were necessary in order to make sophisticated choice applicable to choice problems featuring indifference.

For all choice mechanisms formal definitions were developed. It was furthermore proved that the variety of sophisticated choice which we denoted as perfect choice can be viewed as the dynamic choice counterpart to the game theoretic notion of subgame perfection.

The various choice mechanisms constitute only one building block for the subsequent analysis. The other block is represented by the properties characterizing actual choices. We focussed on two properties which we labelled as ordinality and stability. It was proved that their joint satisfaction is necessary and sufficient for the satisfaction of the property introduced as contractibility. The latter ensures that the dynamic decision problem can be represented by suitably specified static decision problem. The preference ordering associated with the static version was denoted as a shadow ordering.

Moreover, it was argued that this shadow ordering can be viewed as a valid yardstick of an agent's overall preferences. In other words, even in the presence of changing preferences one may judge an individual's welfare.

We then merged the two building blocks (choice mechanisms and properties of choice) and derived for each mechanism necessary and sufficient conditions for the joint and separate satisfaction of ordinality and stability. As a result, we know precisely what the decision tree and the associated preference structure must look like in order to generate contractible choices. Our findings show that these conditions partly depend on the applied choice mechanism. Remarkably, the conditions coincide for naive and three of the sophisticated varieties of choice (sagacious, lenient, and cautious choice). The conditions are necessary though not sufficient for contractibility of the fourth variety of sophisticated choice which was denoted as dogmatic choice. Resolute choice exhibits contractibility if and only if preferences are constant over time.

Finally, uncertainty was introduced into the analysis. It was demonstrated that this extension does not change the fundamentals of the analysis. All results could be easily generalized. The only modification worth pointing out occured with respect to the derivation of shadow preferences. In contractible decision problems featuring uncertainty the shadow preferences may not necessarily form a shadow ordering but merely a shadow quasi-ordering.

Appendix A

In this appendix we state that part of Theorem 10.11's proof which is related to sagacious choice. Below, we arrange the list of conditions different from the theorem's original formulation. For simplicity, in the proof we write $x \in A(n_t)$ instead of $x(n_t) \in A(n_t)$.

Theorem 10.11 Sagacious choice is ordinal if and only if no triple of options $\{a(n_0), b(n_0), c(n_0)\}$ exists, such that:

$\quad\quad$ (i) $aP(n_t^{ac})cR(n_t^{ac})b$,
$\quad\quad$ (ii) $bP(n_s^{ab})a$,

or

$\quad\quad$ (iii) $aI(n_t^{ac})cR(n_t^{ac})b$,
$\quad\quad$ (iv) $bP(n_s^{ab})a$,

or

$\quad\quad$ (v) $aP(n_t^{ac})bI(n_t^{ac})c$,
$\quad\quad$ (vi) $aI(n_s^{ab})b$,

or

$\quad\quad$ (vii) $aR(n_t^{ac})cP(n_t^{ac})b$,
$\quad\quad$ (viii) $aI(n_s^{ab})b$, $\quad s > t$.

First, the proof derives necessary and sufficient conditions for a violation of property α. Then, necessary and sufficient conditions are derived for a violation of property β under the premise that no violation of property α occurs.

PROOF:

Property α:

[65] Let $\tilde{A} = \{a, c\}$ and $A = \{a, b, c\}$. Then, $c \notin C(\tilde{A})(n_t^{ac})$, but $c \in C(A)(n_t^{ac})$. Hence, (i) and (ii) are sufficient for a violation of property α.

[66] In view of Lemma 10.1, a violation of property α requires that some option $c \in \tilde{A}(n_q)$ and $c \notin C(\tilde{A})(n_q)$ exists, such that adding some option g to $\tilde{A}$, leads to $c \in C(A)(n_q)$, with $A \backslash \tilde{A} = g$, $q < t$.

[67] For $c \notin C(\tilde{A})(n_q)$ to be true, some option $a \in C(\tilde{A})(n_{t+1})$ must exist, such that $aP(n_t^{ac})c$ [$\Longrightarrow$ first relation of (i)].

[68] A violation of property α at node n_q implies a violation at node n_t^{ac}. For $c \in C(A)(n_t^{ac})$, adding g to $\tilde{A}$ must result in some option b becoming a member of $C(A)(n_s)$, $s > t$, with $bP(n_s^{ab})a$ [$\Longrightarrow$ (ii)].

[69] Suppose $b \neq g$. Since $b \in C(A)(n_s^{ab})$, $b \notin C(\tilde{A})(n_s^{ab})$ would imply a violation of property α. Re–labelling b as c brings us back to [67]. That $\{a, b\} \subseteq C(\tilde{A})(n_s^{ab})$, however, is not reconcilable with $bP(n_s^{ab})a$. Hence, it must be true that $b = g$.

[70] We get either $cR(n_t^{ac})b$ [$\Longrightarrow$ second relation of (i)] or $bP(n_t^{ac})c$.

[71] If $bP(n_t^{ac})c$, some option $d \in \tilde{A}$ must exist, such that $dP(n_r^{ad})b$, $t < r < s$. Since $a \in C(\tilde{A})(n_{t+1})$, we know that $aR(n_r^{ad})d$. Re–label d as b and b as a, and start again at [70] until $cR(n_t^{ac})b$.

[72] Hence, (i) and (ii) are also necessary for a violation of property α.

Property β:

[73] Let $\tilde{A} = \{a, c\}$ and $A = \{a, b, c\}$. Then, according to (iii) and (iv), $\{a, c\} \subseteq C(\tilde{A})(n_t)$, $c \in C(A)(n_t)$, but $a \notin C(A)(n_t)$. Let $\tilde{A} = \{b, c\}$ and $A = \{a, b, c\}$. Then, according to (v) and

(vi), $\{b,c\} \subseteq C(\tilde{A})(n_t)$, $c \notin C(A)(n_t)$, but $b \in C(A)(n_t)$. Let $\tilde{A} = \{a,b\}$ and $A = \{a,b,c\}$. Then, according to (vii) and $(viii)$, $\{a,b\} \subseteq C(\tilde{A})(n_t)$, $a \in C(A)(n_t)$, but $b \notin C(A)(n_t)$. Hence, (iii) and (iv), or (v) and (vi), or (vii) and $(viii)$ are sufficient for a violation of property β. They do not generate a violation of property α.

[74] Let $c \in C(\tilde{A})(n_q)$ and $c \in C(A)(n_q)$, $\tilde{A} \subset A$, $q < t$. A violation of property β requires that by adding some option g to $\tilde{A}$ $(A \backslash \tilde{A} = g)$ there is some option a such that $a \in C(\tilde{A})(n_q)$, but $a \notin C(A)(n_q)$. Let options a and c split at the beginning of period t: n_t^{ac}.

[75] Then, for $\{a,c\} \subseteq C(\tilde{A})(n_q)$, it must hold that $\{a,c\} \subseteq C(\tilde{A})(n_t^{ac})$, which necessitates that $aI(n_t^{ac})c$ [$\Longrightarrow$ first relation of (iii)].

[76] $a \notin C(A)(n_q)$ and $c \in C(A)(n_q)$ necessitates that adding g to $\tilde{A}$ results in some option $b \in C(A)(n_s)$, such that $bP(n_s^{ab})a$ [$\Longrightarrow$ (iv)].

[77] Suppose $b \neq g$. Since $b \in C(A)(n_s^{ab})$, $b \notin C(\tilde{A})(n_s^{ab})$ would imply a violation of property α. That $\{a,b\} \subseteq C(\tilde{A})(n_s^{ab})$, however, is not reconcilable with $bP(n_s^{ab})a$. Hence, it must be true that $b = g$. Let options b and c split in period r: n_r^{bc}. Now, we have to discriminate between three cases.

[78] Case 1: $s > t$ $(r = t)$.
Either $cR(n_t^{ac})b$ [$\Longrightarrow$ second relation of (iii)], or $bP(n_t^{ac})c$. If the latter applies, then some option $d \in \tilde{A}$ must exist, such that $dP(n_u^{ad})b$, $t < u < s$. Since $a \in C(\tilde{A})(n_s^{ab})$, we know that $aR(n_u^{ad})d$. Re-label d as c. For $aI(n_t^{ac})c$, we get (iii) and (iv), and for $aP(n_t^{ac})c$ we get a violation of property α.

[79] Case 2: $s = t$ $(r > t)$.
For $c \in C(A)(n_t^{ac})$ and $b \in C(A)(n_t^{ac})$, it is required that $cI(n_r^{bc})b$. Re-label a as c, c as b, and b as a [$\Longrightarrow$ (v), (vi)].

[80] Case 3: $s = r < t$.
For $c \in C(A)(n_t^{ac})$, it must be true that $cR(n_s^{ab})b$. Re-label c as a, a as b, b as c, s as t, and t as s [$\Longrightarrow$ (vii), $(viii)$].

[81] Hence, either (iii) and (iv), or (v) and (vi), or (vii) and $(viii)$ are necessary for a violation of property β. $\|$

Appendix B

In this appendix we state the proof of Theorem 10.12. Below, we arrange the list of conditions slightly different from the theorem's original formulation. For simplicity, in the proof we write $x \in A(n_t)$ instead of $x(n_t) \in A(n_t)$.

Theorem 10.12 Dogmatic choice is ordinal if and only if no triple of options $\{a(n_0), b(n_0), c(n_0)\}$ exists, such that either

$\quad\quad$ (i) $aP(n_t^{ac})cR(n_t^{ac})b$,
$\quad\quad$ (ii) $bP(n_s^{ab})a$,

or

$\quad\quad$ (iii) $aP(n_t^{ac})cR(n_t^{ac})b$,
$\quad\quad$ (iv) $bP(n_r)a$,
$\quad\quad$ (v) $aI(n_s^{ab})b$,

or

$\quad\quad$ (vi) $aI(n_t^{ac})cR(n_t^{ac})b$,
$\quad\quad$ (vii) $bP(n_s^{ab})a$,

or

$\quad\quad$ (viii) $aI(n_t^{ac})cR(n_t^{ac})b$,
$\quad\quad$ (ix) $bP(n_r)a$,
$\quad\quad$ (x) $aI(n_s^{ab})b$, $\quad s > r > t$.

Conditions (i) and (ii) as well as (iii) to (v) of Theorem 10.12 generate a violation of property α (but not a violation of property β), whereas a violation of property β (though not a violation of property α) is generated by (vi) and (vii) as well as by $(viii)$ to (x). In the first stage of the proof we derive necessary and sufficient conditions for a violation of property α under the premise that no violation of property β occurs. This yields conditions (i) to (v). In the second stage necessary and sufficient conditions are derived for a violation of property β under the premise that no set of options exists as specified in (i) to (v). This yields conditions (vi) to (x). Since (i) to (v) cannot lead to a violation of property β. (vi) to (x) are necessary and sufficient conditions for a violation of property β. Similarly, (vi) to (x) do not lead to a violation of property α. Thus, (i) to (v) represent necessary and sufficient conditions for a violation of property α.

PROOF:

Property α:

[82] Let $\tilde{A}(n_0) = \{a, c\}$ and $A(n_0) = \{a, b, c\}$. For (i) and (ii) as well as for (iii) to (v), we get that $c \notin C(\tilde{A})(n_t^{ac})$, but $c \in C(A)(n_t^{ac})$. Hence, (i) and (ii), or (iii) to (v) are sufficient for a violation of property α. They do not generate a violation of property β.

[83] In view of Lemma 10.1, a violation of property α requires that some option $c \in \tilde{A}(n_0)$ and $c \notin C(\tilde{A})(n_p)$ exists, such that adding some option $g(n_0)$ to $\tilde{A}(n_0)$, leads to $c \in C(A)(n_p)$, $A(n_0)\backslash\tilde{A}(n_0) = g(n_0)$.

[84] For $c \notin C(\tilde{A})(n_p)$ to be true, some option $a \in C(\tilde{A})(n_{p+1})$ must exist, such that $aP(n_v)c$, $p \leq v \leq t$, where n_v is the last node for this strict preference to hold and options $a(n_0)$ and $c(n_0)$ split at node n_t^{ac}.

[85] For $c \in C(A)(n_t^{ac})$, adding $g(n_0)$ to $\tilde{A}(n_0)$ must result in some option $b(n_q)$ becoming a member of $C(A)(n_q)$, $q > t$, with $bP(n_q)a$. Let n_q denote the last node for this strict preference

to hold and let options $a(n_0)$ and $b(n_0)$ split in period s $(s \geq q)$: n_s^{ab}.

[86] Suppose $b(n_q) \neq g(n_q)$. Since $b \in C(A)(n_q)$, $b \notin C(\tilde{A})(n_q)$ would imply a violation of property α. Re–labelling b as c brings us back to [84]. $\{a, b\} \subseteq C(\tilde{A})(n_q)$ is not reconcilable with $bP(n_q)a$. Hence, it must be true that $b(n_q) = g(n_q)$. We now have to discriminate between two cases.

Case 1: $v < t$

[87] Since $aI(n_t^{ac})c$ and $a \notin C(A)(n_t^{ac})$, we would generate a violation of property β by adding $\bar{A}(n_t^{ac}) = A(n_t^{ac}) \backslash \{a(n_t^{ac}), c(n_t^{ac})\}$ to $\{a(n_t^{ac}), c(n_t^{ac})\}$.

Case 2: $v = t$.

[88] Thus, we get in [84] that $aP(n_t^{ac})c$ [$\Longrightarrow$ first relation of (i) and (iii)].

Subcase 2.1: $q = s$.

[89] From [85] [$\Longrightarrow$ (ii)]. Either we get $cR(n_t^{ac})b$ [$\Longrightarrow$ second relation of (i)], or $bP(n_t^{ac})c$. If the latter applies, then $c \in C(A)(n_t^{ac})$ requires that $b \notin C(A)(n_{t+1})$. This stipulates some option $d \in C(\tilde{A})(n_w)$, such that $dP(n_w)b$, $t < w < s$, where n_w is the latest node for this strict preference to hold. Re–labelling d as b and b as a brings us back to [88].

Subcase 2.2: $q < s$.

[90] Then, $aI(n_s^{ab})b$. Either we get $cR(n_t^{ac})b$ [$\Longrightarrow$ second relation of (iii)], or $bP(n_t^{ac})c$. If the latter applies, then $c \in C(A)(n_t^{ac})$ requires that $b \notin C(A)(n_{t+1})$. This stipulates some option $e \in \tilde{A}(n_0)$, such that $eP(n_r)b$, $t < r < q$, where n_r is the latest node for this strict preference to hold. Re–labelling e as b and b as a brings us back to [88].

Property β:

[91] Let $\tilde{A}(n_0) = \{a, c\}$ and $A(n_0) = \{a, b, c\}$. For (vi) and (vii) as well as for $(viii)$ to (x) we get that $\{a, c\} \subseteq C(\tilde{A})(n_t^{ac})$, $c \in C(A)(n_t^{ac})$, but $a \notin C(A)(n_t^{ac})$. Hence, (vi) and (vii), or $(viii)$ to (x) are sufficient for a violation of property β.

[92] Let $c \in C(\tilde{A})(n_q)$ and $c \in C(A)(n_q)$, $\tilde{A}(n_0) \subset A(n_0)$, $q < t$. A violation of property β requires that by adding some

option $g(n_0)$ to $\tilde{A}(n_0)$ $(A(n_0)\backslash\tilde{A}(n_0) = g(n_0))$, there is some option $a(n_0)$ such that $a \in C(\tilde{A})(n_q)$, but $a \notin C(A)(n_q)$. Let options $a(n_0)$ and $c(n_0)$ split at the beginning of period t: n_t^{ac}.

[93] For $\{a, c\} \subseteq C(\tilde{A})(n_q)$, it must be true that $aI(n_t^{ac})c$ [$\Longrightarrow$ first relation of (vi) and $(viii)$].

[94] Then, $a \notin C(A)(n_q)$ and $c \in C(A)(n_q)$ necessitates that adding $g(n_0)$ to $\tilde{A}(n_0)$ results in some option $b \in C(A)(n_{r+1})$, such that $bP(n_r)a$, $r > t$. Let n_r^a denote the last node for this strict preference to hold and let options $a(n_0)$ and $b(n_0)$ split in period s $(s \geq r)$: n_s^{ab}.

[95] Suppose $b(n_0) \neq g(n_0)$. Since $b \in C(A)(n_r^{ab})$, $b \notin C(\tilde{A})(n_r^{ab})$ would imply a violation of property α. Re–labelling b as c brings us back to [84]. That $\{a, b\} \subseteq C(\tilde{A})(n_r^{ab})$, however, is not reconcilable with $bP(n_r^{ab})a$. Hence, it must be true that $b(n_0) = g(n_0)$. Now we have to discriminate between two cases.

Case 1: $s = r$.

[96] From [94] [$\Longrightarrow$ (vii)]. Either we get $cR(n_t^{ac})b$ [$\Longrightarrow$ second relation of (vi)], or $bP(n_t^{ac})c$. If the latter applies, then $c \in C(A)(n_t^{ac})$ requires that $b \notin C(A)(n_{t+1})$. This stipulates some option $d \in \tilde{A}(n_0)$, such that $dP(n_w)b$, $t < w < s$.

[97] Let options $d(n_0)$ and $a(n_0)$ (and thus $b(n_0)$) split in period u, $w \leq u < s$: n_u^{ad}. We know that $dR(n_u^{ad})b$. Since $a \in C(\tilde{A})(n_t^{ac})$, we also know that $aR(n_u^{ad})d$. If $aP(n_u^{ad})d$, then a violation of property α occurs at node n_u^{ad}. This case is covered by (i) and (ii). If $aI(n_u^{ad})d$, then we can generate a violation of property β (which is covered by (vi) and (vii)) by adding $b(n_0)$ to $a(n_0)$ and $d(n_0)$.

Case 2: $s > r$.

[98] Then, $aI(n_s^{ab})b$ [$\Longrightarrow$ (ix), (x)].

[99] Either we get $cR(n_t^{ac})b$ [$\Longrightarrow$ second relation of $(viii)$], or $bP(n_t^{ac})c$. If the latter applies, then $c \in C(A)(n_t^{ac})$ requires that $b \notin C(A)(n_{t+1})$. This stipulates some option $e \in \tilde{A}(n_0)$, such that $eP(n_v)b$, $t < v < r$.

[100] Let options $e(n_0)$ and $a(n_0)$ (and thus $b(n_0)$) split in period w. We know that $w < r$ and $eR(n_w^{ae})b$.

[101] We also know that $aR(n_w^{ae})e$. If $eI(n_w^{ae})a$, then adding $b(n_0)$ to $\{a(n_0), e(n_0)\}$ generates a violation of property β at

node n_w^{ae}. This case is covered by $(viii)$ to (x). If $aP(n_w^{ae})e$, then adding $b(n_0)$ to $\{a(n_0), e(n_0)\}$ generates a violation of property α at node n_w^{ae}. This case is covered by (iii) to (v).

[102] Hence, either (i) and (ii), or (iii) to (v), or (vi) and (vii), or $(viii)$ to (x) are necessary for a violation of ordinality.

$\parallel$

References

Ainslie, G. (1975), "Specious Reward: A Behavioral Theory of Impulsiveness and Impuls Control", *Psychological Bulletin*, 82, 463–496.

Ainslie, G. (1991), "Derivation of 'Rational' Economic Behavior from Hyperbolic Discount Curves", *American Economic Review, Papers and Proceedings*, 81, 334–340.

Arrow, K. J. (1959), "Rational Choice Functions and Orderings," *Economica*, 26, 121–127.

Auer, L. von (1998), "Dynamic Choice Mechanisms," *Theory and Decision*, forthcoming.

Becker, G. S. (1992), "Habits, Addictions, and Traditions," *Kyklos*, 45, 327–346.

Becker, G. S., K. M. Murphy (1988), "A Theory of Rational Addiction," *Journal of Political Economy*, 96, 675–700.

Becker, G. S., G. Grossman, and K. M. Murphy (1991), "Rational Addiction and the Effect of Price on Consumption," *American Economic Review, Papers and Proceedings*, 81, 237–241.

Becker, R. A. (1980), "On the Long–Run Steady State in a Simple Dynamic Model of Equilibrium with Heterogenous Households;" *Quarterly Journal of Economics*, 96, 375–382.

Becker, R. A., J. H. Boyd (1993), "Recursive Utility: Discrete Time Theory," *Hitotsubashi Journal of Economics*, 34 (Special Issue), 49–98.

Becker, R. A., J. H. Boyd, and B. Y. Sung (1989), "Recursive Utility and Optimal Capital Accumulation. I. Existence," *Journal of Economic Theory*, 47, 76–100.

Bell, D. E. (1982), "Regret in Decision Making under Uncertainty," *Operations Research*, 30, 961–981.

Benhabib, J., M. Majumdar, and K. Nishimura (1987), "Global Equilibrium Dynamics with Stationary Recursive Preferences," *Journal of Economic Behavior and Organization*, 8, 429–452.

Benzion, U., A. Rapoport, and J. Yagil (1989), "Discount Rates Inferred from Decisions: An Experimental Study," *Management Science*, 35, 270–284.

Blackorby, C., D. Nissen, D. Primont, and R. R. Russell (1973), "Consistent Intertemporal Decision Making," *Review of Economic Studies*, 40(2), 239–248.

Bover, O. (1991), "Relaxing Intertemporal Separability: A Rational Habits Model of Labor Supply, Estimated from Panel Data," *Journal of Labor Economics*, 9(1), 85–100.

Boyd, J. H. III (1990), "Recursive Utility and the Ramsey Problem," *Journal of Economic Theory*, 50, 326–345.

Boyer, M. (1978), "A Habit Forming Optimal Growth Model," *International Economic Review*, 19, 585–609.

Boyer, M. (1983), "Rational Demand and Expenditure Patterns under Habit Formation," *Journal of Economic Theory*, 31, 27–53.

Calvo, G. A., R. Findlay (1978), "On the Optimal Acquisition of Foreign Capital Through Investment of Oil Export Revenues," *Journal of International Economics*, 8, 513–524.

Chakravarty, S., A. S. Manne (1968), "Optimal Growth When the Instantaneous Utility Function Depends Upon the Rate of Change in Consumption," *American Economic Review*, 58, 1351–1354.

Chernoff, H. (1954), "Rational Selection of Decision Functions," *Econometrica*, 22, 422–443.

Chew, S. H., L. G. Epstein (1989), "The Structure of Preferences and Attitudes Towards the Timing of the Resolution of Uncertainty," *International Economic Review*, 30(1), 103–117.

Cowen, T. (1989), "Are All Tastes Constant and Identical," *Journal of Economic Behavior and Organization*, 11, 127–135.

Debreu, G. (1954), "Representation of a Preference Ordering by a Numerical Function," in R. M. Thrall, G. H. Coombs, and R. L. Davis (eds.), *Decision Processes*, New York: Wiley & Sons, 159–165.

Debreu, G. (1959), *Theory of Value*, New York: Wiley & Sons.

Dolmas, J. (1995), "Time–Additive Representations of Preferences when Consumption Grows without Bound," *Economics Letters*, 47, 317–325.

Dolmas, J. (1996), "Balanced–Growth–Consistent Recursive Utility," *Journal of Economic Dynamics and Control*, 20, 657–680.

El–Safty, A. E. (1976a), "Adaptive Behavior, Demand and Preferences," *Journal of Economic Theory*, 13, 298–318.

El–Safty, A. E. (1976b), "Adaptive Behavior and the Existence of Weizsäcker's Long–Run Indifference Curves," *Journal of Economic Theory*, 13, 319–328.

Epstein, L. G. (1987), "A Simple Dynamic General Equilibrium Model," *Journal of Economy Theory*, 41, 68–95.

Epstein, L. G., J. A. Hynes (1983), "The Rate of Time Preference and Dynamic Economic Analysis," *Journal of Political Economy*, 91, 611–635.

Epstein, L. G., S. E. Zin (1989), "Substitution, Risk Aversion, and the Temporal Behavior of Consumption and Asset Returns: A Theoretical Framework," *Econometrica*, 57(4), 937–969.

Epstein, L. G., A. Melino (1995), "A Revealed Preference Analysis of Asset Pricing Under Recursive Utility," *Review of Economic Studies*, 62, 597–618.

Findlay, R. (1978), "An Austrian Model of International Trade and Interest Rate Equalization," *Journal of Political Economy*, 86(6), 989–1007.

Fishburn, P. C., A. Rubinstein (1982), "Time Preference," *International Economic Review*, 23, 677–694.

Fisher, I. (1930), *The Theory of Interest*, New York: The Macmillan Company.

Gandolfo, G. (1996), *Economic Dynamics*, 3rd ed., Berlin: Springer.

Goldman, S. M. (1979), "Intertemporally Inconsistent Preferences and the Rate of Consumption," *Econometrica*, 47(3), 621–626.

Goldman, S. M. (1980), "Consistent Plans," *Review of Economic Studies*, 47, 533–537.

Gorman, W. M. (1967), "Tastes, Habits and Choices," *International Economic Review*, 8, 218–222.

Greenberg, J. (1990), *The Theory of Social Situations*, Cambridge: Cambridge University Press.

Hammond, P. J. (1976a), "Changing Tastes and Coherent Dynamic Choice," *Review of Economic Studies*, 43, 159–173.

Hammond, P. J. (1976b), "Endogenous Tastes and Stable Long–Run Choice," *Journal of Economic Theory*, 13, 329–340.

Hammond, P. J. (1977), "Dynamic Restrictions on Metastatic Choice," *Economica*, 44, 337–350.

Hammond, P. J. (1988), "Consequentialist Foundations of Expected Utility," *Theory and Decision*, 25, 25–78.

Hammond, P. J. (1989), "Consistent Plans, Consequentialism, and Expected Utility," *Econometrica*, 57(6), 1445–1449.

Harvey, C. M. (1986), "Value Functions for Infinite–Period Planning," *Management Science*, 32(9), 1123–1139.

Hayakawa, H., S. Ishizawa (1993), "The Fundamental Principle of Intertemporal Optimization," *Economics Letters*, 41, 273–280.

Hayek, F. A. (1941), *The Pure Theory of Capital*, Chicago: University of Chicago Press.

Hertzendorf, M. N. (1995), "Recursive Utility and the Rate of Impatience," *Economic Theory*, 5, 51–65.

Hotz, V. J., F. E. Kydland, and G. L. Sedlacek (1988), "Intertemporal Preferences and Labor Supply," *Econometrica*, 56(2), 335–360.

Houthakker, H. S., L. D. Taylor (1970), *Consumer Demand in the US: Analysis and Projections*, 2nd ed., Cambridge MA: Harvard University Press.

Iannaccone, L. R. (1984), *Consumption Capital and Habit Formation, with an Application to Religous Participation*, PhD dissertation, Chicago IL, University of Chicago.

Iannaccone, L. R. (1986), "Addiction and Satiation," *Economics Letters*, 21, 95–99.

Johnsen, T. H., Donaldson, J. B. (1985), "The Structure of Intertemporal Preferences under Uncertainty and Time Consistent Plans," *Econometrica*, 53(6), 1451–1458.

Joshi, S. (1995), "Recursive Utility and Optimal Growth under Uncertainty," *Journal of Mathematical Economics*, 24, 601–617.

Karni, E., D. Schmeidler (1991), "Atemporal Dynamic Consistency and Expected Utility Theory," *Journal of Economic Theory*, 54, 401–408.

Kennan, J. (1988), "An Econometric Analysis of Fluctuations in Aggregate Labor Supply and Demand," *Econometrica*, 56(2), 317–333.

Koopmans, T. C. (1960), "Stationary Ordinal Utility and Impatience," *Econometrica*, 28, 287–309.

Koopmans, T. C. (1972), "Representation of Preference Orderings over Time," in C. B. McGuire and R. Radner (eds.), *Decision and Organization*, Amsterdam: North-Holland Publishing Company, 79–100.

Koopmans, T. C., P. A. Diamond, and R. E. Williamson (1964), "Stationary Utility and Time Perspective," *Econometrica*, 32, 82–100.

Kreps, M. D., E. L. Porteus (1978), "Temporal Resolution of Uncertainty and Dynamic Choice Theory," *Econometrica*, 32, 185–200.

LaValle, I., P. Fishburn (1987), "Equivalent Decision Trees and Their Associated Strategy Sets," *Theory and Decision*, 23(1), 37–63.

Léonard, D. (1981), "The Signs of the Co–State Variables and Sufficiency Conditions in a Class of Optimal Control Problems," *Economics Letters*, 10, 321–325.

Lluch, C. (1973), "The Extended Linear Expenditure System," *European Economic Review*, 15, 786–797.

Lluch, C. (1974), "Expenditures Savings and Habit Formation," *International Economic Review*, 15, 786–797.

Loewenstein, G. F. (1987), "Anticipation and the Valuation of Delayed Consumption," *The Economic Journal*, 97, 666–684.

Loewenstein, G. F. (1988), "Frames of Mind in Intertemporal Choice," *Management Science*, 34, 200–214.

Loewenstein, G. F., D. Prelec (1991), "Negative Time Preference," *American Economic Review, Papers and Proceedings*, 81, 347–351.

Loewenstein, G. F., D. Prelec (1992), "Anomalies in Intertemporal Choice: Evidence and Interpretation," *The Quarterly Journal of Economics*, 107, 573–597.

Loewenstein, G. F., N. Sicherman (1991), "Do Workers Prefer Increasing Wage Profiles?," *Journal of Labor Economics*, 9, 67–84.

Loewenstein, G. F., R. H. Thaler (1989), "Anomalies: Intertemporal Choice," *Journal of Economic Perspectives*, 3(4), 181–193.

Loomes, G., R. Sugden (1982), "Regret Theory: An Alternative Theory of Rational Choice," *Economic Journal*, 92, 805–824.

Loomes, G., R. Sugden (1986), "Disappointment and Dynamic Consistency in Choice under Uncertainty," *Review of Economic Studies*, 92, 271–282.

Lucas, R. E. Jr., N. L. Stokey (1984), "Optimal Growth with Many Consumers," *Journal of Economic Theory*, 32, 139–171.

Ma, C. (1993), "Market Equilibrium with Heterogenous Recursive–Utility–Maximizing Agents," *Economic Theory*, 3, 243–266.

Machina, M. J. (1989), "Dynamic Consistency and Non–Expected Utility Models of Choice Under Uncertainty," *Journal of Economic Literature*, 27, 1622–1668.

Majumdar, M. (1975), "Some Remarks on Optimal Growth with Intertemporally Dependent Preferences in the Neoclassical Model," *Review of Economic Studies*, 42(1), 147–153.

McCarthy, M. (1974), "On the Stability of Dynamic Demand Functions," *International Economic Review*, 15, 256–259.

McClennen, E. F. (1988), "Dynamic Choice and Rationality," in B. R. Munier (ed.), *Risk, Decision, and Rationality*, Dordrecht: D. Reidel Publishing Company, 517–536.

McClennen, E. F. (1990), *Rationality and Dynamic Choice*, Cambridge: Cambridge University Press.

Obstfeld, M. (1981), "Macroeconomic Policy, Exchange–Rate Dynamics, and Optimal Asset Accumulation," *Journal of Political Economy*, 89, 1142–1161.

Obstfeld, M. (1982), "Aggregate Spending and the Terms of Trade: Is there a Laursen–Metzler Effect?," *Quaterly Journal of Economics*, 97, 251–270.

Obstfeld, M. (1990), "Intertemporal Dependence, Impatience, and Dynamics," *Journal of Monetary Economics*, 26, 45–75.

Orphanides, A., D. Zervos (1994), "Optimal Consumption Dynamics with Non–Concave Habit–Forming Utility," *Economics Letters*, 44, 67–72.

Orphanides, A., D. Zervos (1995), "Rational Addiction with Learning and Regret," *Journal of Political Economy*, 103(4), 739–758.

Pashardes, P. (1986), "Myopic and Forward Looking Behavior in a Dynamic Demand System," *International Economic Review*, 27(2), 387–397.

Peleg, B., M. E. Yaari (1973), "On the Existence of a Consistent Course of Action when Tastes are Changing," *Review of Economic Studies*, 40, 391–401.

Peston, M. (1967), "Changing Utility Functions," in M. Shubik (ed.), *Essays in Mathematical Economics, in Honor of Oskar Morgenstern*, Princeton N.J.: Princeton University Press, 233–236.

Phelps, E. S., R. A. Pollak (1968), "On Second–Best National Saving and Game–Equilibrium Growth," *Review of Economic Studies*, 35(2), 185–199.

Phlips, L. (1978), "The Demand for Leisure and Money," *Econometrica*, 46, 1025–1043.

Phlips, L. (1983), *Applied Consumption Analysis*, 2nd ed., Amsterdam: North Holland.

Phlips, L., F. Spinnewyn (1982), "Rationality versus Myopia in Dynamic Demand Analysis," in R. L. Basmann, G. F. Rhodes (eds.), *Advances in Econometrics*, vol. 1, Greenwich, Connecticut: JAI Press, 3–33.

Pollak, R. A. (1968), "Consistent Planning," *Review of Economic Studies*, 35(2), 201–208.

Pollak, R. A. (1970), "Habit Formation and Dynamic Demand Functions," *Journal of Political Economy*, 78, 745–763.

Pollak, R. A. (1971), "Additive Utility Functions and Linear Engel Curves," *Review of Economic Studies*, 38, 401–414.

Pollak, R. A. (1975), "The Intertemporal Cost of Living Index," *Annals of Economic and Social Measurement*, 4, 179–195.

Pollak, R. A. (1976), "Habit Formation and Long–Run Utility Functions," *Journal of Economic Theory*, 13, 272–297.

Pollak, R. A., R. Wales (1969), "Estimation of the Linear Expenditure System," *Econometrica*, 37, 611–628.

Ryder, H. E. Jr., G. M. Heal (1973), "Optimal Growth with Intertemporally Dependent Preferences," *Review of Economic Studies*, 40(2), 1–33.

Samuelson, P. A. (1937), "A Note on Measurement of Utility," *Review of Economic Studies*, 4, 155–161.

Samuelson, P. A. (1971), "Turnpike Theorems even though Tastes are Intertemporally Dependent," *Western Economic Journal*, 9, 21–26.

Seidl, C. (1996a), "Experimental and Empirical Research on Utility I: Riskless Utility," in S. Barbera, P. J. Hammond, C. Seidl (eds.), *Handbook of Utility Theory*, Dordrecht: Kluwer Academic Publishers, forthcoming.

Seidl, C. (1996b), "Experimental and Empirical Research on Utility II: Utility under Risk," in S. Barbera, P. J. Hammond, C. Seidl (eds.), *Handbook of Utility Theory*, Dordrecht: Kluwer Academic Publishers, forthcoming.

Selden, L. (1978), "A New Representation of Preferences over 'Certain × Uncertain' Consumption Pairs: The 'Ordinal Certainty Equivalent' Hypothesis," *Econometrica*, 46, 103–118.

Selten, R. (1965), "Spieltheoretische Behandlung eines Oligopolmodells mit Nachfrageträgheit.," *Zeitschrift für die Gesamte Staatswissenschaft*, 12, 301–324.

Sen, A. K. (1969), "Quasi–Transitivity, Rational Choice, and Collective Decisions," *Review of Economic Studies*, 36(3), 381–393.

Sen, A. K. (1971), "Choice Functions and Revealed Preference," *Review of Economic Studies*, 38, 307–317.

Shefrin, H. M. (1996), "Changing Utility Functions," in S. Barbera, P. J. Hammond, C. Seidl (eds.), *Handbook of Utility Theory*, Dordrecht: Kluwer Academic Publishers, forthcoming.

Shi, S., L. G. Epstein (1993), "Habits and Time Preference," *International Economic Review*, 34, 61–84.

Spinnewyn, F. (1981), "Rational Habit Formation," *European Economic Review*, 15, 91–109.

Stigler, G. J., G. S. Becker (1977), "De Gustibus non est Disputandum," *American Economic Review*, 67(2), 76–90.

Streufert, P. A. (1990), "Stationary Recursive Utility and Dynamic Programming under the Assumption of Biconvergence," *Review of Economic Studies*, 57, 79–97.

Streufert, P. A. (1996), "Recursive Utility and Dynamic Programming," in S. Barbera, P. J. Hammond, C. Seidl (eds.), *Handbook of Utility Theory*, Dordrecht: Kluwer Academic Publishers, forthcoming.

Strotz, R. H. (1955/56), "Myopia and Inconsistency in Dynamic Utility Maximization," *Review of Economic Studies*, 23(3), 165–180.

Taylor, L. D., D. Weiserbs (1972), "On the Estimation of Dynamic Demand Functions," *Review of Economics and Statistics*, 54, 459–465.

Thaler, R. H. (1981), "Some Empirical Evidence on Dynamic Inconsistency," *Economics Letters*, 8, 201–207.

Thaler, R. H., H. M. Shefrin (1981), "An Economic Theory of Self Control," *Journal of Political Economy*, 89(2), 392–406.

Uzawa, H. (1968), "Time Preference, the Consumption Function, and Optimum Asset Holdings," in J. N. Wolfe (ed.) *Value, Capital, and Growth: Papers in Honour of Sir John Hicks*, Chicago: Aldine, 485–504.

Wan, H. Y. (1970), "Optimal Saving Programs under Intertemporally Dependent Preferences," *International Economic Review*, 11(3), 521–547.

Weizsäcker, C. C. von (1971), "Notes on Endogenous Change of Tastes," *Journal of Economic Theory*, 3, 345–372.

Weller, P. (1978), "Consistent Intertemporal Decision Making under Uncertainty," *Review of Economic Studies*, 45, 263–266.

Yaari, M. E. (1977), "Endogenous Changes in Tastes: A Philosophical Discussion," in H. W. Gottinger and W. Leinfellner (eds.), *Decision Theory and Social Ethics, Issues in Social Choice*, Dordrecht: D. Reidel Publishing Company, 59–98.

List of Symbols

A	opportunity set (set of available consumption profiles)
$A(n_t)$, $\tilde{A}(n_t)$, $\hat{A}(n_t)$	opportunity sets at n_t
$aR(n_t)b$	at n_t "$a(n_t)$ weakly preferred to $b(n_t)$"
$aP(n_t)b$	at n_t "$a(n_t)$ strictly preferred to $b(n_t)$"
$aI(n_t)b$	at n_t "$a(n_t)$ indifferent to $b(n_t)$"
α^i	positive coefficient
$\alpha(n_t)$	lottery beginning at n_t
B	matrix of coefficients
B_{ii}	diagonal element i of matrix B
b	column vector of coefficients
$\beta(n_t)$	lottery beginning at node n_t
β^i, $\tilde{\beta}^i$	positive coefficients
C	matrix of coefficients
$C(A)(n_t)$	choice set indicating choices from $A(n_t)$
$C(G)(n_t)$	choice set indicating choices from $G(n_t)$
$C(n_t)$	choice function related to n_t
$\hat{C}_{x_{t-1}}(A)$	short–run choice set
$\hat{C}(A)$	long–run choice set

D	diagonal depreciation matrix
D_{ii}	diagonal element i of matrix D
δ	depreciation rate (constant)
δ^i	depreciation rate of commodity i (constant)
ε	positive constant
$F(\cdot)$	monotonic transformation
$f^i(x,h)$, f^i	short–hand notation for $f^i[x(t),h(t)]$: gross additions to $h^i(t)$ (continuous time)
$f(x,h)$, f	vector with elements $f^i(x,h)$
$f^i_{x^j}$	partial derivative of f^i with respect to x^j
f_{x^j}	vector with elements $f^i_{x^j}$
f_x	vector with elements f_{x^j}
$f^i_{h^j}$	partial derivative of f^i with respect to h^j
$f^i_{h^j h^j}$	second order partial derivative of f^i with respect to h^j
$G(n_t)$	opportunity set of lotteries at n_t
g^i_t, $g^i(t)$	weighted average of past consumption
$g(t)$	vector with elements $g^i(t)$
γ^i	positive coefficient
H	current–value Hamiltonian
H_x	partial derivative of H with respect to $x(t)$
H_w	partial derivative of H with respect to $w(t)$
$h^i(\bar{h}_t)$	stationary habit function related to commodity i
$h(\bar{h}_t)$	vector with elements $h^i(\bar{h}_t)$
h^i_t, $h^i(t)$	habits in period (at date) t affecting commodity i
$h(t)$	vector with elements $h^i(t)$
$\bar{h}_t = (\ldots, x_{t-2}, x_{t-1})$	vector of past consumption
h	short–hand notation for $h(t)$
h^i	short–hand notation for $h^i(t)$

$\dot{h}$	partial derivative of $h(t)$ with respect to time
h'	transposed h
$\tilde{h}^i$	positive coefficient
K	diagonal matrix of coefficients
K^{-1}	inverse of matrix K
K_{ii}	diagonal element i of matrix K
k	column vector of coefficients
$\bar{k}, k^i$	positive coefficients
$L(n_t)$	set of all possible lotteries at node n_t
l, l^i	positive constants
l_t	chance node
λ	Lagrange multiplier
m_t	income in period t
m	constant periodic income
μ	current–value shadow price of habits
$\dot{\mu}$	partial derivative of μ with respect to time
N_t	set of decision nodes in $X(n_0)$ related to period t
N	set of all decision nodes in $X(n_0)$
n	number of commodities
n_0	initial decision node
n_t, n_t'	decision nodes related to period t
n_t^{ab}	discrimination node of $a(n_0)$ and $b(n_0)$
$n_t^{\alpha\beta}$	discrimination node of $\alpha(n_0)$ and $\beta(n_0)$
$\hat{P}$	long–run preference relation
p_t^i	price of commodity i in period t
$p_t = (p_t^1, p_t^2, \ldots)$	price vector in period t
$p = (p^1, p^2, \ldots)$	constant price vector
p'	transpose of p
$\pi[\cdot]$	a monotonic transformation
q	number of habit forming commodities
$Q(\bar{x})$	long–run demand indicator
$R(n_t)$	preference ordering related to n_t
$\mathsf{R}(\mathsf{n_t})$	shadow ordering related to n_t
R	shadow ordering

r	interest rate
ρ	rate of time preference
ϱ	discount factor
s	period or date of time
$sgn(\cdot)$	signum
σ^i	elasticity of intertemporal substitution
T	time horizon
t	period or date of time
$\theta_{s,t}(\cdot)$	discount function for period s depending on period of evaluation t
$U_{\bar{h}_t}(\cdot)$	intertemporal utility function conditional on $\bar{h}_t$
$U_t(\cdot)$	intertemporal utility function in period t
$U(\cdot)$	stationary $U_t(\cdot)$
$\hat{U}_t(x_{t+1}, x_{t+2}, \ldots)$	intertemporal sub–utility function from periods $t+1$, $t+2$, $\ldots$ as evaluated in period t
$u_s(\cdot)$	instantaneous utility function in period s
$u_{s,t}(\cdot)$	instantaneous utility function in period s depending on time of evaluation t
$u(\cdot)$	stationary instantaneous utility function
$u(x, h)$	short–hand notation for $u[x(t), h(t)]$: stationary instantaneous utility function (continuous time)
u_{x^i}	partial derivative of $u(x, h)$ with respect to x^i
u_x	vector of partial derivatives u_{x^i}
$u_{x^i h^i}$	second order cross derivative of $u(x, h)$ with respect to x^i and h^i
u_{xh}	vector of second order cross derivatives $u_{x^i h^i}$
$\tilde{u}_{xh}$	vector of approximations of $u_{x^i h^i}$ near a steady state
$u_{x^i x^i}$	second order partial derivative of $u(x, h)$

	with respect to x^i
$u_{h^i h^i}$	second order partial derivative of $u(x, h)$ with respect to h^i
$\tilde{u}_{hh}$	vector of approximations of $u_{h^i h^i}$ near a steady state
u_{h_i}	partial derivative of $u(x, h)$ with respect to h^i
u_{z^i}	partial derivative of $u(x, h)$ with respect to z^i
$u_{z^i z^i}$	second order partial derivative of $u(x, h)$ with respect to z^i
$v(\cdot)$	instantaneous utility function
W_t	aggregator in the recursive utility functional $U_t(\cdot)$
w	short–hand notation for $w(t)$
$w_t, w(t)$	wealth in period (at date) t
$\dot{w}$	partial derivative of $w(t)$ with respect to time
$X = \{a, b, c, \ldots\}$	set of all existing options
$X(n_0)$	set of all options (complete decision tree)
$X(n_t)$	set of all options beginning in n_t (subtree of $X(n_0)$)
X_t	in part I: set of all feasible x_t
	in part II: set of all portions x_t in $X(n_0)$ related to period t
$x = (.., x_{-1}, x_0, x_1, ..)$	in discrete time models: complete consumption profile and terminal node
	in continuous time models: short–hand notation for $x(t)$
x^i	short–hand notation for $x^i(t)$: consumption of commodity i at date t (continuous time)
$x(t)$	vector with elements x^i
$\dot{x}$	partial derivative of $x(t)$ with respect to time

$x_t = (x_t^1, x_t^2, \ldots)$ in part I: consumption bundle in period t and vector of short–run demand in period t
in part II: portion of branch $x(n_0)$ related to period t

x' transposed x

$\tilde{x}_t = (\tilde{x}_t^1, \tilde{x}_t^2, \ldots)$ consumption bundle in period t and vector of short–run demand in period t

x_s^{*t} optimal consumption bundle for period s as evaluated in period $t \le s$

x_t^i short–run demand for commodity i in period t

$\bar{x}^i$ long–run demand for commodity i

$x(n_t)$ truncated branch (option) available at n_t

ξ current–value shadow price of wealth

$\xi(n_t)$ lottery beginning at n_t

$\dot{\xi}$ partial derivative of ξ with respect to time

$z(x, h)$ short–hand notation for $z[x(t), h(t)]$: stationary "z-function" or "utility production function" (continuous time)

$z^i(x_t^i, h_t^i),\ z^i$ commodity i's instantaneous sub–utility function in period t

List of Figures